D1315501

VOLUME 14

DISCOVERING ANTIQUES

THE STORY OF WORLD ANTIQUES

GREYSTONE PRESS/NEW YORK · TORONTO · LONDON

This superb full-color work is brought to you in its entirety from the original publisher, The British Publishing Corporation. Only the arrangement has been slightly altered. In fact, rather than disturb the text in any way, you will find the English monetary system used throughout the set. Here is a handy conversion table showing the value of a Pound (£) in terms of U.S. dollars.

DATES	U.S. Dollars equal to one Pound (£)
1939	$3.92 to 4.68
1940 to Sept. 1949	4.03
Sept. 1949 to Nov. 1967	2.80
Nov. 1967 to Aug. 1971	2.40
Aug. 1971 to June 1972	2.60
June 1972 to present	2.45 (floating rate)

20 shillings = one Pound (£)
21 shillings = one guinea

In February, 1971, the guinea was taken out of circulation.

TITLE PAGE PHOTO CREDIT: *Tankard* by Daniel Mylius, Danzig, c. 1700. Silver-gilt with embossed scenes. (Victoria and Albert Museum, London.) *Photo: K. Hoddle*

Published by the Greystone Press
225 Park Avenue South
New York, N.Y. 10003

Library of Congress Catalog Card Number: 72-90688

Cover Design: Harold Franklin

MANUFACTURED IN THE UNITED STATES OF AMERICA.

Contents

Maximilian and the arts in Germany

Michael Kauffmann

MAXIMILIAN I
Holy Roman Emperor (1493–1519)
CHARLES V
Holy Roman Emperor (1519–56)
FERDINAND I
Holy Roman Emperor (1556–64)
MAXIMILIAN II
Holy Roman Emperor (1564–76)
RUDOLPH II
Holy Roman Emperor (1576–1612)

Fig. 1 *(frontispiece)* ***Maximilian I with his Family*** *by Bernhard Strigel (1460–1528), 1515. Painted on the occasion of the double Habsburg-Hungarian wedding of 1515, this portrait includes Mary of Burgundy (right). The child in the centre is the future Charles V. (Kunsthistorisches Museum, Vienna.)*

2

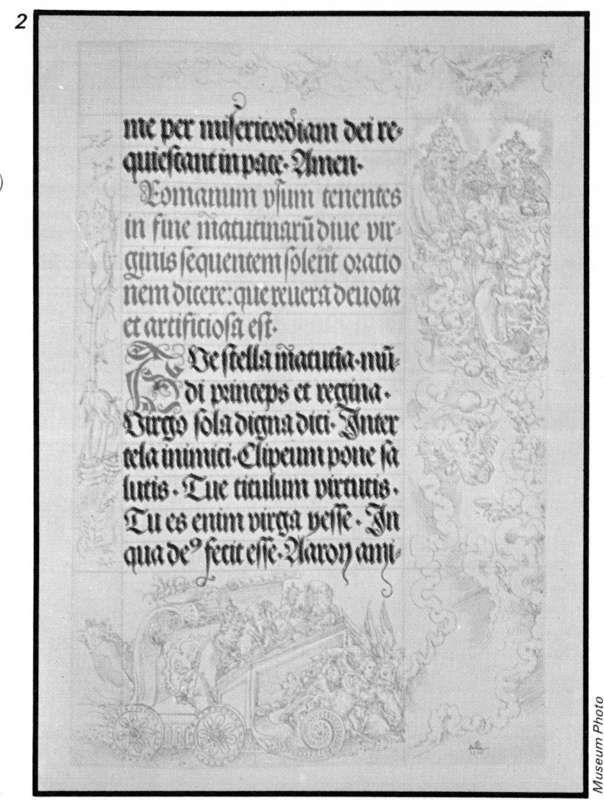

me per misericordiam dei re-
quiescant in pace. Amen.
Romanum usum tenentes
in fine matutinarũ diue vir-
ginis sequentem solent oratio
nem dicere: que reuera deuota
et artificiosa est.
De stella matutina mun-
di princeps et regina.
Virgo sola digna dici. Inter
tela inimici. Clipeum pone sa
lutis. Tue titulum virtutis.
Tu es enim virga yesse. In
qua deus fecit esse. Aaron ami-

Museum Photo

3

Museum Photo

Reigning throughout the German Renaissance, and surrounded by some of the greatest artists of his day, Maximilian I was at heart a romantic knight whose projects never quite worked out.

In Germany in the late fourteenth and fifteenth centuries, when royal authority was on the verge of extinction, social predominance belonged to the towns; by the sixteenth century this ascendancy had passed to the secular princes.

This situation was reflected in the patronage of the arts. The history of German art in the fifteenth century can be written in terms of the burgher classes of the great cities – Cologne, Hamburg, Nuremberg, Ulm, Augsburg, to name but a few. Of course, burgher patronage remained an important factor in the sixteenth century – for Augsburg in particular this was a golden age – yet the great artists of the period worked primarily for the nobility. Dürer was employed by merchants as well as princes, but his most consistent patron was Frederick the Wise of Saxony. Grünewald produced his masterpiece, the great altar-piece now at Colmar, for the Anthonite monastery at Isenheim, but he was essentially in the employ first of Uriel von Gemmingen, Archbishop of Mainz, and then of Albrecht of Brandenburg. Lucas Cranach became painter to the Saxon Court of Wittenberg at the age of thirty-three in 1505, and remained in the service of Frederick the Wise and his successor until his death in 1553. Albrecht Altdorfer, the leading representative of the Danube School, received most of his commissions in the city of Regensburg, but his closest follower, Wolf Huber, was court painter to the Bishop of Passau.

A period preoccupied with romantic nostalgia for the medieval past

These names alone suffice to indicate that Maximilian's reign coincided with one of the high-water marks of artistic achievement in Germany, and this was also the great age of German Humanism. Just as the leading German artists of 1500 introduced renaissance forms from Italy, so her poets and philosophers concerned themselves with the classical heritage. Willibald Pirckheimer, Dürer's great friend, advised Maximilian on some of his decorative schemes and it was the Emperor himself who crowned Ulrich von Hutten, poet laureate in 1517. Maximilian's reign coincides with the German Renaissance, but it was also a period much preoccupied with a romantic nostalgia for the medieval past. Maximilian himself, with his prowess in the tournament and the hunt, has gone down in history as the 'last knight'; his autobiographical writings are modelled on Caesar, but it was as a worthy successor to King Arthur that he really liked to see himself.

Neither '*Ritterromantik*' nor Humanism long survived his reign. On 31 October, 1517, Luther nailed his ninety-five theses to the door of the Wittenberg Schlosskirche. Maximilian did not take

Fig. 2 ***Page from Maximilian's Prayer Book**, Augsburg, 1513. The margin illustrations are by Lucas Cranach (1472–1553). Dürer also contributed forty-five of the drawings to this superb book. (Bayerische Staatsbibliothek, Munich.)*

Fig. 3 ***Maximilian Hunting** by Jörg Kölderer, page from the **Tiroler Jagdbuch** of 1500. Water-colour. This scene comes from an early hunting manual written for Maximilian. (Bibliothèque Royale, Brussels.)*

4

Mansell Collection

Fig. 4 ***The Emperor Maximilian I** by Albrecht Dürer (1471–1528), signed and dated 1519. Woodcut. This portrait of the 'Last of the Knights' was made in the year of his death.*

Fig. 5 ***Detail of The Triumph of Maximilian** by Hans Burgkmair. (1473–1531). Woodcut. This detail shows the opening of the procession with a herald, riding on a griffin announcing the triumph.*

5

K. Hoddle

this event very seriously, but it was to unleash the forces of civil war and social revolution in Germany. Luther's teachings, with their incitement to question established principles, were applied to social, as well as religious affairs. A rising of the depressed class of smaller knights in 1522 and 1523 was followed by the Peasants' Revolt in 1524 which was harshly crushed by the military power of the nobility. If Maximilian's reign was the age of the Romantic Knight and Humanism, that of his successor, Charles V, was essentially the period of the Reformation and Counter-Reformation.

Politically, Maximilian's reign is characterised by grandiose aims matched by paucity of achievement. As a young man of eighteen he married Mary (d.1482), daughter of Charles the Bold of Burgundy, and was thereby drawn into a series of fruitless wars against Louis XI of France. The endless wars in Italy from 1496 to 1518 drained his exchequer without achieving anything.

Only in his marriage projects did Maximilian enjoy the success denied him elsewhere. His son Philip married Joanna of Castile in 1496; their son Charles was to become the ruler of Spain, the Netherlands and Germany. In 1515 Charles' brother Ferdinand married Anne of Bohemia and Hungary, thereby extending the Habsburg domain in the east. Yet it may be argued that Maximilian's grandiose dynastic plans were a factor standing in the way of far-reaching internal reform which alone could have saved Germany from remaining a loose federation of small principalities.

A strong desire for immortality and a keen artistic sense

With his political ambitions, Maximilian combined a strong desire for immortality and a keen artistic sense. His patronage came into being to ensure his own immortality and for this purpose he employed, at different times between about 1500 and his death in 1519, most of the leading artists of his day.

His greatest monument was to be his tomb in the Hofkirche at Innsbruck, to which he gave his attention from 1502. The intention was that it should consist of forty life-size bronze statues of his ancestors which were to surround the great tomb itself. Unfortunately, financial and other difficulties prevented its completion. Only eleven bronze figures of the twenty-eight now surrounding the tomb were completed by 1519; the others were added by his successors.

The process of making these figures was complex and it should be remembered that the final appearance was dependent on the quality of workmanship at each stage rather than on the creative powers of a single artist – as was the case with contemporary Italian bronzes. In the first place, the preliminary drawing was carried out by an artist who need not himself take any further part in the process. At least two of the drawings for the tomb figures are by Dürer (Liverpool and Berlin); others are the work of Gilg Sesselschreiber, who was in charge of the bronze-casting workshop at Innsbruck. A sculptor then made the full-scale wooden model from which the mould for the bronze was prepared. He clearly played a leading part in the process, but for many of the figures the name of the sculptor is unknown. Concerning the final stage of the process we are better informed, for we know that four workshops were responsible for the casting of the following figures:

1. Peter Vischer the Elder, Nuremberg: King Arthur and Theodoric the Ostrogoth (1513)
2. Stefan Godl, Nuremberg: Albrecht of Habsburg (1518)
3. Peter Löffler, Innsbruck: Ferdinand of Portugal (1509)
4. Gilg Sesselschreiber, Innsbruck: the remaining seven, of which Elizabeth of Görz, Zimburgis of Masovia and Kunigunde of Bavaria are appreciably better than the rest.

In both artistic quality and technical achievement the Nuremberg workshops were far superior to those at Innsbruck. Their figures are cast in one piece and are faultless; Sesselschreiber's were cast in separate pieces. The outstanding workshop was Peter Vischer's which produced the best two figures of the series: Arthur (Fig. 9) and Theodoric. Sesselschreiber's workshop was responsible for figures of widely differing quality, doubtless due to their derivation from models by different sculptors. Zimburgis of Masovia (Fig. 8), for example, is characterised by heavy, gothic folds, with an over-all shape not unlike that of a screw, features which do not appear on any of the other figures. She – or rather the wooden model on which the bronze is based – has been tentatively attributed by Karl Oettinger to Veit Stoss of Nuremberg. The figures of Arthur and Theodoric are elegant examples of German renaissance sculpture.

Maximilian had planned the greatest tomb of his time and some of the figures finally achieved rank among the great masterpieces of German sculpture, but the story of their production at times verged on pure farce. Gilg Sesselschreiber, essentially a painter, proved quite incapable of either organising a workshop or mastering the technique of bronze-casting. He continually failed to fulfil his contract and Maximilian came close to withdrawing the commission from him at various times until finally, in 1516, Maximilian lost patience and Sesselschreiber was dismissed from his workshop, to be succeeded by his sons.

Until the funds arrived the goldsmith refused to start work

The scheme's ultimate failure was due to Maximilian's misjudgment in attempting to base it on an untried workshop in Innsbruck. As a centre for the manufacture of armour, however, Innsbruck was – thanks to Maximilian's patronage – second only to Augsburg. In 1511 Maximilian intended to present armours to Henry VIII, to the English ambassador and to his grandson, the Archduke Charles, and here the Emperor's patronage ran into difficulties. They were to be made in the workshop of Conrad and Hans Seusenhofer at Innsbruck and decorated at Augsburg, but Maximilian had the greatest difficulty in obtaining the necessary funds from the Innsbruck administration and, in July 1512, the Augsburg goldsmith who was to carry out the decoration refused to start work until he had secured the necessary gold and silver.

Of all Maximilian's schemes that never materialised perhaps the saddest loss is his equestrian monument, which was to have adorned the choir of

16th century Germany

the church of St. Ulrich at Augsburg. The Emperor commissioned Hans Burgkmair of Augsburg to design the monument and Burgkmair's drawing still exists in the Albertina, Vienna.

Like the sculpture he commissioned, Maximilian's patronage of painters was inspired by his desire to create a memorial to himself. Above all, there are the portraits of him by painters such as Dürer, Lucas van Leyden, Bernhard Strigel and Ambrogío de Predis. Outstanding among these is Dürer's portrait of 1519 – the last year of Maximilian's life. The oil paintings in the Vienna and Nuremberg museums are based on a charcoal drawing in the Albertina, Vienna, which is a masterpiece of portraiture, depicting Maximilian with an expression of sadness, weariness and disillusionment.

Dürer's portrait outshines all the others and served as a model for several artists, including Lucas van Leyden. But the painter whose name is most closely associated with that of Maximilian is Bernhard Strigel (1460–1528), a native of Memmingen in Swabia. Essentially a painter of religious subjects, he was introduced to Italian renaissance naturalism through the influence of Hans Holbein the Elder of Augsburg in the opening years of the sixteenth century. His earliest portrait of Maximilian (Berlin-Dahlem) is dated 1504, but this inscription is corrupt and there is no firm evidence that he portrayed the Emperor from the life until they met at Augsburg in 1507. The painting that resulted from this meeting shows Maximilian in three-quarter profile, arrayed in armour, crowned and carrying sword and sceptre. Strigel achieved a more intimate kind of portraiture in his full profile view of the Emperor in cloak and beret. These stress Maximilian's prominent nose and Habsburg lower lip and chin almost to the point of caricature. A characteristic portrait of this kind reappears in the family group painted on the occasion of the double Habsburg-Hungarian wedding of 1515 (Fig. 1). Mary of Burgundy, who had died thirty-three years earlier, appears on the right; the child in the middle is the future Charles V.

6

K. Hoddle

Fig. 6 ***The Triumphal Arch of Maximilian I*** *(detail) by Albrecht Dürer, dated 1515 but actually printed in 1517. Woodcut printed from one hundred and ninety-two blocks. Overall size 11½ x 9¾ ft. The three portals are dedicated to Fame, Honour and Power, and Nobility, and are decorated with Maximilian's ancestors and scenes from his life. The architectural ornament is full of symbols from medieval heraldry and classical mythology and 'Egyptian hieroglyphs'.*

Strigel's portrayals of the Emperor were not limited to these official portraits. Indeed, he appears with regularity in Strigel's works. In 1507 Maximilian commissioned Strigel to paint an altarpiece of the Holy Cross (Kynžvart, Czechoslovakia) to present to San Paolo Fuori le Mura in Rome in connection with his proposed coronation in 1508, and he himself is portrayed next to Constantine – clearly as a worthy successor to the first Christian emperor. In the *Adoration of the Magi* at Schloss Salem, Maximilian appears in the guise of one of the kings, and he is shown as the donor in the splendid *Death of the Virgin* which he gave to the church of St. Mary at Hietzing, near Vienna, in 1518.

Yet the bulk of Maximilian's patronage had a literary or illustrative rather than a strictly pictorial basis. His own copy of a prayer-book printed at Augsburg in 1513 contains forty-five drawings by Dürer and others by Cranach, Burgkmair, Hans Baldung Grien and Jörg Breu (Fig. 2). It was a co-operative venture of great distinction; the drawings were presumably intended for reproduction as woodcuts, but this plan was never put into effect.

Overcoming obstacles with knightly virtues and God's help

It was in his autobiographical works that Maximilian's search for a fitting memorial and his artistic sense were most fruitfully combined. The *Weisskunig* – a pun on the 'white' or 'wise' king – is an allegorical autobiography, written in prose, modelled on the lives of Caesar and Alexander. Begun in about 1506, it was dictated by Maximilian to his secretary Marx Treitzsaurwein, but remained incomplete in 1519 and was not printed until 1775. It tells the story of his parents' marriage, his own youth and actions in war in terms of the 'white king's' heroism and courtly virtues. Hans Burgkmair, who ranks second only to Dürer among the great graphic artists of the time, contributed one hundred and seventeen of the book's two hundred and fifty-one woodcuts.

At the same time as Maximilian was dictating the *Weisskunig*, Melchior Pfinzing, incumbent of St. Sebald, Nuremberg, was composing a long poem on Maximilian's youth and his courtship of Mary of Burgundy. Theuerdank, the fearless knight who is the poem's hero, is accompanied by his faithful servant Ehrenhold, with whom he journeys in search of his bride, overcoming the obstacles placed in his way by the devil, with knightly virtues and God's help. Many of Theuerdank's adventures serve to demonstrate his prowess as a huntsman and the illustrations recall the water-colours of Maximilian's earlier hunting manuals, such as the *Tiroler Jagdbuch* (Fig. 3). In the *Theuerdank* there are one hundred and eighteen woodcuts, mainly by Hans Schäufelein and Leonhard Beck, which serve to underline the superior quality and more effective use of the medium of the thirteen woodcuts contributed by Burgkmair.

The third work of this group, the *Freydal*, deals with the tournaments and masquerades of Maximilian's life in Burgundy at the time of his marriage in 1477. The original manuscript, which is in the

K. Hoddle

Fig. 7 **Weisskunig** *by Hans Burgkmair, c.1514–16, published 1775. Woodcut. Maximilian caused to be written – and probably contributed to –* Weisskunig, *a prose poem, of which he is the hero.*

Kunsthistorisches Museum, Vienna, contains two hundred and fifty-five water-colours, but the text was never completed and only a few woodcuts were ever made. Five of these were produced by Dürer in 1516.

Perhaps the most ambitious enterprise was the famous *Triumphal Arch*, a mammoth woodcut printed in 1517 from one hundred and ninety-two blocks and measuring $11\frac{1}{2}$ by $9\frac{3}{4}$ feet (Fig. 6). Johann Stabius, the Emperor's astronomer and poet, devised the programme and wrote the explanations; Jörg Kölderer, the Innsbruck architect, designed the architectural framework and Dürer, assisted by the humanist Pirckheimer in matters of iconography, acted as designer-in-chief and was personally responsible for much of the ornament. The three portals are dedicated to Fame, Honour and Power, and Nobility, and decorated with Maximilian's ancestors and scenes from his life. The architectural ornament is suffused with symbols drawn from medieval heraldry and classical mythology and 'Egyptian hieroglyphs', as they were then interpreted. The complexity of the symbolism and of the ornamentation alike announce the arrival of Mannerism in northern art. In Panofsky's phrase, it is to be 'read like a book, decoded like a cryptogram and yet be enjoyed like a collection of quaint sparkling jewellery'.

The Triumphal Arch was supplemented by a *Triumphal Procession* which was printed only in 1526, after Maximilian's death. The procession contains hunts, tournaments, music, artillery, soldiers and machines of siege, and each scene is almost overburdened with symbolic content. Jörg Kölderer did the preliminary designs; the woodcuts are the work of the leading artists of Augsburg and Nuremberg with Burgkmair at their head. Literary in content, complex in its symbolism and decoration and a masterpiece of graphic art, The *Triumph* is a fitting memorial to Maximilian, Europe's 'last knight' and the Emperor of Germany in the Renaissance.

8

J. Bethel

Fig. 8 **Zimburgis of Masovia** *(d.1492), cast in the workshop of Gilg Sesselschreiber, Innsbruck. Bronze. This sculpture of Maximilian's grandmother is part of Maximilian's tomb. (Innsbruck, Hofkirche.)*

9

J. Bethel

Fig. 9 **King Arthur** *from Maximilian's tomb. Bronze. Cast in the workshop of Peter Vischer the Elder, 1513. (Innsbruck, Hofkirche.)*

Fig. 1 ***Cabinet** known as the Wrangelschrank, Augsburg, 1566. Marquetry of various woods with boxwood carvings and alabaster columns. This extraordinary cabinet received its name during the Thirty Years' War, when it was taken as booty by the Swedish commander, Count Wrangel. Behind the inlaid doors lies an inner cupboard, where curios and other small objects would have been kept. The Augsburg intarsia workers consulted engraved designs in the creations of such complicated compositions. (Landesmuseum, Münster.)*

Museum Photo

Developments in German furniture

Eric Mercer

Increasingly a symbol of wealth and status, furniture in sixteenth-century Germany introduced a profusion of exotic woods, ivory, gold and silver, and semi-precious stones or metals.

In Germany as in other countries of western Europe the sixteenth century saw a revolution in housing standards among the upper classes and in their furniture. Medieval magnates had spent much of their time progressing from one gloomy and inconvenient castle to another, carrying much of their furniture with them and making do at every lodging with remarkably little of it. A bed, not always upon a bedstead, a bench, a chest for valuables and a rod hung between two walls for hanging clothes – this represented a high standard of furnishing in a well-appointed house.

When, at the end of the Middle Ages, feudal vassals were transformed into royal courtiers and ministers, they set about adapting themselves to their new role by increasing their creature comforts. They built gorgeous palaces, filling them with magnificent furniture. They did this at a time when gothic architecture and ornament were being displaced by the classical concepts and motifs of the Renaissance and when many men of less exalted status were either growing richer from trade and industry or putting fewer of their riches back into business and more into comforts and luxuries.

As a result, men of all ranks, from kings and kaisers down to gentlemen and wealthy burgesses, were buying and commissioning expensive furniture designed in a new way and enriched with a new kind of ornament. Furniture-makers, in consequence, achieved a new prestige and from the sixteenth century onwards the names of many such as Tilman Riemenschneider, Peter Flötner and the master who signed his pieces with the monogram HS, have come down to us, together with a few of their authenticated works.

In discussing surviving pieces and those which are known to us from illustrations, it is important to distinguish between northern and southern productions. The distinction was geophysical: northern Germany was part of the north European plain and amply supplied with hard woods, especially oak; southern Germany was, in the main, part of the *Alpenlände* and its commonest timbers were soft woods such as larch and pine. The northern furniture resembled that of England, of the Netherlands and of north France, while the affinities of the south were with northern Italy and Lombardy.

The hard woods of northern Europe were well

2

Museum Photo

3

Ullstein Bilderdienst

Fig. 2 **Chest,** *known as the Erasmus chest, by Veltin Redner and Jacob Steiner, Basle, 1539. Limewood and ash. This marvellous piece of renaissance carving is traditionally said to have been made in memory of Erasmus of Rotterdam, to the order of his heir, Dr. Bonifazius Amerbach. The left-hand medallion contains a portrait of Erasmus, while that on the right depicts Aristotle. (Historisches Museum, Basle.)*

Fig. 3 **Cupboard,** *Kärnten, southern Austria, 1539. Carved and painted wood. (Schloss Charlottenburg, Berlin.)*

4

Ullstein Bilderdienst

Fig. 4 **Wardrobe,** *Tyrolean, 1478. Carved wood with the inscription:* 'Maria Hubert anno 1478'. *This wardrobe and the cupboard in Fig. 3 are excellent examples of southern furniture decoration. Because soft woods such as larch and pine were used, carving had to be shallow, and motifs of twisted vines or ribbons often run along the structural members. (Museum für Deutsche Volkskunde, Berlin.)*

adapted to deep under-cutting and modelling in imitation of, or in sympathy with, the contemporary productions of stone-masons and sculptors. The soft woods of the south were not suited to such treatment, but rather lent themselves to shallow carving and low relief. From these physical differences arose others in the disposition and form of ornament. Northern craftsmen worked in an architectural manner, often treating the uprights of large pieces in a way which emphasised their structural role – as gothic buttresses or as classical pilasters. Like late gothic masons and carpenters, they conceived of the intervening spaces as non-structural curtaining and as a field for ornament. It was therefore upon the intermediate panels that the main decorative interest was concentrated, often in the form of crowded and lively sculptural scenes. The south Germans, tied by their material to a flat presentation, tended to cover the uprights and cross-pieces with shallow motifs of twisted ribbons or running vine-leaves and to leave undecorated most of the panel surfaces.

A bed of 1512 now in the Historisches Museum, Basle (Fig. 7), provides a good example of southern practice. The canopy, or tester, and the side-pieces of the bedstead, and the ribs outlining the panels of the head-board, are covered with ornament; the panels themselves are untouched by any form of decoration whatever.

A national style began to emerge and wider markets opened

North and south differed not only in decorative techniques but also in furniture forms: broadly speaking, it may be said that in the north the chest of medieval derivation continued throughout the century to be a very common piece of furniture for storage purposes, while in the south it was rapidly supplanted by the cupboard which had appeared late in the fifteenth century. In the north, and especially in the Luneburg-Bremen area, chests of almost medieval shape were made in large numbers up to the end of the sixteenth century. Although late examples had abandoned gothic ornament they made little direct concession to renaissance taste. All the interest apart from the owner's arms was upon a main panel often decorated with figured scenes from Old and New Testament history. Some of them combine the busts and roundels of *quattrocento* origin with gothic motifs, while the flowing ornament of southern decoration is markedly absent.

It is necessary to emphasise the differences between these two furniture provinces for until that is made clear 'sixteenth-century German' can be a very ambiguous label. At the same time, one should stress the elements which were common to both regions for, by the mid-sixteenth century, the most costly pieces were beginning to show a certain national character that was neither wholly northern nor wholly southern. By then, too, there was to a far greater extent than ever before, a national market and an international one, too, for that matter.

Each piece was treated as a small-scale architectural construction

A development common to both areas was the change from a gothic repertoire of motifs and mouldings to a classical, or would-be classical, one. Early pieces from north or south are prodigal of the crocketing, the finials, the flamboyant tracery, the battlementing that were the stock-in-trade of late gothic masons. By about the second quarter of the century this was giving way, as in the works of Peter Flötner, to the vases, the laurel-wreath roundels, and the silhouette busts of *quattrocento* ornament. By the mid-century a more correct and up-to-date style was appearing in which the piece was treated as though it were a small-scale architectural construction.

At this time, too, a variety of tables also came into use in the houses of the wealthy. The old *table dormant*, with its massive central supports, and the movable trestle table were superseded by others, generally of lighter construction and with legs at the corners or arranged along the sides rather than with central supports. These presented an easy opportunity for classical ornament, and in a more appropriate form than was usually the case, as load-bearing columns. In the last years of the century, and in sympathy with the publications of men like De Vries in the Low Countries and Wendel Dietterlein in Germany, the correctly classical columns and arcades of the middle years were increasingly superseded by such debased forms as herms and diminishing pilasters.

At this stage, however, one should perhaps

5

Stadtarchive

6

K. Jung

emphasise that although the renaissance style was dominant by the middle of the century, the gothic still lingered on for a surprising time and in some surprising places. In the town museum at Ulm there is a cupboard of 1569 (Fig. 6), almost certainly a product of the fashionable local school, which combines the most up-to-date motifs in marquetry of many different coloured woods upon the main panels, with a profusion of deeply undercut flamboyant tracery upon the styles and uprights beneath a battlemented top. Apart from its other merits, it serves as a warning against over-confidence in dating any individual piece to a narrow period.

A large foreign market for the more easily portable products

The change from gothic to renaissance ornament was not peculiar to Germany; neither was the increasing fondness as the century progressed for inlay and marquetry. What became a very marked feature was the technical skill of the German craftsmen and the style and quality of their wares. This was appreciated by contemporaries and there was a large foreign market for the more easily portable products. When Catherine de' Medici died in 1589, she had a large number of '*cabinets d'Allemagne*'; German cabinets early found their way to Denmark; and the oddly-misnamed Nonsuch chests, so popular in England, originated in Germany, even if some of the later ones were made here by refugee craftsmen. At this time the export traffic reached a new intensity both in the number of objects and in the value of individual pieces.

The spread of education, and in the circumstances of the age it was necessarily renaissance education, was creating a demand among the laity for small portable cabinets and writing tills and desks to hold the curios, valuables, and writing instruments that were now indispensable to the *élite*.

Perhaps the least accomplished of these new productions are the Nonsuch chests. Many of them are carried out in the somewhat less difficult technique of parquetry – thin pieces of different coloured woods assembled into a pattern and neither inlaid into the solid nor yet, as in marquetry, into a veneer ground, but affixed directly to the body. These pieces are distinguished by the use of light-coloured woods against a darker ground and by a fondness for architectural compositions of tall pavilion-like buildings with domes and turrets which owe something to classical concepts and much to romantic fancy. They seem to belong to the latter half of the century and by then they were perhaps rather out of date in their ornament.

Of a higher standard of craftsmanship, more sophisticated in their choice of motifs, more versatile in their combination of marquetry and high-relief carving, more exotic in their use of materials, and far more expensive, were the cabinets which were being produced by the mid-century in such famous centres as Augsburg, Ulm and Würzburg. It is not possible to draw a sharp line between these and their less esteemed fellows, and it would be wrong to suggest that they ran to a standard pattern, but the qualities of a very distinctive group which embody all the most up-to-date motifs and most developed techniques of the age are epitomised in the Wrangelschrank of 1566.

This famous cabinet, now in the Landesmuseum

16th century German Furniture

Fig. 5 *(far left, above).* **Cupboard,** *from the workshop of Melchior von Rheydt, Cologne, c.1600. Marquetry of various woods. This intricate piece shows the final development of the style shown in its transitional form in Fig. 6. The body of the cupboard is entirely covered by* intarsia *work and decorative motifs – the illusionistic panels and the caryatids – and the overall proportions of the piece are entirely renaissance. (Rheinisches Landesmuseum, Bonn.)*

Fig. 6 *(far left, below),* ***Two-tiered cupboard,*** *1569. The frame of pine and oak, the marquetry panels of various woods. This beautiful piece shows a combination of decorative motifs typical of the period. The carving at the top and bottom, with its flamboyant tracery and crenellations, is totally gothic, while the marquetry is in the most up-to-date renaissance style. (Museum der Stadt, Ulm.)*

Fig. 7 **Canopy Bed,** *from the Carthusian Monastery, Basle, 1512. The frame of oak and beech, the flat carving in pine. As on the pieces in Figs. 3 and 4, this bed shows the shallow carving in soft wood, typical of southern Germany. The side-pieces of the bedstead, the ribs outlining the panels of the head-board, and the surface of the canopy are covered in ornament, while the panels have been left completely plain. (Historisches Museum, Basle.)*

7

Museum Photo

at Münster (Fig. 1), is remarkable for the technical virtuosity of its intarsia work and for its iconography. On the exterior and interiors of the main doors and of the leaves of the inner compartments are medleys of classical ruins, trophies of arms, astronomical instruments, grotesque birds and beasts, strap-work, and many other elements in exploding mannerist scenes reminiscent, on an infinitely smaller scale, of some of Guilio Romano's work at the Palazzo del Tè.

The north was less fond of mannerist tricks than the south

In most matters, north and south Germany were one province by this time, but there was still a difference between them both in the amount of marquetry and inlay they used and in the choice of motifs. The north was on the whole less profuse in its display of applied ornament, less fond of classical ruins and mannerist tricks than the south; it was beginning in the last years of the century to develop a style distinguished by a greater use of arabesque and a liking for near-naturalistic floral designs.

As the sixteenth century drew to a close, the use of ever richer materials and ever more elaborate processes was making furniture far more expensive. The increased skill of furniture-makers was resulting in the appearance of articles whose body was wholly hidden beneath veneers and inlays, and whose decorative qualities therefore were no longer derived from exploiting the properties of the basic material, but from the application of ornament carried out in other materials. The more fashionable it became to expend large sums in this way, the more easily the earlier applied ornament of different coloured woods, or other reasonably cheap substances, was superseded by more expensive ones, by ivory or precious or semi-precious stones or metals. As this happened, the goldsmiths and silversmiths began to take a hand and such well-known craftsmen in metal as Wenzel Jamnitzer and Matthias Wallbaum turned their attention to furniture, particularly to small and potentially precious objects.

MUSEUMS AND COLLECTIONS

German furniture of the sixteenth century is on view at the following:

Germany: Germanisches Nationalmuseum, Nuremberg
Kunstgewerbe Museum, West Berlin
Bayerisches Nationalmuseum, Munich

Great Britain: Holyrood Palace, Edinburgh
Luton Hoo, Bedfordshire
Victoria and Albert Museum, London

FURTHER READING

A Social History of Furniture Design by J. Gloag, London, 1966.
Deutsche Möbel aus sieben Jahrhunderten by G. Schade, Leipzig, 1966.
World Furniture ed. by Helena Hayward, London, 1965.
Alte Möbel vom Mittelalter bis zum Jugenstil by S. Muller-Christensen, Munich, 1957.

The Stoneware of Germany

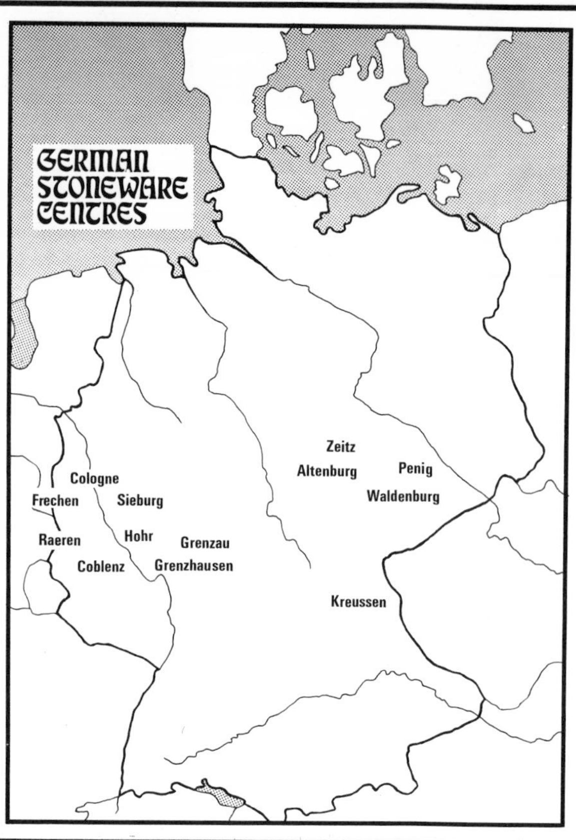

Geoffrey Wills

Stoneware, the characteristic pottery of the Rhineland and east Germany, was shaped and ornamented to suit the taste of many export markets.

Fig. 1 ***Jug***, *Cologne or Frechen, c.1570.*
This type of mottled brown-glazed stoneware is known as tigerware because its appearance resembles a tiger's coat. The jug was mounted in England with a silver-gilt cover, handle and base. (Victoria and Albert Museum, London.)

1

Museum Photo

Stoneware is a type of pottery made from clay, which is fired at a high temperature to produce a very hard material impervious to most liquids. The kilns in which it is baked have to be raised to between 1200° and 1400° centigrade and thus its manufacture is dependent on ample supplies of fuel. In Germany, the well-wooded slopes bordering the river Rhine provided not only sufficient timber to establish and maintain this important industry, but also deposits of suitable clay.

Stoneware naturally has a completely matt surface, but a finishing coat of glaze was usually added. This was applied in spite of the fact that stoneware vessels are watertight and it must be assumed that it was given a shiny appearance for reasons of decoration.

Pottery with the surface texture of the skin of an orange

The lead-based glazes normally employed on pottery would not withstand a high temperature. For stoneware it was discovered that common salt, introduced into the kiln at the time of greatest heat, resulted in a thin, colourless, even glaze. The pieces so treated almost always have a distinctively glossy and slightly wrinkled surface, which has the texture of the skin of an orange.

A small range of colours was available, either covering the whole article or emphasising some feature, by dipping in or brushing on a wash containing iron (for brown), cobalt (for blue), or manganese (for purple or black). The most popular was an all-over brown, which sometimes resulted in the mottled skin resembling miniature animal-markings seen on tigerware (Fig. 1). Equally characteristic is a deeply toned bright blue applied in contrast to the greyish background (Fig. 7).

Further embellishment took the form of silver or silver-gilt mounts, which demonstrate how highly their original owners valued the pieces. Jugs of tigerware were especially favoured for this treatment and many surviving examples have covers and foot-rims bearing date-letters of the late sixteenth century (Fig. 1).

The stoneware industry was established in the Rhineland by the late Middle Ages and reached its peak of production there in the fifteenth and sixteenth centuries. The numerous factories were situated in an area bordering the river between Cologne and Coblenz and there were other, smaller, centres in the east of the country. Much of the considerable output was exported throughout Europe, with inscriptions and decoration to suit the market, causing confusion as to the place of its manufacture.

One of the most important centres of stoneware production was Raeren where, in the second half of the sixteenth century, Jan Emens was active. He has been described as 'perhaps the greatest figure in the history of Rhenish stoneware'. A typical example of Emens's relief designs is the tall tankard, or *Schnelle*, (Fig. 2), which bears scenes from the story of Samson – Samson carrying off the gates of Gaza, Manoah's sacrifice, and Delilah cutting off the hair of Samson. His work is often signed with his initials, I.E., and is sometimes dated.

In about 1586 Emens began to produce a series of large jugs with rounded bodies and short necks, ornamented with bands of figures. These depict biblical and mythological scenes and in designing them he made use of contemporary engravings by Hans Sebald Beham, Etienne de Laune, Adrian

2

Museum Photo

3

Sotheby Photo

Fig. 2 ***Tankard, or Schnelle,*** *Raeren, c. 1570. Height 10 ins. This tankard is coated with a wash of brown, salt-glazed and decorated with reliefs depicting the story of Samson. (Fitzwilliam Museum, Cambridge. Glaisher Collection.)*

Fig. 3 ***As the old sing, so the young pipe*** *by Jacob Jordaens (1593–1678), Flemish. Oil on canvas, $57\frac{1}{4}$ x $85\frac{3}{4}$ ins. (Private Collection.)*

Fig. 4 ***Brown-glazed jug,*** *Cologne, Maximinenstrasse factory, c.1530. Height $4\frac{1}{8}$ ins. (Fitzwilliam Museum, Glaisher Collection.)*

Fig. 5 ***Inkstand,*** *Westerwald, c.1730. Height $15\frac{1}{2}$ ins. This inkstand is typical of the rather fanciful later wares produced in the Westerwald. (Fitzwilliam Museum, Glaisher Collection.)*

4

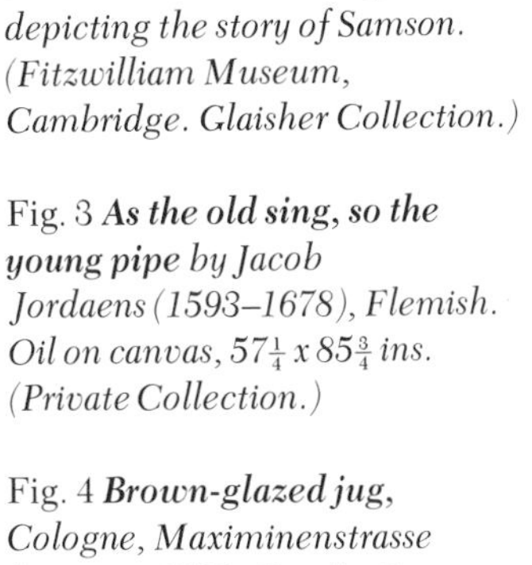

Museum Photo

5

Museum Photo

Collaert and others.

Early Raeren stoneware was brown in colour and while the production of this continued, a new type, with a grey body, to which decoration in blue was added, made its appearance. The ornament on it was often of a higher quality than hitherto, with the relief modelling showing notable clarity.

In addition to those of Jan Emens, initials found on the ware include those of members of the Mennicken family, of whom Baldem Mennicken has left dated work of between 1575 and 1584. As the letters were cut with the pattern of the mould when it was first made, and the mould might have remained in use for a hundred years or more, their presence, and that of a date, is no guarantee that a piece bearing them is of early manufacture.

At Siegburg, potteries were active from at least the fourteenth century and had been formed into a guild by about 1450. The majority of their output was in a near-white material that was frequently left unglazed. Some of the early pieces show patches of reddish-brown which were acquired by accident, while others bear an all-over faint tint of pink or pale brown.

Jugs and drinking-vessels of all kinds were made, but the most typical at Siegburg was the *schnelle*. Its distinctive tall and slender form was followed in the shaping of many other pieces, both at the time and for long afterwards.

As was commonplace in other centres, the Siegburg industry was confined to a few families, and the names of the Knütgens, Symons, Flachs and Omians were prominent over the years. In 1590, Anno Knütgen, with his sons Bertram and Rütger, left Siegburg and established themselves at Höhr, in the Westerwald, where they continued their craft. Their departure anticipated the virtual extinction of potting both at Siegburg and Raeren. In the course of the Thirty Years' War, which ravaged parts of Germany between 1618 and 1648, both these towns were sacked in 1632 by the army

16th century
German Pottery

Fig. 6 ***Wine-bottle or 'Bellarmine'**, partly brown, made either in Cologne or Frechen, second half of the sixteenth century. Height 7⅝ ins. The bottle is decorated with a bearded mask at the neck and five star-like medallions enclosing the head of a Roman soldier. (Fitzwilliam Museum, Glaisher Collection.)*

Fig. 7 ***Grey stoneware tankard,** Westerwald, 1700. Height 6 ins. From the 'Land of the Pot-bakers', this grey stoneware tankard is decorated in blue and manganese. (Fitzwilliam Museum, Glaisher Collection.)*

Fig. 8 ***Jug,** Bunzlau, mid-eighteenth century. Height 7⅛ ins. This jug is decorated with reliefs of flowers and leaves and has a Prussian eagle bearing the cypher of Frederick the Great. (Fitzwilliam Museum, Glaisher Collection.)*

Fig. 9 ***Tankard, or Schnelle,** bearing the initials L.W. Siegburg, c.1576. Height 9⅜ ins. Tankards were often decorated with religious scenes or scenes from history, like this suicide of Lucretia. (Fitzwilliam Museum, Glaisher Collection.)*

6

Museum Photo

7

Museum Photo

9

Museum Photo

of Gustavus of Sweden. Although some of the potteries were re-started, they never recovered their former prosperity.

Cologne, the important city and port on the Rhine, boasted three stoneware potteries, which were at the height of their production in the middle of the sixteenth century. All of them produced a grey-bodied material coated with a wash of brown and an overall glaze. Most examples have the speckled or mottled appearance that has earned the variety the name of tigerware.

The biggest of the potteries was situated in the Maximinenstrasse, where excavations have revealed evidence of the various types of articles that were made there. In particular, this factory was the source of many of the so-called 'Bellarmines', known also as Greybeards, *Bartmannskrüge* or *Barbmans*. They acquired the name by which they are best-known in England because of their supposed caricature-likeness to the Italian Catholic divine, Cardinal Roberto Bellarmino (1542–1621), whose publications incited anger among Protestants. The 'Bellarmine', with its bearded mask on the short neck was sometimes decorated with scrolled stems of oak leaves and roses, and occasionally patterns copied from published engravings were employed (Fig. 6).

The Komödiengasse factory, under the direction of Herman Wollters, made similar types of ware, but at a slightly later date. Excavations on the site in 1890 or 1891 laid bare a kiln and 'round about the ruins was heaped an accumulation of fragments and castaway pieces'. The third, the Eigelstein, factory differed little in its general output from the others. Some pieces bearing dates in the 1560s have been attributed to it.

The Cologne potters quarrelled for many years with the city authorities, and finally the latter triumphed. The kilns were closed and by the end of the sixteenth century the industry had been transferred to nearby Frechen.

Pottery of one kind or another was made at Frechen, about eight miles to the west of Cologne, from the Middle Ages. By the fifteenth century, stoneware was being produced in large quantities and, following the arrival of the Cologne potters in about 1600, the town attained considerable importance. However, its reputation rests more on the quantity of goods produced than on their artistic quality.

'Eat, drink and obey the Ten Commandments'

Although many types of vessels were made there, it would seem that the larger proportion comprised 'Bellarmines'. They were frequently made more attractive for foreign buyers by the addition of armorial shields. In some instances German inscriptions were translated for the benefit of distant buyers, but perfect accuracy was not always achieved, and the carelessness or illiteracy of the potters resulted in garbled lines like the injunction 'Drinck und Eate, Got and His Commandement nic not Vergeat', a version of 'Eat, drink and obey the Ten Commandments'.

The Westerwald district, because of the number of potteries in it, was named *Kännerbackerland* (literally, 'The Land of Pot-bakers'). It lay on the Rhine, opposite Coblenz, and the most important of the group of towns in it concerned with potting were Höhr, Grenzau and Grenzhausen. The industry began to assume consequence with the arrival there from Siegburg in 1590 of Anno Knütgen and his sons, and later, members of the Mennicken family from Raeren.

The former settled at Höhr and although they began predictably, making wares of the off-white Siegburg type, they later turned to producing a grey-coloured stoneware with painted blue decoration. It was a typical manufacture of all the potteries of the area, and few examples are traceable to any particular source.

The Mennickens went to Grenzhausen and, again, made the shapes and used the patterns with which they were already familiar. The initials of Johann are said to be 'perhaps the commonest on

Museum Photo

all Rhenish stoneware'. They brought with them the moulds used originally by Jan Emens and other Raeren craftsmen, retaining their initials.

The use of delicate relief ornaments waned towards the close of the seventeenth century. Decoration then took the form of applied rosettes, lion masks and other devices in conjunction with bands of incised lines and raised dots, all emphasised with blue, and sometimes purple, against the grey background. The furrows restrained the colour from flowing and in addition formed part of the basic pattern. As at Cologne, much of the production was made for export, and was suitably ornamented for the intended market. For England, the initials *G.R.* for Guglielmus Rex (William III of Orange), were the same as for the three Georges, so they are no indication of date.

In the mid-eighteenth century, fanciful pieces were produced, and the inkstand shown in Fig. 5 is representative of such elaborate essays. Birds and animals were similarly rendered and standing figures of men holding small pots, probably intended for use as salt-cellars, have been recorded.

Outside the Rhineland, a distinctive stoneware was manufactured at Kreussen, near Bayreuth, in Bavaria. Long known as a source of pottery stoves *(Haffner)*, stoneware became an important part of the output for most of the seventeenth century. The material is a light brown-grey, but it was invariably given a coating of colour, usually chocolate-brown but occasionally lighter in shade.

In the most distinctive articles the patterns are picked out in white and opaque colours against their sombre background. Alternatively, the designs were painted on a smooth surface, where the effect is no less telling. It has been mentioned that there is a strong resemblance between specimens of Kreussen stoneware and contemporary Bohemian glass, which was painted with enamels of the same kind. It is not unlikely that the same artists decorated both, as the glass industry was located at no great distance from the potteries.

Jugs, flasks and tankards were among the pieces made, and they were often decorated in stock patterns which have given their name to the type. They include *Planetenkrüge*, painted with figures representing the Planets; *Apostolenkrüge* (Fig. 10), with figures of the Apostles; and *Hochzeitkrüge*, with marriage scenes.

In the south and south-east of Germany were a number of potteries which made interesting stoneware from the sixteenth century onwards. At Penig, Zeitz and Waldenburg (Saxony) distinctive types were made, the latter decorating dark brown-coloured jugs with bands of incised dots and zig-zags. However, the various potteries copied one another, and precise allocation of specimens is not always possible.

At Altenburg (Thuringia) brown-surfaced pieces were also ornamented by means of a roulette, while in the Voigtland area, in the south-west corner of Saxony, coloured painting in the manner of Kreussen was used. From there also came tankards *(Perlkrüge)* decorated with simple patterns of flowers, figures and other subjects formed from small dots of clay in a contrasting colour to that of the background.

At Bunzlau, in the province of Silesia, now part of Poland, an old-established pottery produced stoneware from the eighteenth century. The grey body was disguised by a coating of coffee or rust-colour, which was often decorated with applied reliefs in a yellowish clay (Fig. 8). Sometimes painting was added, and this was further embellished with gilding.

It may be noted that some of the above-mentioned potteries continued in operation, or were revived, in comparatively modern times. They made articles of traditional types, and these are not always easy to differentiate from the truly old. For instance, it is known that in the late nineteenth century, forgeries of early Siegburg pieces were made at Höhr.

Museum Photo

Fig. 10 ***Tankard, or Apostolenkrüge,*** *Kreussen, first half of the seventeenth century. Height* $7\frac{1}{8}$ *ins. (Fitzwilliam Museum, Glaisher Collection.)*

FURTHER READING

World Ceramics ed. by R. J. Charleston, Chapter IV, 'Stoneware', Germany, by F. A. Dreier, London, 1968.

European Ceramic Art by W. B. Honey, 'Rhenish Stoneware', London, 1952.

The Ancient Art Stoneware of the Low Countries and Germany by M. L. E. Solon, London, 1892.

Jamnitzer & German traditions in Bronze and Silver

Anthony Radcliffe

The German flair for metalwork combined with the new forms of the Italian Renaissance to create pieces of an exceptional ingenuity, intricacy and magnificence.

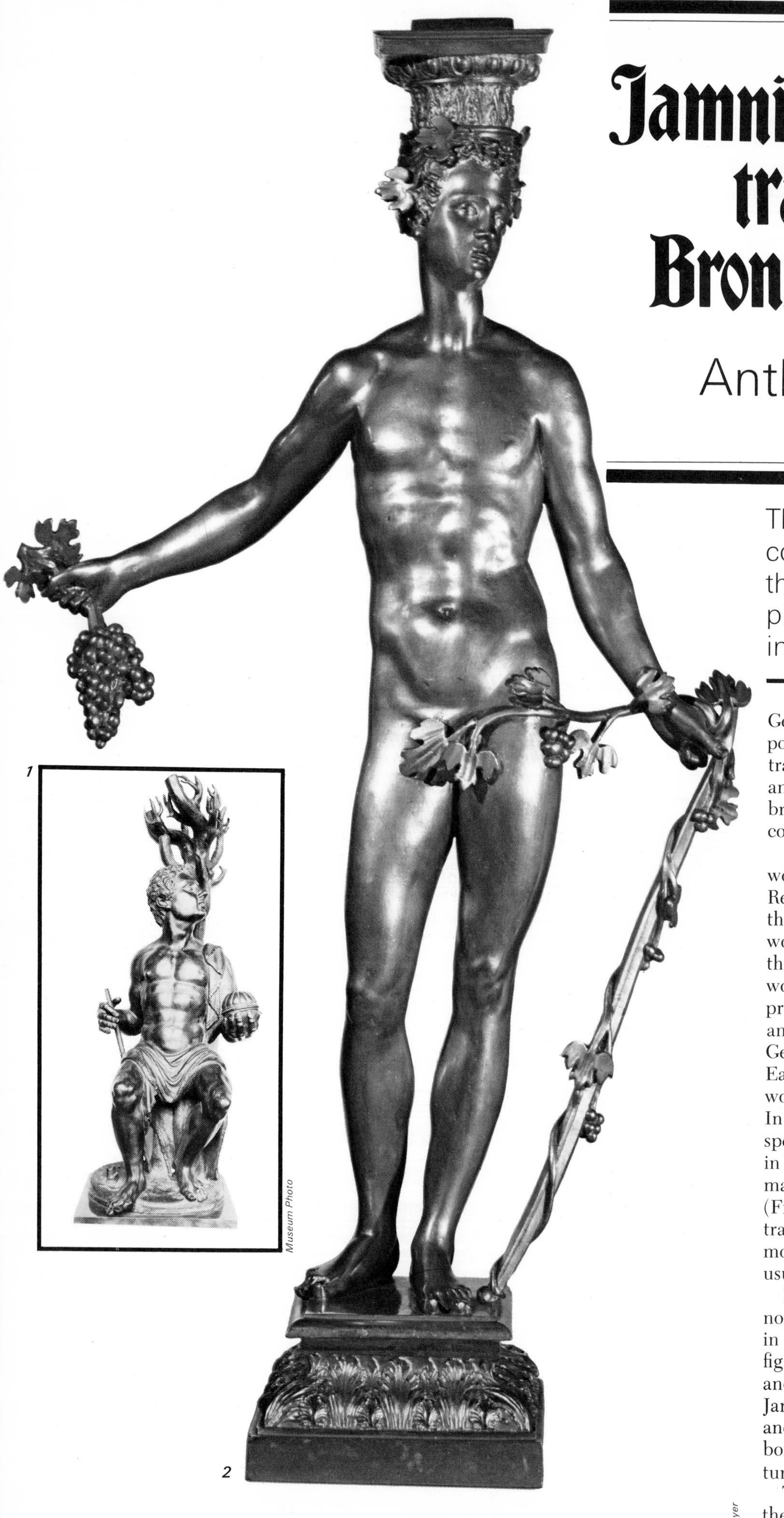

1

Museum Photo

2

Photo Meyer

Germany in the early sixteenth century was the possessor of a long-standing and vigorous native tradition of craftsmanship in metal. Its work in silver and gold was famous throughout Europe, and its bronze and brass foundries were the heirs to a continuous line of figure-work in the base metals.

It was to be expected that German metalwork would come to reflect the new forms of the Italian Renaissance, but there were certain factors besides the weight of native tradition which ensured that it would retain a distinct national character. One of these was the guild system. Whereas in Italy a single workshop, such as that of Verrocchio, might produce paintings, sculpture in stone and bronze, and vessels and figure-work in silver and gold, in Germany all these crafts were rigidly separated. Each craft had its own specialist practitioners who would not trespass on the territory of another craft. In the case of sculptural work in metal this had special repercussions: the production of a statue in bronze required the collaboration of a sculptor to make the model and a bronze-founder to cast it (Fig. 4), and, since in Germany the sculptural tradition was one of carving rather than of modelling, the model provided for the founder was usually of wood.

In Italy at this time a bronze statue would normally have been modelled in wax and then cast in bronze by the sculptor himself. In the case of figure-work in silver, the same practice prevailed, and even a supreme artist like the great Wenzel Jamnitzer who minutely designed his own pieces and is believed to have had recourse to a carver for boxwood models from his drawings which he, in turn, could cast in silver.

The renaissance style in German metalwork was therefore in the nature of an Italian graft on to a thriving native stock. The influence was felt earliest and most powerfully in the two wealthy south

Fig. 1 *(far left)* ***Paris**, probably cast in the foundry of Marx Labenwolf the Younger, Augsburg, c.1570. Bronze, height 21 ins. This statuette is the only surviving component of a fountain with figures depicting the Judgement of Paris, which once stood in the garden of the Duke of Württemberg in Stuttgart. Augsburg founders specialised in making complex bronze garden fountains in the second half of the sixteenth century. (Württembergisches Landesmuseum, Stuttgart.)*

Fig. 2 *(middle left)* ***Autumn** by Wenzel Jamnitzer (1508–85), Nuremberg, c.1575. Gilt-bronze, height 28 ins. This figure of Bacchus, representing Autumn, is one of four classical deities symbolising the four seasons which formerly supported an elaborate ten-foot high table fountain supplied to the Emperor Rudolf II in 1578. The rest of the fountain, made entirely of silver, was melted down for its metal in 1747. This sophisticated statuette demonstrates Jamnitzer's familiarity with the Italian high renaissance sculptural idiom. (Kunsthistorisches Museum, Vienna.)*

Fig. 3 ***Mars and Venus** by Konrad Meit (c.1475/80-after 1536), Malines, c.1520. Bronze, height 13½ ins. Meit, a distinguished boxwood carver, also made a few bronzes while he was working for Margaret of Austria. These are the nearest approximation by a German artist to Italian bronzes of the time. (Germanisches Nationalmuseum, Nuremberg.)*

Fig. 4 ***Nude warrior**, cast by Stephan Godl (active early sixteenth century) probably from a model by Leonhard Magt (died 1532), Innsbruck, 1525–26. Bronze, height 20⅞ ins. This remarkable statuette is the result of a wager made by the Archduke Ferdinand of Tyrol. Godl was required to cast a figure so perfectly that it needed no chiselling. (Alten Galerie au Landesmuseum Joanneum, Graz.)*

3

Museum Photo

4

Museum Photo

German commercial cities of Nuremberg and Augsburg lying on the trade-route from Venice to the North, both of which possessed vigorous metal-working industries. In Nuremberg the great bronze foundry of the Vischer family provides a striking example of the gradual assimilation of the new Italian style into the indigenous craft tradition.

The Vischer workshop had been founded in Nuremberg in 1453 by Hermann Vischer the Elder and under his mastership and, from 1489, that of his son Peter the Elder, it had specialised in providing magnificent funerary monuments in bronze throughout southern Germany. In 1488 it received its most important commission, a canopy for the shrine of Saint Sebaldus in the Sebalduskirche in Nuremberg the design for which was produced by Peter. His drawing still survives, conceived in an unadulterated late gothic style. The project was shelved for twenty years and when work eventually started in 1508 it was initially to the original design. At about this time, Peter's second son, Peter the Younger, made a journey to Italy. His journey must have followed fairly closely on Dürer's return to Nuremberg in February 1507 from his second visit to Venice, and, although little is known about it, we may assume that, like Dürer, he would have visited Venice and Padua, both of which were at that time thriving centres of bronze sculpture. Some of his surviving drawings testify to a close study of Italian bronze statuettes.

Putti clambering all over the canopy and occupying every possible foothold

Over the next few years there seems to have been a struggle for ascendancy between the new ideas brought back from Italy by the son and the traditional outlook of the father and, in 1514, the commission for the canopy was removed from the elder Peter and transferred to his eldest son, Hermann the Younger. But although Hermann was now nominally in charge, it was the younger Peter who seems to have been the controlling mind in the modification of the design. By this time the base of the structure, signed by the father, was already completed but, outside and above this, new types of figures appear which are unmistakably of Italian origin – allegorical male and female figures, satyrs, mermaids, tritons, grotesques and above all *putti*, the ubiquitous nude winged boys of the Italian Renaissance, who clamber all over the canopy and seem to occupy every possible foothold on it. The figures of the Sebaldus shrine, particularly the *putti*, had a considerable issue in bronze statuettes on the Italian model from the Vischer workshop, and later works in bronze by the younger Hermann and Peter show a strong Italian influence.

The clear outlines and smooth surfaces proclaim the German origin of the inkwell

Two inkwells in bronze by Peter the Younger, both today in the Ashmolean Museum, Oxford, show a clear progression in German interpretation of a north Italian type of object. One is dated 1525 and the other, which bears no date, must have been made some ten years earlier. The earlier inkwell (Fig. 8), even though the basic composition is entirely Italian and the figure imitated from one on the reverse of an Italian medal, could not be taken for anything but a German production. The hard clear outlines and smooth surfaces of the figure, the form of the urn and the light colour of the unpatinated surface, all proclaim this. The later inkwell (Fig. 9), however, represents a serious attempt on the part of the artist to approximate as nearly as he was able to a Paduan bronze of the time. In this inkwell the modelling of the figure is much more subtle, the form of the urn more restrained and classical and the surface is covered with the dense black lacquer used in Padua.

The closest approximation by a German artist of this time to the independent bronze statuettes of Italy, which were made to stand beside actual classical bronzes, is to be found in the work of Konrad Meit, a native of Worms. In his group of Mars and Venus of about 1520 (Fig. 3), the figure of Venus is derived from an engraving by the Italian Cristofano Robetta, while that of Mars is directly based on a north Italian bronze statuette of the early

16th century
German Bronzes

Fig. 5 ***Table fountain with a figure of Actaeon,*** *artist and founder unknown, Nuremberg or Augsburg, c.1550–70. Bronze, height 32½ ins. (Victoria and Albert Museum, London.)*

5

Museum Photo

6

Museum Photo

Fig. 6 ***Christ Child Blessing,*** *cast by Pankraz Labenwolf (1492–1563) from a model by an unknown sculptor, Nuremberg, c.1550–60. Bronze, height 19⅛ ins. (Victoria and Albert Museum.)*

sixteenth century which was itself an imitation of a classical bronze. But the statuettes of Meit and the inkwells of Peter Vischer are exceptional in Germany. Meit, a distinguished sculptor in wood and stone, was, at the time at which he produced his bronzes, attached to the sophisticated and cosmopolitan court of Margaret of Austria, Regent of the Netherlands, at Malines. As a court artist he was free of the restrictions imposed by the guild system on the workshops of Nuremberg and Augsburg, working in an atmosphere of patronage very like that which operated in the courts of Italy. As for Peter Vischer's two inkwells, they were made for his own private use as essays in a genre of which the workshops of Padua retained a virtual monopoly.

Mechanical devices worked by water-power and clockwork

The city of Trent stands mid-way between Venice and the Brenner Pass on the old trade route which leads to the cities of southern Germany, poised, as it were, between the two cultures, and it is significant that when in the 1530s Cardinal Bernhard von Cles, the cultivated Bishop of Trent, wanted bronze desk furniture for his study in his new renaissance palace, the Palazzo Magno – inkwells, pen-caskets and bells – he ordered them from the foundry of the Grandi family in Padua. For the bronze fountain for the courtyard of the palace, however, he placed the order in Nuremberg.

The *Lustbrunnen*, or pleasure-fountain, whether as a feature for the courtyard or the dining-table, was a genre in which the bronze foundries of Nuremberg and Augsburg specialised and excelled in the sixteenth century. The earlier fountains are comparatively simple, but in time they became increasingly complicated and ingenious, incorporating a large number of figures, human and animal, and mechanical devices worked by water-power and clockwork. Many of the German bronze statuettes which survive from the middle and later years of the sixteenth century were originally components of such fountains, all but a very few of which – and all the most complex of which – were dismembered in the course of years.

The fountain for the palace at Trent was ordered in 1531 from the Nuremberg foundry of Pankraz Labenwolf, a former apprentice of the Vischer workshop, who was to dominate the Nuremberg bronze industry through the middle years of the sixteenth century. It was surmounted by a sculptural group of Apollo and Daphne, for which the model was supplied by the sculptor Peter Flötner. This fountain no longer survives, but the fruit of another exactly contemporary collaboration between Flötner and Labenwolf can still be seen today in the Apollo fountain which stands in the courtyard of the Pellerhaus in Nuremberg. The Apollo fountain, surmounted by its superb nude figure, ranks as one of the great sculptural masterpieces of the German Renaissance. It is a sophisticated essay in the Italian style. Flötner's design for the figure was inspired by an engraving by Jacopo de' Barbari, the Venetian whose work was so influential in Germany and whose prints were so eagerly studied by Dürer in his attempt to master the secret of human proportion; the decoration of the pedestal testifies

7

Museum Photo

to a careful study of Paduan decorative bronzes.

Labenwolf himself must be counted among the most accomplished masters of bronze-founding of his time. In terms of technical refinement his work is in no way inferior to the productions of the Italian workshops of that date, and it is superior to those of any contemporary German foundry. But although he contracted himself for the bronzes, he made and signed some of them with his own name; he was not an artist in the sense that Peter Vischer was, and he was dependent upon sculptors to provide him with models. The hands of several other sculptors besides Flötner can be discerned in works which he cast, all of them unknown to us by name. The hand of one such unknown but highly talented sculptor can be seen in a beautiful statuette of the Christ Child of about 1550 (Fig. 6), which at one time was believed to be Italian but which exhibits all the technical characteristics of Labenwolf's shop.

He cluttered his fountains with figures of animals

A restrained Italianate elegance marks most of the works cast by Pankraz Labenwolf in the middle years of the century. Some years later in Augsburg, bronze fountains of much greater complexity but of notably less refinement were produced in the foundries of Hans Reisinger and Marx Labenwolf, a member of another branch of the Labenwolf family. None of these survive, but some are recorded in engravings. A vigorous figure of a unicorn by Reisinger survives in Dresden as a record of the figures of animals with which he cluttered his fountains, and in the museum at Stuttgart is a splendid figure of Paris which is almost certainly the only surviving component of a fountain with a group of the Judgement of Paris made by Marx Labenwolf soon after 1570 for the garden of the Duke of Württemberg at Stuttgart (Fig. 1).

Museum Photo

Fig. 7 ***Design for the Merkel Centrepiece*** *by Wenzel Jamnitzer, Nuremberg, before 1549. Pen and wash, height 36¼ ins. This full-sized working drawing for the most sumptuous of Jamnitzer's surviving works provides a fascinating record of the artist's creative process. A few changes were introduced during the making of the centrepiece, notably in the allegorical female figure, representing Mother Earth, which forms the stem. (Germanisches Nationalmuseum.)*

Fig. 8 ***Inkwell*** *by Peter Vischer the Younger (1487–1528), Nuremberg, c.1515. Bronze, height 6½ ins. The figure, which probably represents Vanity, is imitated from the reverse of an Italian medal of about 1512. The inkwell was almost certainly made for the artist's personal use, and bears his motto* 'Vitam non mortem recogita' *(Reflect on life, not death). (Ashmolean Museum, Oxford.)*

Fig. 9 ***Inkwell*** *by Peter Vischer the Younger, Nuremberg, 1525. Bronze, height 7½ ins. Like the inkwell in Fig. 8, this was made for the artist's own use. Not only does it bear his device of two speared fish and his motto, but also his initials and the date 1525. (Ashmolean Museum.)*

Fountains for the dining-table were made in both Nuremberg and Augsburg. A rare and complete example of a fairly modest bronze table-fountain which might have been made in either city between about 1550 and 1570 is in the Victoria and Albert Museum (Fig. 5). One might imagine that it was made for a prosperous burgher household. But the largest and most complex table fountain ever made was commissioned in 1556 by the Emperor Maximilian II from the great Nuremberg goldsmith Wenzel Jamnitzer. It took twenty-two years to complete and was finally delivered to Maximilian's son and successor the Emperor Rudolf II in Prague in 1578.

Figures symbolic of the great monarchies and the social hierarchy from emperor to peasant

This fountain was made almost entirely of silver, and was melted down for its metal in the eighteenth century, but it was very fully described by a German student who visited Prague in the mid-seventeenth century in terms which today seem hardly credible. Ten feet high by five feet wide, it was designed as a symbol of the empire. The central section was in the form of an imperial crown enclosing several series of symbolic figures, complete modelled landscapes with mountains and flowing rivers which worked models of mills and a representation of the sky with clouds and birds. Surmounting the crown was a celestial globe with sun and moon operated by clockwork. Above this were figures of the archangels and at the apex of the whole structure was a figure of Jupiter seated on an eagle. Outside the crown were figures symbolic of the great monarchies and of all the degrees of social hierarchy from emperor to peasant, and the complex included two scenes of dances operated by water power. This whole fantastic construction was supported on four large figures representing the seasons (Fig. 2), which, since for the sake of strength they were made of the base metal, bronze, are the only components which have survived. These four figures, of extraordinary beauty and sophistication, indicate that the fountain was not only a work of scarcely believable ingenuity but one executed in an advanced style and with great refinement in detail.

The delicacy of Jamnitzer's work in silver is attested by many highly complex works on a more modest scale which have survived intact, of which the most splendid is the so-called Merkel centrepiece (Fig. 7). This piece, which was bought from him in 1549 by the city of Nuremberg, exhibits practically the whole of his decorative repertory, with casts direct from nature of insects and reptiles, and flowers and grasses so fine that they react to a draught, the surfaces enriched in parts with both fired and unfired enamelling. Like the imperial fountain it is designed to a philosophical programme. Throughout his career Jamnitzer oscillated between a wide variety of styles, including gothic, renaissance and mannerist which could either be encrusted with fantastic detail and encumbered with a profusion of naturalistic growths, as in the Merkel centrepiece, or broadly modelled with a comparatively restrained sculptural elegance as in a ewer in Munich of about 1570; the latter is based on two nautilus shells and is possibly his most beautiful and original work.

The accomplished sculptural qualities and advanced style of the four supporting bronze figures for Jamnitzer's imperial fountain have led to speculation as to whether they might have been modelled for him by the Dutch sculptor Johann Gregor von der Schardt, who was in close contact with the latest sculptural developments in Italy and who was for a time resident in Nuremberg, but this cannot be proved.

Whether or not Schardt modelled the figures for Jamnitzer's fountain, they herald the arrival of a new high renaissance sculptural style in south Germany, just as Schardt's presence in Nuremberg in the early 1570s foreshadows a new era in south German bronze sculpture which was to be dominated by Netherlanders like himself. Schardt, a native of Nijmegen, was a close contemporary of the great Flemish sculptor who settled in Florence, Giovanni Bologna, and he was soon followed to Germany by two younger Netherlandish artists who had been trained in Giovanni Bologna's workshop in Florence. The first to arrive in 1580 was Hubert Gerhard of s'Hertogenbosch who was to work in Augsburg, Munich and Innsbruck, followed by Adriaen de Vries, of the Hague, who from 1601 was established as court sculptor in the service of the Emperor Rudolf II at Prague.

The new style forged by Giovanni Bologna in Florence which Gerhard and de Vries brought with them to Germany was to have tremendous repercussions throughout Europe. In a practical sense in the foundries of southern Germany its impact drastically upset the traditions of generations. Not only did it require considerable technical innovations before it could even be reproduced in metal, but it firmly placed the founder in a subordinate position to the sculptor. It was perhaps only at this point at the very close of the sixteenth century that the German medieval tradition in bronze sculpture finally came to an end.

Silver from Augsburg & Nuremberg

Anthony Radcliffe

1

Gerhard Howald

Fig. 1 **St. Eligius in his workshop** by Niklaus Manuel Deutsch the Elder (*c.*1484–1530), Bern, 1515. Tempera and oil on panel, 47 x 32 ins. St. Eligius (588–660), a goldsmith of legendary skill in the seventh century, was a well-documented figure who worked for Dagobert I, by whom he was appointed Bishop of Noyon and Tournai. After canonisation, he became the patron saint of metalworkers. This painting, signed by the German-Swiss artist Niklaus Manuel Deutsch and dated 1515, shows the interior of a typical German goldsmith's workshop of the early sixteenth century. The Saint and two assistants are depicted at work on chalices with the tools of their craft lying about on the table. In the background a boy works the bellows for the furnace.
(Kunstmuseum, Bern.)

Fig. 3 (right). **Covered goblet** by Friedrich Hillebrandt (d.1608), Nuremberg, 1595. Nautilus shell mounted in silver-gilt, height 15$\frac{1}{8}$ ins. The most distinguished member of a family of goldsmiths in Nuremberg, Friedrich Hillebrandt specialised in the setting of nautilus shells in elaborate silver mounts, although the same art was also practised by other German goldsmiths, among them Wenzel Jamnitzer. This is one of Hillebrandt's most splendid surviving pieces, superbly executed with fine mannerist detail, although it is weaker in design than comparable pieces by Jamnitzer. The shell is supported by a figure of Atlas which shows a strong Venetian influence, and the cover is surmounted by Neptune and his sea-horses. (Germanisches Nationalmuseum, Nuremberg.)

2

Scala

Fig. 2 **Flask** by Hans Karl of Nuremberg (active early seventeenth century), Salzburg, 1602. Enamelled gold, height 8$\frac{7}{8}$ ins. This beautiful flask, which is inscribed '*Hans Karl : fecit : 1602*' on the bottom, bears the arms of Wolf Dietrich von Raitenau, Archbishop of Salzburg, for whom it was made. Formerly in the Treasury at Salzburg, it was acquired by Ferdinand III, Grand Duke of Tuscany, during the period of his exile in the early nineteenth century. On his return to Florence, he brought it with him together with many other superb pieces of German renaissance metalwork which he had appropriated from the Salzburg treasury.
(Museo degli Argenti, Florence.)

Scala

4

Museum Photo

5

K. Hoddle

Fig. 4 **The Schlüsselfelder Nef**, possibly by Hans Krug, Nuremberg, *c.*1503. Silver, parcel-gilt, height 30 ins.
At one time attributed to Albrecht Dürer the Elder, father of the famous artist, this centrepiece, which bears the Nuremberg mark, was probably made just about the time of his death in 1502. It has always, as far as is known, been in the possession of the patrician family of the Schlüsselfelder in Nuremberg, and was probably made for them. The centrepiece in the form of a ship, known as a nef, was an important type in the late gothic goldsmith's work in France and Germany. It was used in the same way as the 'great salt' in England, to mark the place of the host at table. This example is a more accurate representation than most showing the precise nautical detail of an actual ship of the time and its crew. The influence of the Renaissance can be seen in the supporting figure of a siren or mermaid. (Germanisches Nationalmuseum, Nuremberg, lent by the Schlüsselfelder family.)

Fig. 5 **Salt,** Nuremberg, 1550. Silver, parcel-gilt, height $3\frac{1}{4}$ ins. This severely simple salt in the renaissance style is decorated with gilt medallions after the sculptor Peter Flötner, an extremely influential artist in the German Renaissance, who died in 1546, a few years before the salt was made. (S. J. Phillips, Ltd., London.)

Dürer and the print-makers

Professor Ettlinger

1

Giraudon

Fig. 1 ***Self-Portrait*** *by Albrecht Dürer (1471–1528), dated 1493. Dürer's earliest painted self-portrait was executed when he was twenty-two years old to celebrate his betrothal. Even at this early stage in his career he had mastered the drawing of structure and anatomy which were so important to his graphic style, as we can see from his particularly sensitive treatment of the hands. In the detailed study of the plant he holds, Dürer shows the keen interest in nature that was to last throughout his life. (Louvre, Paris.)*

Dürer brought to print-making not only new techniques but a fertile imagination. For the first time woodcuts and engravings provided more than just information and instruction; they became works of art in their own right.

Our attitude to prints differs fundamentally from that current in the days of their inception. The modern collector looks for the hand of some individual master, for evidence of technical skill and refinement, for good impressions – in short, he regards the print as a work of art and an object of beauty. But such was not the case in the early-fifteenth century when they were first circulated. Originally their role was both humbler and more significant, for they served as a means of communication and a source of information. As long as prints – like all other forms of art – were, so to speak, an 'applied art', it was their social function which mattered, not their aesthetic value; artistic perfection, let alone originality, counted only when it enhanced their efficiency as a means of communication. One may say that, as a method of disseminating knowledge and ideas, the graphic arts were at that time closer to the letter-press than to painting and it should be remembered that the origins of both belong to the same epoch, though prints preceded books by a few decades.

The immense and ever-growing popularity of prints

If prints originally had specific and practical uses, we can say – and with a happy degree of certainty not always allowed to the historian – that the first artist to make prints for art's sake was Albrecht Dürer and this at a significant moment. In order to understand Dürer's revolutionary attitude to print-making, it is first of all necessary to look at fifteenth-century techniques. We can neither date nor localize exactly the beginnings of the woodcut and the engraving, beyond saying that they must have originated in south Germany around the year 1400. In spite of the fact that the techniques employed in the making of woodcuts and engravings had been known for centuries, we may still speak of their 'invention', since before this period nobody had hit on the idea of applying these techniques to the mass-production of images on paper.

In order to make a woodcut the design is drawn on, or transferred to, the surface of a wood-block (Fig. 4). The parts which are to appear white are cut out with a knife, or graver, and the block is then inked over and can be printed by hand or on an ordinary printing-press. Woodcuts are usually referred to as 'relief prints' since the impression is made by the high ridges left standing after the cutting-out process. The earliest examples are somewhat primitive outline cuts but, as the technique became more refined, increasingly complex patterns of hatching were used to indicate modelling, light and shade. The basic method had already been used by the Egyptians for fabric-printing and it was fairly commonly used during the Middle Ages for the same purpose and also for decorating wallpaper.

An engraving, by contrast, is an 'intaglio print'. The impression is produced by the ink from the grooves cut into a metal plate, usually of copper. Again, the basic methods of engraving in metal had been practised by goldsmiths and armourers since antiquity but never before for the printing of pictures, though pulls may occasionally have been made in order to record a pattern. On account of the more costly material and the rather intricate technique involved, engravings were more expensive than woodcuts and hence directed at the more affluent classes.

The historian must be intrigued by the cause of the immense and ever-growing popularity of prints during the fifteenth century, which extended well into the sixteenth, for it cannot be attributed only to the romantic notion of the alleged religious fervour of the epoch around 1500, when mankind once again expected apocalyptic happenings.

A purely material but nevertheless decisive factor was that paper became widely available during the fifteenth century. It had been known, of course, for a long time in the Orient and some did find its way to Europe. The first paper-mill was established in Germany in 1391, though there were earlier ones in Italy and France. The introduction of paper made the manufacture of cheap prints possible since parchment was costly.

More important, however, was the mentality

which demanded cheap images in plenty. If we look at the surviving prints of the fifteenth century – and it is certain that only a fraction survive – we are struck by the fact that the majority (but by no means all) depict religious subjects of a particular kind. Biblical narratives – a regular feature of medieval illustration – are rare, except for scenes from the Passion and from the Life of Mary. Instead we find Christ, the Saints, the Virgin. Clearly such images, however crude, were made for contemplation and devotion. Their original function is also evident from the fact that many of them were discovered stuck into religious books, on pews and choir-stalls. And this devotional purpose persisted well into the sixteenth century, as a glance through the output of Dürer or Cranach shows. These prints served a religion which had become more private and personal since the days of the monumental cycles of sculpture adorning gothic cathedrals. Of this general tendency there is, of course, ample evidence in the theological literature of the period.

2

Courtauld Institute of Art

Fig. 2 ***Sea-monster** by Dürer*, c.*1501*.
Engraving *The significance of this strange scene has never come to light but it is quite possible that it illustrated an old folk legend.*

But devotion was not the only purpose for which prints were produced. The age was one of great curiosity and a growing hunger for information and instruction. The catch-phrase 'The Discovery of the World and of Man' has become a commonplace in characterising the aspirations of the epoch, and in this quest, too, the print was a popular aid. The unlettered could understand it and, for those who could read, it provided something in addition to the letter-press. Hence we find woodcuts and engravings with views of towns, with plants or animals, with portraits of the famous; but we also encounter the forerunner of the news-sheet with its depiction of monsters, marvels from afar, catastrophes. Finally, the many satirical prints – particularly of the Reformation period – must be mentioned, when for the first time in history visual political propaganda was widely used and even artists such as Dürer, Cranach and Altdorfer did not find it beneath their dignity to contribute.

The centres of production were the larger towns such as Nuremberg, Basle, Strasbourg or Ulm – places also famous as centres of early book production and publishing. The maker of prints is described as *Briefmaler* or *Formschneider*, the former term designating the craftsman who decorated documents, edicts, broadsheets and indulgences and who, on account of experience, could also provide images of saints and the very popular playing-cards. A contemporary chronicler reports that in the fifteenth century the Ulm *Briefmaler* used to send crates full of cards to Italy, Sicily and the farthest corners of the earth.

Prints were sold in churches and at markets and fairs

Engravers always worked their own plates, but we do not know whether the designer and cutter for a woodcut were always the same person. The *Formschneider*, as his name implies, was a specialist who cut the wood-blocks, and he was probably a carpenter by training. In towns where he did not have his own guild he belonged to that of the carpenters and this led sometimes to conflicts reminiscent of today's union squabbles. One rather independent practitioner of the craft insisted that he had really nothing to do with the making of furniture, that the cutting of wood-blocks for illustrations was an altogether different task and that above all he collaborated with the clergy. Trade-unionism was stronger, however, and he did not get away with this excuse. Incidentally, the reference to working with the clergy is an important pointer to the source of the imagery of these devotional prints. They were not spontaneous folk art (as has been claimed) but made to order under the direction of educated men.

Religious prints seem to have been distributed in churches, monasteries and pilgrimage centres. A charming Flemish annunciation of the fifteenth century – derived from the *Mérode Altar-piece* attributed to Robert Campin – shows such a print prominently displayed over the mantelpiece. This usage introduces an interesting social phenomenon, for cheap prints in the home must have been substitutes for expensive paintings. The wealthy and powerful would have small painted altar-pieces in their private chapels – they owned lavishly decorated breviaries, or books of hours, illuminated by some famous artist – but poorer people had to make do with mass-produced and often inferior prints. It is therefore interesting to note that these – like the

'Penny Plain', 'Two-penny Coloured' of the nineteenth century – were sometimes crudely tinted, to increase their effect and simulate a painting.

While prints could certainly be obtained in churches – in some, a *Briefkapelle* was set aside for their sale – they were also traded at markets and fairs. Dürer's correspondence and diaries give an interesting insight into the trading of them and it seems likely that in this respect he followed accepted practice. From a letter we hear that old Frau Dürer sold the *Kunstware* at a fair held on a religious feast day and that Dürer's wife travelled to the big Frankfurt fair to sell prints there. But by the sixteenth century there were also agents or print dealers. Dürer, always a good businessman, laments the death of his agent in Rome because he lost stock and money with him.

Dürer's employment of an agent in Rome is surely an indication of his international standing, but we should also remember that the export of prints from Germany had flourished since the fifteenth century. As early as 1441 we hear of a petition addressed by the Venetian woodcutters to the Signoria asking for protection against imports threatening their business.

A few points peculiar to engraving should be noted. Since engravers had at their command a more pliable technique, they were able to use a richer vocabulary in figure drawing, light and shade, perspective and design. It is significant that they never formed their own guilds but joined those of the goldsmiths or more often of the painters. An engraving such as the *Judgment of Solomon*, from the hand of the mid-fifteenth-century Master ES, shows complete familiarity with the subtleties of contemporary Flemish painting, replacing colour by an amazing skill in the use of the burin, the tool used for engraving on copper.

One further use of engravings must be mentioned. A print like Martin Schongauer's *Censer* (Fig. 7), can only have been made to serve as a model for goldsmiths and there are other examples which prove that engravings were circulated in workshops, taking the place of medieval pattern-books.

Dürer's graphic work served for devotion, instruction and information

Dürer (Fig. 1) was the son of a goldsmith, the godson of a publisher and the pupil of an artist who was both a painter and illustrator. He was an admirer of Schongauer, and after his training in Nuremberg worked for a while in Basle, supplying woodcut book-illustrations. Moreover, he improved his technique as a draughtsman by copying, or rather tracing, Italian engravings. Most important of all, his work brought him into contact with publishers and scholars; he visited Italy and was thus in touch with the aims and achievements of renaissance artists and critics.

Dürer's graphic work may still be divided into the familiar categories for it serves for devotion, instruction and information. The celebrated *St. Jerome* engraving – a miracle of its kind – firmly belongs to the tradition of the print showing a popular saint; and a woodcut such as *The Penitent*, though showing David chastising himself before the Ark, has an obvious devotional character since the

Fig. 3 ***St. John's vision of Christ and the seven candlesticks*** *by Dürer, from* The Apocalypse, *1498. Woodcut.*
Dürer's visual imagery was completely revolutionary. If one compares this visionary scene from the Apocalypse *with the earlier fifteenth-century Apocalyptic representation in Fig. 8, the extent of his originality can be realised.*

3

Courtauld Institute of Art

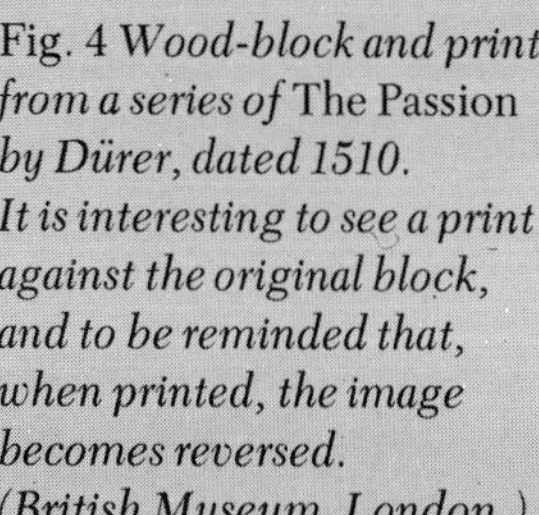

Fig. 4 *Wood-block and print from a series of* The Passion *by Dürer, dated 1510.*
It is interesting to see a print against the original block, and to be reminded that, when printed, the image becomes reversed. (British Museum, London.)

4

R. B. Fleming

Fig. 5 ***The artist drawing a reclining woman*** *by Dürer. Woodcut. Dürer made several studies showing techniques for drawing perspectives. This one shows how, by translating what he sees through the upright graph on to the equivalent squares of his working paper, he will be able to represent the awkward perspective accurately.*

5

Courtauld Institute of Art

Fig. 6 ***St. Christopher***, *German, 1423. Woodcut. Woodcuts were often tinted and hung on the walls of houses as the poor man's substitute for expensive paintings. (John Rylands Library, Manchester.)*

Fig. 7 ***Censer*** *by Martin Schongauer (1445?–1491). Engraving. Prints such as this were often used in the same way as pattern books and were circulated as models for goldsmiths' use. (British Museum, London.)*

Fig. 8 ***Scene from the Apocalypse*** *by an unknown artist, Netherlands or south Germany, c.1465. (John Rylands Library, Manchester).*

6

Library Photo

7

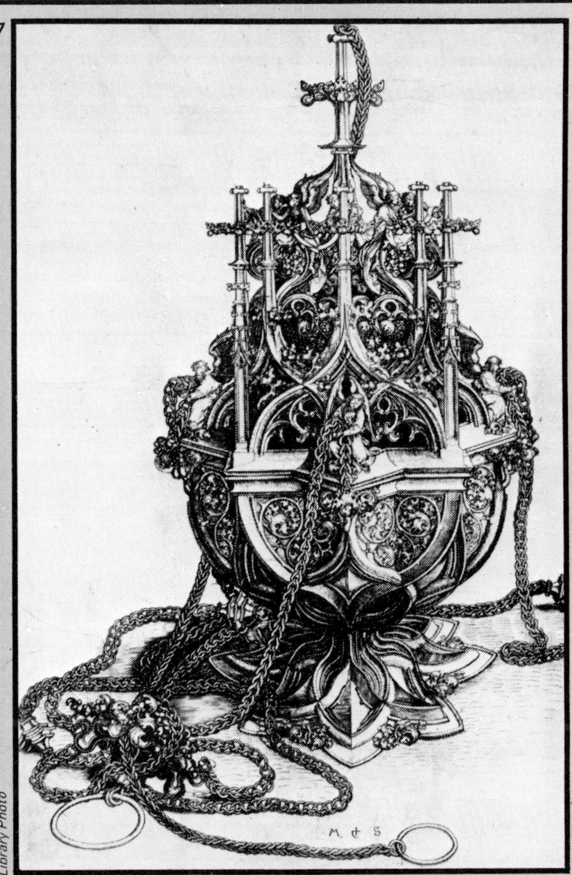

R. B. Fleming

8

Library Photo

flagellant unmistakably bears Dürer's own features. Instruction is provided, for example, by the woodcuts which Dürer made to illustrate his own theoretical writings, and the impressive engraved portrait of *Erasmus* – to quote again but one example of many – tells the curious what the great humanist looked like.

But the character and appearance of Dürer's graphic art differs from that of his predecessors, for he radically changed the processes of woodcutting and engraving; one has only to compare a page from his *Apocalypse* (Fig. 3) with a comparable print of thirty years earlier (Fig. 8) in order to realise the fundamental difference. Later, when working for the Emperor Maximilian, Dürer employed a *Formschneider* whom he had trained, but for the *Apocalypse* (and other works of the same early period) he cut the blocks himself because nobody brought up in the traditional methods would have been able to cope with his demands. Clearly Dürer now conceived the woodcut as a print in black and white only. He refined outline and hatching, emulating subtleties hitherto the prerogative of the engraver.

9

Courtauld Institute of Art

Fig. 9 ***Amorous Couple on a bench*** *by Master ES, mid-fifteenth century. Engraving. This engraving of a young couple in a garden is very delicately handled and the Master ES obviously took great care in depicting the delights of the garden. The variety of plants and small creatures which surround the amorous pair adds much to the charm of this composition.*

But Dürer's engravings are also revolutionary in their novel technique. The *Nativity* of 1504, again an early work, becomes a veritable display of skills and refinements, without in the least impairing the intimacy of the scene. As never before, an engraving now serves two purposes: there is the overt religious subject inviting devotion, but there is also art in presenting it and inviting appreciation.

A public fond of reading legends illustrated in an exciting manner

This insistence on 'art' is most obvious in Dürer's secular engravings, of which the so-called *Sea-monster* (Fig. 2) is a particularly splendid example. In this case it does not really matter what is represented here – and nobody has succeeded in giving a wholly satisfactory explanation – but Dürer is addressing a public fond of reading legends and keen on having them depicted in a really exciting manner. The eye has a lot to see, and the mind may admire the manner of representation and invention.

Dürer was a deeply religious man who upheld tradition in everything. He had not been in touch with Humanism and the Renaissance for nothing, and the originality after which he strove had for him a deep double meaning. It allowed him to give personal expression to his subjects, and to do so in the best possible manner artistically. He was no longer a craftsman mass-producing prints, but a creative individual giving his version of Holy Writ or telling a story meaningful to himself.

When Erasmus of Rotterdam wished to erect a verbal monument to the memory of Albrecht Dürer, he called him an Apelles who had achieved through black lines alone what the celebrated painter of classical antiquity had done with the help of colours, adding that one would destroy the work were one to add tints. Dürer himself knew that his painting had gained him respect, but that his prints were copied and even pirated. His most interesting remark in this respect is an admission, and at the same time an indication of the social and economic standing of his graphic art: 'From now on I shall concentrate on engraving. Had I done so all my life I should today be richer'.

MUSEUMS AND LIBRARIES

The following museums are among the best collections in the world for prints. You may go to these print rooms although it is often necessary first to make an appointment, order the prints as you would a book in a library and inspect them at your leisure on the premises.

Austria:	Graphische Sammlung Albertina, Vienna
France:	Bibliothèque Nationale, Paris
Germany:	Albrecht-Dürer Haus, Nuremberg Kupferstichkabinett, West Berlin
Great Britain:	British Museum, London National Gallery of Scotland, Edinburgh Victoria and Albert Museum, London
U.S.A:	Boston Museum of Fine Arts, Boston William Hayes Fogg Art Museum, Cambridge Metropolitan Museum of Art, New York

FURTHER READING

Dürer, das Graphische Werk by Karl-Adolf Knappe, Vienna and Munich, 1964.

Dürer by M. Levey, London, 1964.

German engraving, etching and woodcuts by F. W. H. Hollstein, Amsterdam, 1954.

Albrecht Dürer by Erwin Panofsky, Princeton, 1948.

Pierre Jahan

The Grandeur of the Baroque Palace

William Gaunt

2

A. F. Kersting

3

A. F. Kersting

A love of the ornate and the grandiose, often carried to astonishing extremes, characterised the palaces built in Germany during the era following the end of the Thirty Years' War in 1648

Many of the most amazing products of the Baroque – grandiose palaces, emotionally inspired sculpture, breathtaking feats of interior ornamentation, religious and secular – are to be found in Germany, especially in the south, and in Bohemia and Austria. The flourishing period of this Central European Baroque was the first half of the eighteenth century. This was late in the development of the international style in architecture and decoration that had first been given shape in Rome by the genius of Bernini and Borromini more than half a century before.

The reason for the late arrival of the style, and for its great popularity, is to be found in the Thirty Years' War and its outcome. From 1618 to 1648 the German states and what had been the kingdom of Bohemia were devastated in the confused struggle which expanded with the intermixture of religious and political aims. During that time, the arts received little attention in the Germanic lands; nor were they sufficiently recovered for some time afterwards to indulge in ambitious schemes of reconstruction.

The pilgrimage church of Birnau is so festive that it has been called 'the Good Lord's Ballroom'

The Treaty of Westphalia in 1648 that ended the War replaced the fiction of the Holy Roman Empire by a federation of more than three hundred independent German states. Except in the remaining Habsburg possessions, religious toleration was an accepted principle. In effect, this resulted in a broad division between Protestant and Catholic regions similar to that which had separated the northern from the southern Netherlands.

North Germany, strongly Protestant and sympathetic for a long time past with Protestant Holland in her fight for independence, now pursued a similar cultural path. In architecture, style was restrained and practical, the more important buildings being designed in a modest version of Palladian classicism. South Germany, Catholic for the most part, was a vehicle of the Counter-Reformation and was receptive architecturally to a style that came from Rome; this was approved by the Jesuit advisers to the German courts as a feature of their campaign to restore and extend the authority of the Roman Church.

The union of architecture, sculpture, ornamental detail and mural painting in the interiors of the south German baroque churches – the Wies Kirche in Bavaria, for example, and the pilgrimage church of Birnau which is so festive in aspect that it has been called 'the Good Lord's Ballroom' – was a later development, however, than that of buildings to house secular authority. These

German
Baroque Palaces

Fig. 1 (Frontispiece) ***Staircase well** at Bad Wurzach, tentatively attributed to J. B. Neumann, c.1750.*

Fig. 2 ***Kaiser-saal,** the Imperial Hall in the Residenz, Würzburg, designed by Johann Balthasar Neumann (1687–1753), 1719–20. Decorated by G. B. Tiepolo (1696–1770) 1749–53. Originally commissioned by the Prince-Bishop Philip von Schönborn, Würzburg was built over a period of sixty years. Tiepolo decorated the Imperial Hall with magnificent allegorical paintings alluding to the patronage of the Prince-Bishop Karl Phillip von Greiffenklau.*

Fig. 3 ***First floor Gallery** of the Neue Schloss, Schleissheim, planned by Enrico Zuccalli (c.1642–1724), 1684, completed by Joseph Effner (1687–1745), c.1715–26. Schleissheim was one of the grand palaces designed for the art-loving Elector, Maximilian Emanuel of Bavaria.*

Fig. 4 ***Ceremonial staircase** at Brühl, Cologne, by Neumann, c.1740. Most of the work at Brühl was executed by the Walloon architect Cuvilliés (1695–1769), but Neumann's genius was responsible for the grand staircase.*

Fig. 5 ***Ceremonial staircase** in the Residenz, Würzburg, designed by Neumann and decorated by Tiepolo, 1752–53. Stucco work by Giuseppe Antonio Bossi. The great staircase divides into two as it returns to the first floor landing leading the eye upwards to the magnificent* trompe l'oeil *ceiling by Tiepolo.*

Fig. 6 ***Main Hall** at Nymphenburg, Munich, decorated by J. B. Zimmermann (1680–1758), early eighteenth century. Built for Maximilian Emanuel of Bavaria, the transition from the baroque to the lighter rococo style can be seen here in the variety of decoration.*

had priority in the states recently made independent.

The baroque style expressed the dominance of both the secular ruler in a palace and the spiritual power in a church. The smaller of the states were no less inclined than the larger to this form of display, encouraged, perhaps, by the desire not to be overshadowed by their neighbours. The architectural style was the expression of absolutism. But it did not come exclusively from Italy. The architects and designers of Louis XIV in France had given their own version of the architectural framework proper for despotism. It was inevitable that France, the great power that had emerged from the Thirty Years' War over the wreck of Habsburg ambitions and had set the tone for Europe in so many ways, should do so for these minor despots. This influence brought with it complications in style. French architects in the reign of Louis XIV aimed at a classical grandeur with something of antique severity, though there was an element of the Baroque in the ostentatious formality of an exterior such as that of Versailles. The interiors used all the baroque accessories of decorative scrolls, sculptural ornament and wall and ceiling painting to overwhelm the spectator with the sensation of a superlative magnificence.

In Germany, there is a trace of the French classicism, combined with a certain baroque ornateness in the treatment of interiors, modified during the course of the eighteenth century by the later evolution of the Baroque in France into the Rococo. Versailles gave a model to Frederick the Great, who was ever receptive to French culture, for his own creation Sans Souci, near Potsdam, which was a type of palace outside the urban zone and surrounded by ornamental gardens. It had a prototype in the Italian villa, although the playfulness of design found in those summer retreats was excluded from gardens which were laid out in rigid geometrical patterns and dignified perspectives. Embedded in the centre of this formally planned landscape, the palace was the more suggestive of authoritarian aloofness.

A painting of the story of Frederick Barbarossa, dazzling in its feats of *trompe l'oeil*

Sans Souci, built in 1745–47 by Georg Wenzeslaus von Knobelsdorff from sketches by Frederick himself, had this formidable approach. The interior shows some contrast between the classical severity of the cupola-surmounted hall and the spidery delicacy of rococo ornament in the music-room.

The Dresden Zwinger of 1710–28, designed by Matthäus Daniel Poppelmann for Augustus the Strong of Saxony, wrecked by the bombing of 1945 and restored by 1959, had more of the fanciful splendour of the Italian villa in its outer aspect. To this, Balthasar Permoser added lavish embellishment of decorative sculpture.

The design of staircases received special attention in order to convey a suitable idea of magnificence. There are many remarkable examples, among them Schloss Weissenstein, Pommersfelden (1711–21), basically designed by Lothar Franz von Schönborn, Prince-Bishop of Bamberg and Elector

4

Bildarchiv Foto Marburg

5

Bildarchiv Foto Marburg

6

Bildarchiv Foto Marburg

Fig. 7 ***Residenz,*** *Würzburg, designed by Neumann, begun 1719.*
Like many great palaces of the period, in France and Italy as well as Germany, the exterior is dignified in comparison with the vigour and exuberance of the interior (see Fig. 2*). In its grandeur of conception Würzburg can be paralleled with Versailles.*

of Mainz, but elaborated by Johann Dientzenhofer. A double flight of stairs with elaborate stucco work by Daniel Schenk leads grandly to the open gallery of the first floor. The Residenz of the Prince-Bishop at Würzburg, designed by Johann Balthasar Neumann in 1719, was a spacious conception that took long to complete. The great single staircase that divides into two leads the eye upward to Tiepolo's fresco of 1752–73. The *putti* holding up lamps are the still later addition of J. P. Wagner. Würzburg is one instance among many of the employment of Italian artists and craftsmen in Germany. The combination of the Venetian master's painting of the story of Frederick Barbarossa, dazzling in its feats of *trompe l'oeil*, with the stucco of Giuseppe Antonio Bossi, gives the effect of opera to the Imperial Hall. One of those baroque effects deliberately designed to astonish is the winding staircase of Wurzach surmounted by a perspective ceiling, intended to create the illusion of infinite space.

These were essentially baroque features, although it is scarcely possible to make an absolute division between the baroque and rococo styles, any more than between the French and Italian influences in Germany. In France the Rococo is closely associated with the sense of release and enjoyment at Court in the reign of Louis XV after its release from the oppressive disciplines enforced by his predecessor. Playful fancy began to temper the former seriousness of the Baroque in Germany as elsewhere in Europe. The decorative charm it introduced into Bavarian sculpture is evidenced in the work of Josef Anton Feuchtmayr (1696–1770) who produced stucco figures for many churches. A similar change from the monumental and grandiose to a delicate refinement is apparent in Bohemia in the sculpture of Ignac Miller (active *c.*1730).

The clearest distinction between Baroque and Rococo in sculpture is to be found in the adaptability of Rococo to the fragile elegance of porcelain as seen in the products of the Meissen factory.

7

Bildarchiv Foto Marburg

8

Ludwig Windstosser, Stuttgart

Fig. 8 ***Schloss Ludwigsburg,*** *built for Eberhard Ludwig of Württemberg. It is partly in Italian* palazzo *style and partly east German baroque. (German National Tourist Office.)*

The German love of the ornate sometimes carried to a high pitch of exaggeration

The interplay of French and Italian influences in Germany often made for an inseparable mixture. Thus Eberhard Ludwig of Württemberg wished the Ludwigsburg Palace to emulate Versailles, but although Versailles was the model for the façade, the Italian architects, stucco workers and mural painters who completed the building produced a typically ornate Italian interior. On the other hand, the Schleissheim and Nymphenburg Palaces in Bavaria first planned towards the end of the seventeenth century by Italian architects – Schleissheim by Enrico Zuccalli and Nymphenburg by Agostino Barelli and Giovanni Antonio Viscardi – were completed after an interval of some years by Joseph Effner, trained in France, who gave both palaces the stamp of a French-inspired style. But a native skill in design and a love of the ornate, sometimes carried to a high pitch of exaggeration, also mark this astonishing period. 𝔊𝔎

BAROQUE PALACES IN GERMANY AND AUSTRIA

The following baroque palaces and castles are normally open to the public:

Belvedere	Vienna
Nymphenburg	Munich
Schleissheim	Munich
Schloss Weissenstein	Pommersfelden
Schönbrunn	Vienna
Residenz	Munich
Residenz	Würzburg
Schloss Ludwigsburg	Württemberg
Schloss Brühl	Cologne

A. F. Kersting

Fig. 9 ***Hall at Nymphenburg*** *by J. B. Zimmermann (1680–1758), early eighteenth century.*

10

George Reinhold, London

Fig. 10 ***Interior with Musicians*** *by J. H. Schönfeldt (1609–75). This shows an Italian-inspired gallery. (Gemäldegalerie, Dresden.)*

Fig. 11 ***The Library at Wiblingen Abbey,*** *Ulm, c.1720–24.*

1

A. F. Kersting

Fig. 12 ***Gallery and ceiling at Schloss Weissenstein,*** *Pommersfelden.*

12

Pierre Jahan

Böttger and the Invention of Porcelain

William Hutton

1

Fig. 1 ***Teapot and cup and saucer,*** *1710–15. Polished stoneware. Teapot height $3\frac{3}{4}$ ins; cup height $3\frac{3}{4}$ ins; saucer diameter $5\frac{1}{2}$ ins.*
It was not uncommon for stoneware designs to derive from silver models, as was the case with this teapot.
(Victoria and Albert Museum, London.)

After years of fruitless experiment, the secret of true porcelain was discovered. Böttger's early successes and the subsequent improvements in technique made the name of Meissen synonymous with the finest achievements in European porcelain

The discovery in Europe of how to make true porcelain, and the opening chapter in the art which sprang from this great technical feat, are linked with the name of Johann Friedrich Böttger (1682–1719). These events not only changed the course of European ceramics but also led to one of the most characteristic art forms of the eighteenth century. Both the red stoneware and the white porcelain made at Meissen under Böttger's direction include some of the most admirable examples of German late baroque art, on the same level of inspiration as, for instance, contemporary achievements in glass or architecture. They were, however, precious luxury wares intended for the few, and it was only later that Meissen achieved European celebrity.

From late medieval times, single pieces of Chinese porcelain found their way to the West, where rarity was enhanced by awe and mystery surrounding their substance and origin. The novelty of their designs and brilliant colours, notably the blue and white, caused a revolution in ceramic taste and launched a host of distinguished imitations in tin-glazed earthenware, or faience. While faience might emulate the appearance, it lacked the durable and translucent properties of Oriental porcelain, which was in demand for its decorative splendour and also because its thinness and resistance to heat and staining were particularly

Fig. 2 ***Two teapots or coffee-pots.*** *Stoneware. Left: c.1710–20. Partly polished with silver mounts, height 6¼ ins. Right: c.1712–15. Black glazed and painted with lacquer colours, height 6 ins. (Victoria and Albert Museum.)*

Fig. 3 ***Cup and Saucer,*** *1716–20. Porcelain, lustered and gilded. Cup height 1½ ins; saucer, diameter 4½ ins. Böttger must take the credit for the mother-of-pearl lustre, first derived from gold in 1716. (Victoria and Albert Museum.)*

K. Hoddle

K. Hoddle

K. Hoddle

Fig. 4 ***Teapot,*** *c.1710–13. Stoneware with cut and polished details, height 4⅛ ins. Modelled in the Chinese style, the enamelling of the flower reliefs has been attributed to the Dresden artist, J. F. Meyer. (Victoria and Albert Museum.)*

suited to the exotic new luxury drinks – tea, coffee and chocolate – that first reached Europe in the mid-seventeenth century.

Chinese porcelain is the product of firing a white, refractory or non-fusing clay (*kaolin*) with a related but fusible feldspathic rock (*petuntse*) to produce a white, hard and translucent body.

At first glance, it is surprising that the invention of a porcelain equal to that of the Orient took place outside the great centres, in the central German electorate of Saxony. However, at the outset of the eighteenth century, with the Turkish menace and the disastrous effects of the Thirty Years' War both left behind, the swarm of absolute rulers in Germany now had the means and energy to glorify their princely rank and patronise the luxury arts. None was more intent in this than Augustus the Strong, Elector of Saxony from 1694 to 1733 and King of Poland. The Versailles of Louis XIV was then the universal model of courtly sumptuousness, and French taste generally was the standard in Germany, as elsewhere. In his youth, Augustus' Grand Tour included several months at the French Court. The unrivalled display customary there, added to his own nature, fired an ambition for magnificence, the fruits of which achieved European celebrity even in that extravagant age.

It is sufficient to mention the fantasies of his court goldsmith, Melchior Dinglinger, or one of the glories of baroque architecture, the Dresden Zwinger – a series of pavilions and galleries for court spectacles – built between 1711 and 1722, the years with which we are concerned here. Augustus was also afflicted to an extreme degree with the mania for Oriental porcelain, shared by many of his peers, and early in his reign he laid the foundations of the greatest of all porcelain collections, with an entire building devoted to it, the celebrated Japanese Palace.

Saxony was not rich, and Augustus' need for money was always acute. In 1701 he heard of a young alchemist, J. F. Böttger, who had fled to Saxony from Berlin fearing imprisonment as an impostor by the Prussian king for his failure to make gold from base metal. Augustus took this valuable man into custody and for years he, too, hoped for magical wealth.

From medieval times, minerals were of prime importance in the Saxon economy. There was also a long-established ceramic tradition. These resources attracted the attention of Ehrenfried Walther von Tschirnhaus (1651–1708), a Saxon nobleman who was a mathematician and physicist of international repute. He was an adherent of mercantilism, the theory of national self-sufficiency in industry, and of his king's passion for porcelain he wrote, 'China is the bleeding-bowl of Saxony'. As early as 1675 the great scientist Leibnitz noted that Tschirnhaus was experimenting with clays. Later, these led to investigations into the fusing points of refractory materials. By 1694, Tschirnhaus' research had centred on porcelain. Soon after, his concern for the state of Saxon manufactures led to a survey of mineral resources, and he set up workshops for polishing and cutting semi-precious hardstones and making and engraving glass.

In 1704, exasperated with his luckless goldmaker, Augustus placed him under the supervision of Tschirnhaus, who may well have assessed Böttger's genuine talents and suggested this move to the King, whom he had approached earlier with his porcelain project. In 1705, as costly failures multiplied, Augustus ordered Böttger to be isolated to work in the medieval Albrechtsburg, a castle at Meissen, twelve miles north-west of Dresden. Not until September 1707 was Böttger brought back to Dresden to live in the closely-guarded laboratory that had been built upon the city walls. Böttger had little enthusiasm for porcelain research, which he felt was the province of Tschirnhaus. Nevertheless, he set to work with zeal under the older man's eye, perhaps spurred on by the hope that success of some sort would bring freedom from royal restraint.

In two months Böttger improved upon Tschirnhaus' earlier samples of a red stoneware inspired by the similar but softer Yi-hsing ware and its Dutch imitations, esteemed for their heat-retaining and tea-brewing qualities. This new material was proudly called 'red, or jasper, porcelain', for in the eighteenth century it was mistakenly thought to be a type of true porcelain. Among ceramic bodies it is remarkable for its intense hardness and fine texture.

Development of stoneware had shown that, after firing, some clays remained porous, while others became smooth and vitrified. What was needed was the combination of a white-burning clay with a substance that would vitrify throughout. By July 1708 success was achieved using white Colditz clay, with alabaster as the fluxing agent. Though true porcelain, this paste required even higher firing than the Chinese (1400° as against 1300° C.), thus leading to endless difficulties with colours at a later date. *Kaolin* was gradually substituted between 1711 and 1717, but the feldspathic flux was not introduced until 1720. The inventors and their staff were now sworn to secrecy on all matters concerning materials, processing and firing;

5

Museum Photo

Fig. 5 ***Teapot,*** *c.1715–20. White porcelain with applied porcelain roses, height $4\frac{7}{8}$ ins. Applied decoration is characteristic of the earliest Meissen porcelain. The rose motif is carried right through into the handle and lid. (Victoria and Albert Museum.)*

Fig. 6 ***Two teapots,*** *1710–15. Stoneware. Left: polished and engraved with silver mounts, height $3\frac{3}{4}$ ins. Right: facet-cut and polished, height $3\frac{7}{8}$ ins. Designs could be engraved into the red body (left) or the whole surface could be cut with light-reflecting facets (right). (Victoria and Albert Museum.)*

6

K. Hoddle

7

Museum Photo

9

Museum Photo

Fig. 7 ***Pair of stoppered flasks,*** c.*1717–19. Porcelain painted with enamel colours, height 9 ins. Deriving their shape from Japanese* sake *bottles, these spirit, or cordial, flasks pre-date the great enamel colour innovations made at Meissen in the 1720s. (Victoria and Albert Museum.)*

Fig. 8 ***Vase,*** c.*1715–20. Porcelain, height 9 ins. This fine early example of Meissen porcelain employs another favourite motif, the grape-vine. Like so many of the pieces produced at Meissen, it is based on a silver model. (Victoria and Albert Museum.)*

Fig. 9 ***Bust of a child,*** c.*1710–20. Polished stoneware, height 5¾ ins. (Victoria and Albert Museum.)*

to a large extent the method remained a Saxon monopoly for some fifty years.

Tschirnhaus died in October 1708, at the moment of victory. The next year, working alone, Böttger developed the glaze indispensable to the completion of the invention. It is remarkably close-fitting and flawless. The ivory tone common to both it and the paste are a hallmark of Böttger porcelain. While Tschirnhaus the theorist deserves credit for having set events in motion and sustaining them, it was Böttger whose practical sense achieved both workable formulae and the design of high-temperature kilns. He now petitioned the King to found a 'red and white porcelain manufactory'. Sensing prestige, possible profit and the glory of his own porcelain supply, this was decreed by Augustus in January 1710, and two months later established in the Albrechtsburg at Meissen. Though not for sale, a few small pieces of the Saxon porcelain were first shown to the public at the Leipzig trade fair in May of that year.

At the same time, a proclamation listed several ways of embellishing the red stoneware that was now offered to Leipzig buyers. As this includes all the kinds of decoration now known, it is clear that this ware had received much thought since its invention. In its natural state it had a matt, slightly granular surface, the austerity of which usually called for further treatment. Both its red-brown colour and the degree of hardness were varied by fluctuations in composition or firing heat. When underfired the texture is porous and the colour paler. When overfired the surface tends toward black. In rare cases, clays of several different colours were mixed to produce effects simulating agate or jasper.

Böttger was not an artist, and for his forms and decoration he looked to the many skilled craftsmen attracted to the Dresden Court. Stoneware shapes were partly taken from Yi-hsing models (Figs. 2 and 4), but the main influence on their design was the court silversmith Johann Jakob Irminger (*c.*1660–1726), attached to the factory from 1710 until after 1720.

Irminger had an admirable sense of proportion and restraint, and the high distinction of the Böttger wares, as well as their freedom from undue Oriental influence, is largely due to his work. Used to working with cast and relief ornament, he found that the highly plastic stoneware and porcelain could be wheel-thrown and mould-shaped with metallic sharpness. His crisp profiled mouldings, gadroons, leaves and masks, drawn from the international repertoire of Régence ornament, are admirable foils to the plain surfaces of often quasi-architectural forms. While some designs derive directly from silver models (Fig. 1), others recall vessels cut from hardstones, with the glittering surfaces of which they have understandably been mistaken.

The most characteristic decoration was polishing and engraving. For this, glass craftsmen were retained in Dresden and Bohemia, as well as Meissen, and they applied to the new materials the techniques and styles used for Bohemian glass drinking-vessels. Most often this was plain polishing, the dull outer surface being ground away to a brilliant finish. The surface might also be wheel-engraved with formal designs or scattered flowers.

Effective contrast was gained by engraving through a black glazed surface on to the red body or the entire piece was cut with light-reflecting concave facets (Fig. 6). To make saleable underfired wares from his undependable kilns, Böttger in 1710 perfected a shining black glaze (from cobalt and manganese) which was painted with unfired gold, silver and colours in the style of Oriental lacquer (Fig. 2). The court lacquerer, Martin Schnell, was highly paid for this sort of work. Certain rare pieces were enamelled with the kind of fired colours used on Saxon glass and pottery. The teapot (Fig. 4) has enamel painting of great refinement, possibly by the Dresden artist J. F. Meyer. There are even others whose preciousness, a quality inherent in much of the stoneware, has been further enhanced by garnets set into the flower reliefs.

Figures in stoneware are not numerous. There was no factory figure-modeller until 1727. Both in the round and as low relief plaques, they largely stem from the small-scale sculpture in ivory, box-wood and bronze long favoured in Germany. While some are clearly after works in those materials, the sources of others remain in question. It is reasonable to suppose that models were furnished by some of the men assisting Balthasar Permoser in the vast programme of sculptural decoration of the Zwinger. The polished bust of a child (Fig. 9) may have been cast from a renaissance bronze. It was in production by 1711 and must have been successful, as several examples are known.

In vessels, only single pieces for the tea-table and for ornamental purposes were made. Superb as it is, the stoneware required too much costly labour for finishing, and its colour was not really suited to tablewares. The material itself, and the ultimate products, were probably too essentially German in taste to interest a wider market. Nonetheless, the basic artistic vitality of Meissen was clearly shown from the very start in the astonishing variety of shapes, and by the fertility of invention applied to the decoration of even the same model: both these points underlie the remarkable later history of Meissen.

Mother of pearl lustre derived from gold was a Meissen secret

Serious problems plagued production of the porcelain, and not until 1713 could the first pieces be placed on sale. Porcelain is liable to collapse in firing, and constant efforts were made to cut the huge kiln losses. Firing cracks and warping scar many Böttger pieces seen today. Only in 1715 could porcelain be made in enough quantity to replace the stoneware, production of which now declined. Chinese vessel shapes, particularly Fukien *blanc-de-Chine* were adapted to Böttger porcelain, but here, also, Irminger provided the more consequential designs. Some stoneware forms were repeated in porcelain, but a range of shapes and decorations exists only in the latter. Moulded and applied reliefs of grape-vine, chrysanthemum and feathery foliage (Fig. 8), or fully modelled and applied rose sprays (Fig. 10), are characteristic.

Even before the factory's foundation Augustus had ambitions for splendid colours to rival the Oriental decoration, but Böttger was no colour chemist. He failed to produce a workable under-glaze blue, greatly desired by the King, owing to the excessively high heat his paste required. His enamel colours are mostly dull, uneven and intractable under the brush. The problem involved finding enamels that would stand the temperature needed to fuse them into the glaze, and much Böttger porcelain is white for this reason. Quite a few pieces of both porcelain and stoneware have delicate strap-work designs or formal borders in gold attributed to the gilder J. G. Funke. The pair of spirit or cordial flasks, a favourite shape, are modelled after Japanese *sake* bottles (Fig. 7). They may date from *c*.1717–19, when the colour problem was again taken up; in any case, their dry-looking enamels precede the reform of the Meissen palette in the early 1720s. A colour of which Böttger could be justly proud, however, is the mother of pearl lustre, derived from gold in 1716 (Fig. 3). This remained a Meissen secret, and it was later employed with striking effects.

Porcelain production comprised chiefly wares for tea, coffee and chocolate, and some of these were apparently assembled in services. Many single pieces such as vases and bowls were also made. Böttger had no luck with plates, which warped, and dining-table wares, much wanted by the King, remained for the future. Figures are few, and they present questions of date as well as of authorship. Fukien Kuan-Yins were copied, and in the Chinese style are the more original squatting and grinning 'pagods'. Judging from surviving figures, often showing the whiter paste of the 1720s, many of the 'pagods', and also the well-known dwarfs in the style of Callot, were made in the post-Böttger period.

Böttger tea-table shapes were continued with little change into the 1720s, and without applied reliefs they furnished ideal surfaces for painting. Much Böttger porcelain found its way unpainted into the hands of independent artists outside the factory (*Hausmaler* painters), notably in Silesia, Bohemia and Augsburg, who supplied distinctive decorations of their own devising.

Böttger had been kept under guard until 1714. The years of confinement, plus excessive drinking and tobacco, ruined his health. He was no administrator. The factory, not yet showing a profit, was at the mercy of a captious ruler who refused to build the improved kilns projected by Böttger, and there was constant intrigue among his staff. Early in 1719 his arcanist, Samuel Stöltzel, conveyed the secrets of paste and kilns to Vienna, where they enabled Du Paquier to found Meissen's first rival. At Böttger's death at the age of thirty-seven, in March 1719, the factory staff had fallen by half to some twenty men, and the operation was in disarray.

After Böttger's death one may almost speak of a new beginning. The King reformed management and finance. Within a year paste and kilns were improved and the under-glaze blue achieved. Of chief importance, in April 1720 the repentant Stöltzel returned, bringing with him a young Du Paquier colleague, the enamel painter Johann Gregorius Höroldt (1696–1775). Höroldt quickly perfected an excellent range of over-glaze enamels, and with them created fantastic *Chinoiseries* of his own invention as well as the splendid copies of Oriental wares sought by the King, whose appetite for spectacular porcelain was presently further satisfied by a remarkable series of ground colours.

Both Höroldt's artistic and administrative gifts were recognised, and it was he who first gained European artistic fame and commercial success for Meissen, whose just pride in its productions caused the first use of a factory mark in 1722, altered to the famous crossed swords a year or so later. For fifteen years painted decoration remained paramount, until in the later 1730s, J. J. Kaendler's relief-modelling and figures gave a new direction to European porcelain.

10

Museum Photo

Fig. 10 **Bowl,** *c.1715–20. White porcelain with applied roses, height 4½ ins.*
As in the teapot (Fig. 5), the rose decoration is carried into the handles which curve back into the bowl.
(Victoria and Albert Museum.)

MUSEUMS AND COLLECTIONS

Early Meissen stoneware and porcelain are on view at the following:

GERMANY

Dresden:	Grünes Gewölbe
Cologne:	Kunstgewerbemuseum
Frankfurt:	Museum für Kunsthandwerk
Hamburg:	Museum für Kunst und Gewerbe
Munich:	Bayerisches Nationalmuseum Residenz Museum
Schleissheim:	Schneider Collection (Schloss Lustheim)
Stuttgart:	Landesgewerbemuseum

GREAT BRITAIN

Bedford:	Cecil Higgins Art Gallery
Cambridge:	Fitzwilliam Museum
London:	British Museum Victoria and Albert Museum

U.S.A.

Jacksonville, Florida:	Cummer Gallery of Art
New York:	Metropolitan Museum of Art
Washington:	Smithsonian Institution

FURTHER READING

German Porcelain and Faience by S. Ducret, London, 1962.

Meissen and Other Continental Porcelain, Faience and Enamel in the Irwin Untermyer Collection by Y. Hackenbrock, London, 1956.

German Porcelain by W. B. Honey, London, 1947.

Dresden China by W. B. Honey, London, 1934 and 1954.

Style and Splendour in Baroque Furniture

William Collier

Walter Steinkopf

Fig. 1 **Guéridon,** *Berlin, late seventeenth or early eighteenth century. Carved and gilt wood. The vigorous design of the curving leaf-work shows strong Italian influence. (Schloss Charlottenburg, Berlin.)*

2

Museum Photo

Fig. 2 **Bridal bed,** *Tyrolean, 1771. Carved and painted wood. It was a Tyrolean custom to provide a decorative bed for a marriage. This one is a delightful example of the painted woodwork which was executed throughout the eighteenth century in the remoter parts of Austria and south Germany. It is traditionally baroque in design and is decorated with typical scroll-work. The bride's name is painted on the headboard. (Tiroler Volkskunstmuseum, Innsbruck.)*

German, Austrian and Bohemian craftsmen gradually developed a strangely eclectic style of furniture design. This persisted in all its extravagance into the eighteenth century and finally mellowed into the charming folk pieces of the Alpine provinces

Fig. 3 **Stool**, *German, late seventeenth century. Such stools were used at Court and in the homes of the nobility. This example shows carving employed in the characteristic spiral form combined with richly carved foliage. (Rijksmuseum, Amsterdam.)*

3

Museum Photo

Baroque furniture of the late seventeenth and early eighteenth centuries in Germany shows a strong sense of style and an absence of narrow cultural nationalism. Initiative in art patronage had passed to the virtually independent German princes, freed by the Thirty Years' War from all but a shadow of central control. This war had, by impoverishing towns and peasantry, removed any threat to them from the populace. The cosmopolitan outlook of the aristocracy is illustrated by Prince Eugene of Savoy, one of the foremost patrons of baroque art who signed his name in Italian, German and French: 'Eugenio von Savoie'.

A spate of palace-building and furnishing during this period involved the creation or enlargement of special court workshops. These helped to end the monopoly of the furniture-makers' guilds, whose careful system of apprenticeship and strict terms of promotion to the rank of master craftsman had been partially responsible for the technical excellence of German furniture. This system tended, however, to cut the craftsman off from the decorator and architect who provided the setting for the furniture. The guild craftsmen, including the specialist inlay workers of Eger (Fig. 12) and the makers of highly ornamented cabinets and clocks at Augsburg, continued to produce much fine furniture; but working at Court could free men from guild conservatism and give them a better chance to experiment with new styles. Even where these opportunities were not taken, the German princes at least provided generous, even extravagant, patronage in terms of the country's resources as well as a new status for the furniture-maker. Hermann Korb, for example, in the service of the Duke of Brunswick, rose from cabinet-maker to superintendent of all architecture in the Duchy, and designer of much of it. It is also significant that new forms of furniture – commodes, writing-cabinets and bureaux – first appeared in the early 1700s.

Fig. 4 **Upholstered armchair,** *Vienna, c.1730. Made for Prince Eugene of Savoy's hunting-lodge at Schlosshof, this chair is typical of the transitional period between Baroque and Rococo and shows French stylistic influence in the lighter curving forms. (Österreichisches Museum für Angewandte Kunst, Vienna.)*

4

Foto Ritter

Solid, imposing furniture was well suited to the homes of the wealthier merchants

The Thirty Years' War coincided with the formative period of the Baroque in Italy and with a period of prosperity and artistic activity in Holland. There, some of the favourite baroque motifs of twisted columns and curved panel mouldings were being applied to cabinets and cupboards without as yet altering their otherwise mainly rectangular forms. This nascent baroque style spread by the 1660s to the north German ports which traded with the Dutch, and soon north German furniture, often in walnut, combined this Dutch influence with the bold outlines of traditional north German oak carving. This solid, imposing furniture was well suited to the homes of the wealthier merchants and found its counterparts in the larger inland trading centres such as Leipzig and Frankfurt (Fig. 9).

In south Germany, where towns already in decline from the decay of their Venetian trade had suffered heavily from the war, the Catholics favoured the infiltration of Italian art and artists. By 1679 we find the painter Matthias Echter publishing in Italian a book of baroque designs, *Collection of Caprices and New Designs*, and a few years later the new style was boosted by the need to rebuild the suburbs of Vienna destroyed by the Turks. As the capital of the Habsburg emperors, hereditary rivals of the Bourbons, Vienna was averse to French styles and all the more ready to accept Italian ones. But though many court painters and some sculptors were Italian, furniture-making remained largely in native hands.

Some of the best productions were sent as gifts to placate those in authority

Austrian baroque furniture consequently differs from Italian in two important respects. It never wholly accepts as worthy of imitation that essential baroque fusion of the fine arts of architecture, painting and sculpture; hence cabinets are seldom miniature palaces or chair legs formed sculpturally from curving foliage, nor is the better furniture usually painted. Conversely, it has that quality which we tend to think of as typically Germanic – careful, thorough workmanship paying attention to the nature of the materials employed. Often Austrian furniture of this period has, despite its massiveness, a certain elegance and restraint, perhaps derived from the character of the Habsburg Court – assured, intent on form but hardly needing to *épater le bourgeois*, as did the more calculating ostentation of Louis XIV.

Some French influence nevertheless crept in when the arabesque designs of Jean Bérain were used on furniture for the imperial Hofburg palace. There one even finds the tortoise-shell inlay perfected in France by Boulle. Most Austrian inlay and veneer consists of contrasting woods, with walnut as the main ground and panels in maple, cherry or rosewood, sometimes patterned, even occasionally in perspective designs, but often relying for effect simply on the different colours and grain of the woods.

Bohemia, under Habsburg rule, followed the lead of Vienna. Furniture-makers were, for the most part, natives of the country or immigrants from Germany and Austria, but their work had to fit into new palaces designed as often as not by Italians: in 1680 there were no less than twenty-eight Italian architects in Prague and only seven northern ones. In north-western Bohemia the town of Eger continued to produce its cabinets and caskets with pictorial panels of wood inlay carved in low relief (Fig. 12). This especially skilled work, already famous in the sixteenth century, was seriously affected by the Thirty Years' War, since most of the town's inhabitants were Protestants, many of whom were expelled. Others, including the foremost

Fig. 5 **Cabinet,** *Augsburg, 1715. Marquetry of tortoise-shell, metal and mother of pearl. (Victoria and Albert Museum, London.)*

Fig. 6 **Design for a cupboard,** *north German, 1707. There are alternative designs for the central panel, one on each door.*

Fig. 7 **Painted writing-desk** *with* chinoiserie *motifs, Berlin, in the manner of, or possibly by, Gerard Dagly, early eighteenth century. (Schloss Charlottenburg.)*

5

Museum Photo

6

Walter Steinkopf

8

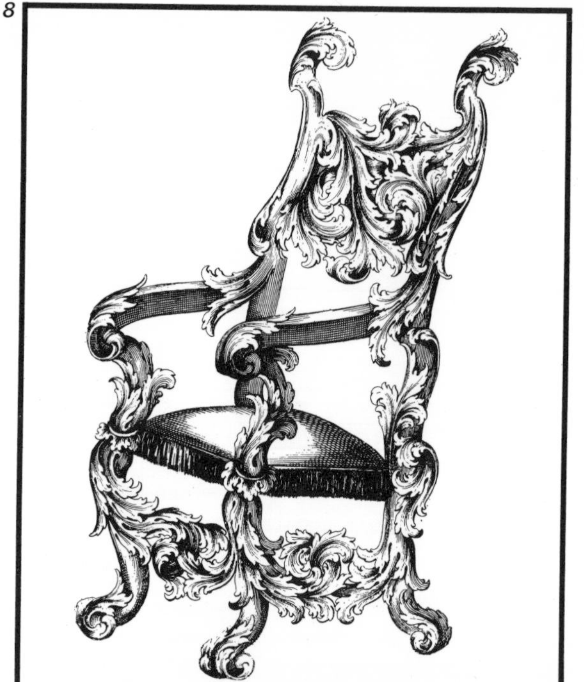

9

Museum Photo

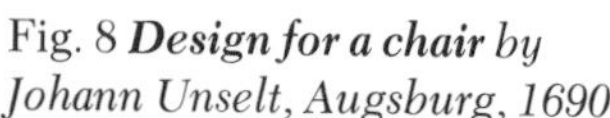

Fig. 8 **Design for a chair** by *Johann Unselt, Augsburg, 1690.*

Fig. 9 **Walnut sideboard** by *J. Friedrich Keller, Basle, 1663. A particularly elaborate example of the early baroque style, this sideboard shows strong Dutch influence in the spiral columns and tightly carved scroll-work. (Kunstgewerbemuseum, Berlin.)*

10

Fig. 10 **Alternative design for a bed** *by Johann Unselt, Augsburg, 1690. Designs of this sort would have been modified in execution.*

11

Museum Photo

Fig. 11 **Marriage chest,** *Tyrolean, 1794. Carved and painted wood. Like the bed in Fig. 2, this follows a traditional design. The motif of the vases of flowers dates back to the sixteenth century. (Tiroler Volkskunstmuseum.)*

craftsman of the time, Hans Georg Fischer (1587–1669) fled. Some of the best productions had to be sent as gifts to placate those in authority at Prague and Vienna, as for example the magnificent cabinet made in 1721 with portraits of all the Habsburg emperors. Usually the inlaid pictures showed allegorical figures or scenes taken from the Bible or classical mythology, which might be copied from the prints by Wenceslaus Hollar or Abraham Bosse.

In central Germany, the Schönborn family, closely allied to the Habsburgs, patronised what one of them termed, in a characteristic mixture of German and Italian, the '*Theutscher Gusto*'. But while the furniture for their Würzburg Residenz was made by the Viennese-trained craftsman Auvera in a German-Italianate style, their Pommersfelden palace has splendid furniture by Ferdinand Plitzner (1678–1724) in a partly French manner. His work is important not only for its co-ordination by one artist of furniture with interior decoration, but also for the quality and particular character of his designs. The bold serpentine fronts of his cabinets are unmistakably German, despite French details such as trellis patterns and the curving legs in the shape of female herms. Similarly, his gilt-brass or ivory inlay, though rich, has not quite the overwhelming lavishness of French Boulle and ormolu work.

Lightly fantastic furniture for Augustus the Strong's new Japanese Palace

Elsewhere in central and southern Germany and in the Rhineland, the prestige of Louis XIV's Court ensured a gradual acceptance of French fashions in furniture design. Dutch examples were being followed in the mid seventeenth century, as shown by the engravings of Friedrich Unteutsch of Frankfurt and Georg Caspar Erasmus of Nuremberg. The decorative detail most commonly found in this furniture is the ear-shaped scroll which gives the style its name of auricular. By the early eighteenth century, however, the designs of Paul Decker were making use of the more flowing French motifs of Daniel Marot. The mirror-frame makers of Augsburg turned from the Italianate style practised by Johann Ulrich Stapf, with its carved foliage and cupids, to the lighter pierced French ornament represented by the work of Albrecht Biller.

The change was most marked at Munich after the Elector Maximilian Emanuel had switched from a Habsburg to a Bourbon alliance. Boulle furniture was imported for the Elector from Paris and his court architect, decorator and furniture-designer, Joseph Effner, was sent in 1706 to Paris for training in art. On his return he was made responsible for all work on and in the many palaces and pavilions built and furnished for the Elector, in much the same way as Lebrun had been made co-ordinator of court art by Louis XIV.

It was at Berlin and Dresden that court patronage produced its most original and interesting results. Other German princes – notably at Bamberg, Munich and Ludwigsburg – followed the French fashion for lacquered *chinoiserie* wall panels and usually imported their lacquered furniture from Holland. The Elector of Brandenburg took the logical step of importing his own maker of lacquer furniture, Gerard Dagly, from the Netherlandish town of Spa. The Elector's son, Frederick I of Prussia, made him *Directeur des Ornéments*, in charge of *chinoiserie* decoration and furniture (Fig. 7). Instead of keeping to the traditional Chinese and Japanese scheme of gilt scenes on black backgrounds, Dagly experimented with vividly coloured scenes and figures, part Oriental and part European in design, on a white background. This decoration was applied to many different types of furniture, such as tables, *guéridons* and clock-cases, and produced highly successful, novel effects not unlike Chinese porcelain. A Saxon pupil of Dagly, Martin Schnell, returned to his native Dresden to make similar but even more lightly fantastic furniture, some of the finest for the Elector's new Japanese palace. His later work, including designs for the Meissen porcelain factory, are in the rococo manner.

Fig. 12 ***Decorative panel of a cabinet***, *Eger, north west Bohemia, late seventeenth century. Wood with low relief inlay. (Victoria and Albert Museum.)*

12

Museum Photo

13

Walter Steinkopf

Fig. 13 ***High-back chair***, *German, early eighteenth century. Carved and inlaid wood. The curved splats or horizontal supports are in the French manner, while the careful detailing of the wood is typical of fine German craftsmanship. This type of chair was used by the Court and the nobility and could be either set against a wall or used at table. (Schloss Charlottenburg.)*

Marriage coffers and bridal beds were painted with the date and the name of the bride

The Baroque lingered on in parts of Germany during the middle and later years of the eighteenth century. The ingenious designs of Johann Jakob Schübler, first published at Augsburg in 1720, went through many editions and probably influenced much of the furniture made for the German nobility. An even longer survival of the Baroque occurred in the peasant furniture of remote districts such as the Austrian Alpine provinces. There the painted designs resembling coloured inlay exhibit flower vase motifs which can be traced back to the sixteenth century. They are combined on bedheads and chests with curved baroque outlines. This folk art is in some respects highly traditional and in others strongly individualistic in that pieces made as marriage chests (Fig. 11) and bridal beds are painted with the date and the name of the bride (Fig. 2). The bed illustrated shows a common feature, a Madonna and Child painted on the bedhead panel. Painting was usually complemented by carving, and pieces made included rocking-cradles, dressers and tall cupboards with one or two doors.

MUSEUMS AND COLLECTIONS

German baroque furniture may be seen at the following:

AUSTRIA

Innsbruck: Tiroler Volkskunstmuseum

Vienna: Österreichisches Museum für Angewandte Kunst

GERMANY

Frankfurt: Museum für Kunsthandwerk

Hamburg: Museum für Kunst und Gewerbe

Munich: Bayerisches Nationalmuseum

GREAT BRITAIN

London: Victoria and Albert Museum

HOLLAND

Amsterdam: Rijksmuseum

FURTHER READING

Cabinet Makers and Furniture Designers by Hugh Honour, London, 1969.

Mobili Tedeschi by Edi Baccheschi, Milan, 1969.

Die Kunst des Deutschen Möbels by Heinrich Kreisel, Munich, 1968.

Egerer Reliefintarsien by Heribert Sturm, Munich, 1961.

ARTHUR NEGUS COLLECTORS' ITEM

HELMETS OF THE GERMAN ARMIES

The First World War brought to an end the era of glamour and romance in battle. The splendour of the uniforms, and many of the traditions that had contributed to their appearance, became a thing of the past. The most colourful and diverse of the armies of 1914 was that of Imperial Germany, whose forces embodied the historical continuity of more than a dozen states. Although the distinctive head-dress of the various armies was largely the same within that army, there was a huge variation in the style and type of plate and ornament. The familiar Prussian spiked helmet was first introduced in 1842 for the infantry. In 1846, a similar helmet surmounted by a ball was in use for the artillery; these two types remained in continuous use until 1918. Early examples were conical in shape, with a high crown and front and rear visors; the crown was successively lowered, and the visors shortened, four times in the lifetime of that pattern of helmet. Until 1857 all helmets were given square-cut visors, after which only the dragoons and general officers wore the square peak. The Bavarian army, however, on the adoption of the spiked helmet in 1871, wore the square visor throughout the service. The Hessians, on the other hand, wore the rounded visor throughout, including Generals. The finest spiked helmets are those for general officers, surmounted by a six-sided fluted spike and carrying the enamelled badge of the State above the visor. Amongst the cavalry, the variety was even greater: Lancers wore the Polish *tschapka* in innumerable colours; Hussars wore the busby or *pelzmutze* of otter or sealskin; Dragoons wore a version of the spiked helmet; the Cuirassiers, or mounted *Jägers*, wore a helmet of burnished steel; the *Garde du Corps* carried a helmet of zinc and copper alloy, surmounted by a silver eagle. The variety and decorative quality of detail is so great that it is imperative to carry with you a good reference book; there are several in English, of which the handiest is Colonel Robert Rankin's *Helmets and Head-dress of the Imperial German Army.*

Notes For The Collector

There are so many variations in the different patterns of helmet and plate that faking a rare unit or type is a comparatively simple matter. Before deciding on a purchase, it is always worth taking the helmet to pieces, and looking closely at stitching and rivets.

Prices

These vary widely: you won't be able to buy a *Garde du Corps* helmet for under £200, but it is possible to pick up infantry helmets of the later pattern for something in the region of £10.

Above: Left ***Prussian artillery officer's helmet*** *with a cannon-ball on the peak.* Right ***Polish tschapka*** *worn by lancers.* Centre ***Prussian dragoon's helmet*** *with a square peak.*

Below right: Left ***Saxon infantry helmet.*** Right ***Bavarian officer's helmet*** *with fluted spike.*

Below left: Left ***Prussian Guard officer's helmet.*** Right ***Prussian 1st Life Hussar's Death's Head pelzmutze.***

Opposite: ***Prussian officer's helmet,*** *1842. (Tradition, Piccadilly, London.)*

Tradition, Piccadilly, London: R. Todd-White

Tradition, Piccadilly, London: R. Todd-White

Distinction in German and Bohemian Glass

Gabriella Gros-Galliner

1

Fig. 1 ***Goblet and cover** engraved by Gottfried Spiller (died 1721), Potsdam, c.1700. The Potsdam factory was founded in 1674 by the Elector Frederick William of Brandenburg. The engraved decoration is of bacchanalia. (Victoria and Albert Museum, London.)*

Throughout the seventeenth century, a distinctive national style was emerging in German and Bohemian glass. New techniques of cutting, enamelling and colouring placed these exquisite wares among the most prized of all Europe

The swelling curves and irregular protuberances of the baroque movement found expression in the interiors of secular and, in particular, ecclesiastical buildings enriched by painted ceilings, intricate metalwork and gilt statues in voluminous, flowing robes. To set off this new splendour, colourful stained glass was ousted and supplanted by a plain, colourless window-pane permitting maximum penetration of undiluted light.

In the early years of the seventeenth century sweeping changes were made in Italian-inspired glass-making in Germany and Bohemia. Venetian and medieval Frankish-Rhenish influences which flourished side by side were gradually allotted their proper niche in the glass-maker's craft, thus encouraging the emergence of a distinctive national style.

Due to the crippling drain on natural and economic resources, and the devastation brought about by the unrestrained violence and plunder committed by armies and foreign mercenaries during the Thirty Years' War, the transition was slow, and remnants of medieval beliefs, superstitions and artistic concepts lingered on.

A significant period in Bohemian glass-making came during the later sixteenth century, when the nobility sought to augment feudal revenues by establishing glass-works on their vast and amply forested estates. This enterprise benefited from an influx of German glass-makers who could no longer tolerate the astronomical price of essential wood fuel brought about by the rapid expansion of the native mining industry. Privileges were granted to these immigrants who grew prosperous, intermarried and soon formed the nucleus of industry.

It was usual practice, if not indeed obligatory, for the continental craftsman to fill in the immediate years after serving his apprenticeship – the *Lehrjahre* – with a period of travel – the *Wanderjahre* – a perfect insurance against stagnation. A somewhat different aspect of the glass trade was represented by the glass-pedlar, who wandered from town to town selling his wares. One such glass-hawker, setting out with his heavy walking-stick, is shown in a woodcut from Georgius Agricola's famous book, *De Re Metallica* (Fig. 10). A huge contraption on the pedlar's back holds glasses of all sorts packed in straw. Glass-maker's tools are lying about untidily, but the focal point in the illustration is the beehive-shaped glass furnace subdivided into the firing chamber, founding chamber and annealing chamber. An open door allows a glimpse of a tavern-like service counter where the glass-worker would quench his thirst – most likely free of charge – a provision still observed in some glass-houses in the nineteenth century.

The glass-hawker was often trained as an engraver and glass-painter

The glass-hawker was often trained as an engraver and glass-painter, well able to decorate a customer's purchase to order. The Bohemian glass-seller Georg Francis Kreybich made about thirty journeys between 1683 and 1721, which took him all over Europe, including Murano and Moscow. The diaries he kept are extremely informative and entertaining.

The mountains and forests of Bohemia, Silesia, Moravia and, on the German side, Bavaria, Thuringia, Saxony and Franconia, were ideal locations for the establishment of glass-houses. Silica, soda (or potash) and lime are the main components of glass. In the forest areas there was an abundance of beechwood supplying fuel and potash, and most other essential raw materials were present in rocks and soil. Apart from window-glass, forest glass-houses produced hollow glass in a thick metal of greenish colour and bubbly consistency.

Museum Photo

3

Sperryn's Ltd., London

4

H. Klein

Forest glass, or *Waldglas*, appears all over Europe with characteristic features common to specimens from different countries (Fig. 6).

A number of medieval vessels were still produced during the seventeenth century. The *Nuppenbecher*, a short straight-sided beaker with applied prunts (blobs of ornamental glass) and incurving rim, was a modified version of the slightly earlier *Krautstrunk* (cabbage stalk), a beaker with plain thorny prunts which, in turn, was related to a small beaker with spiked prunts aptly named the *Igel* (hedgehog), appearing during the sixteenth century. From these medieval forms developed one of the most important vessels of the Rhineland, the *Roemer*, with hollow spun foot, hollow shaft with applied prunts and ovoid bowl.

The *Roemer*, a term possibly derived from the Dutch *roemen* – to praise – retained its popularity in the eighteenth century, when it grew in dimension and, as a presentation glass, incorporated appropriate engraved decoration.

The *Angster*, or *Kuttrolf*, a sprinkler vessel of Eastern origin, achieved a sophisticated renaissance during the seventeenth century. After undergoing a number of transformations, it appeared as a vessel with a capacious, usually bulbous, body and long, often multi-tubular, slightly inclined neck.

Alongside these medieval remainders, the fashion for graceful and airy forms of glass '*à la façon de Venise*' asserted itself. Italian-initiated glass-houses were established in larger cities such as Vienna, Cologne and Dessau, and Venetian artisans were invited to the royal courts in order to produce the brittle, clear *cristallo*. German and Bohemian glass-makers visited Murano to familiarise themselves with Venetian techniques.

The artistic treatment of glass falls into several distinct categories. In its ductile state, it may be blown and manipulated into an endless variety of shapes and forms, a technique to which the fluid soda *cristallo* lent itself admirably. By colouring the glass batch, any number of attractive contrasts may be obtained.

The *Passglas* was passed around the company, each man emptying it down to the next ring

A very different decorative process is the application of paint, or enamel colours, to the finished glass surface. A third, and by many collectors regarded as the most accomplished of all techniques, is that of cutting and engraving. Bohemian and German glass artists have excelled in both the last mentioned decorative forms.

By the early sixteenth century, enamelling had gone out of fashion in Venetian glass-making. The highly fragile *cristallo* proved unsuitable for re-firing – essential for ensuring a permanent fusion of the enamel pigments to the glass surface. Enamelled glass appeared in Bohemia and

Fig. 2 ***Cobalt blue glass jug*** *with enamelling in colour, Bohemian, 1595. (Museum of Applied Art, Prague.)*

Fig. 3 ***Vasenpokal,*** *or covered goblet, with diamond engraving, enamelling and gilding, Innsbruck, c.1580. (Sotheby's, London.)*

Fig. 4 ***Humpen*** *with hunter and woman, Bohemian, 1594. (Kunstmuseum, Dusseldorf.)*

17th century German and Bohemian Glass

Museum Photo

Museum Photo

Fig. 5 **Goblet,** *Nuremburg, late seventeenth century. Coloured and clear glass are satisfactorily combined in this piece. (British Museum, London.)*

Fig. 6 **Stangenglas,** *or tall glass, south Netherlandish or Rhenish, late sixteenth or early seventeenth century. Green forest glass, or* Waldglas. *(British Museum.)*

Fig. 7 **Footed beaker,** *probably decorated by Johann Schaper, Nuremburg, 1660–70. The central medallion has an enamelled portrait of Johann Georg, Elector of Saxony. (British Museum.)*

Museum Photo

Fig. 8 **Beaker,** *engraved by Caspar Lehman (1570–1622), signed and dated 1605. The engraved decoration depicts allegorical Figures of Power, Liberty and Nobility. (Museum of Applied Art, Prague.)*

Germany about 1575 and was soon produced in all the important glass centres with increasing popularity until the early eighteenth century. The work or influence of *émigré* Venetians is apparent in late sixteenth-century specimens which show decorative borders of brilliantly coloured or white dots and designs with gilding, reminiscent of fifteenth-century enamelled Venetian glass. However, a distinct national character emerges quite soon in both theme and painting technique, which is in the manner of peasant art with gay colours of thick opaque enamel and delightfully naive pictorial representation. Preferred glass forms for this decorative technique are of substantial dimension, such as the *Humpen* or *Vilkum* (German: *Willkomm*), a very large, more or less cylindrical beaker with applied foot-ring or hollow foot, and a pronounced kick (indentation) in the base (Figs. 4 and 9). Equally popular was the *Stangenglas* (Fig. 6), a tall, narrow, cylindrical beaker, and its more important near relation, the *Passglas*. When full, the *Passglas* was passed around the company, each man emptying it down to the next ring.

A *Humpen* portraying a pastor with his first and second wives separated in two registers

Vessels of this time reflect the vogue for beer drinking, and pewter-mounted tankards, jugs and ewers were given colourful enamelling. The glass metal used is colourless, of greenish tint, and may show striations and impurities. Towards the end of the sixteenth century, Christof Schürer rediscovered the technique of producing blue transparent glass by the addition of cobalt, and this looked most effective when enamelled in glowing orange-red. Decorative motifs are abundant, and glasses are grouped accordingly. The *Reichsadler* (Fig. 12) and the *Kurfürsten Humpen* show allegories of the Holy Roman Empire and its electors, with the double eagle emblem and coats of arms. Particular events during the reign of local elector-palatines, hunting scenes, sporting and domestic events such as marriages and christenings, are commemorated by illustration and inscription. Toasting glasses enamelled with trade insignia and mottoes for various guilds became highly popular. A most delightful seventeenth-century Saxon *Humpen* in the Toledo Museum of Art, Ohio, amusingly portrays a pastor, Salomon Hartzer, with his first and second wives, duly separated in two registers, and their nine children, each one identified by name. *Humpen* are usually inscribed with the date and region of provenance. A popular local glass is the *Ochsenkopf Humpen* made in the glass-houses of the Fichtelgebirge. It is so named after the locality's second highest mountain, represented by an ox head in a mountainous landscape and the rivers springing therefrom. Many of these glasses which have survived, usually without their original cover, were cold-enamelled and the applied colour pigments treated with a lacquer fixative.

During the second half of the seventeenth century, a far more sophisticated enamelling technique came to Bohemia by way of Germany. This was particularly associated with the *Schwarzlot* (a low viscosity mixture prepared from copper oxide and powdered glass, and fused to the surface by firing) painting developed by Johann Schaper (1621–70) of Nuremberg, whose techniques were based on the medieval stained glass process. Schaper's work, carried out in transparent *grisaille* with the help of a magnifying lens, is of the highest artistic quality. His subjects include portraits and landscapes, and he particularly delighted in representing characters from the *Commedia dell'Arte* popularised in the engravings of Jacques Callot (1592–1635). A small cylindrical beaker on three bun feet remained Schaper's most favoured vessel (Fig. 7).

At the end of the sixteenth century, the short-lived glass-houses at Innsbruck and Hall-in-Tyrol produced diamond-engraved glass '*à la façon de*

Fig. 9 ***Humpen** presented to Caspar Steiner of Volpersdorf by Christian Preussler, Bohemian, 1680. Decorated with enamelling. The decoration depicts the glassworks at Zeilberg. The Preusslers were a large family of glass-makers and this* Humpen *would have been made in the Zeilberg works which they owned. (Museum of Arts and Crafts, Prague.)*

Gabriel Urbanek

Venise', comparable to specimens made at Verzelini's London glass-house. However, it is in seventeenth-century Prague that the art of glass engraving and cutting by the wheel received a new and unparalleled significance. The abundance of rock-crystal and other minerals caused the art of the lapidary to flourish, and the art-loving monarchs, Rudolf II at Prague, Wilhelm V of Bavaria and Christian II of Saxony, vied with each other in engaging the finest artisans from far and near. At the Bavarian Court, the work of famous Milanese lapidaries had a significant influence on the Strasbourg cutter Valentin Drausch, who may well have been the master of that great artist innovator, Caspar Lehman (1570–1622).

By way of Munich and Saxony, Lehman arrived in Prague in 1588, already an experienced cutter of gems, rock-crystal and glass. Lehman's astonishing achievements in transferring lapidary techniques to the thin, hard brittleness of Venetian *cristallo* represents one of the marvels of artistic glass-making and when a robust glass metal was at last developed successfully, Lehman had been dead for over half a century. Early cutting techniques were shallow and broad, but Lehman's work has a vigorous quality far advanced of his time, and his designs were frequently based on contemporary Flemish and Italian engravings. After a quarrel with the Emperor's adjutant, Lehman left Prague in 1606 to work at the Court in Dresden, but returned in 1608. He was knighted by the appreciative Rudolf, and in 1609 was granted a monopoly for the application of glass engraving. After his death, the monopoly was inherited by a gifted pupil, Georg Schwanhardt.

The effects of the Thirty Years' War and the Counter-Reformation prompted Schwanhardt to settle in Nuremberg, a free city, and lay the foundation for a flourishing centre of glass decorators and engravers. A number of Lehman's pupils established workshops elsewhere, as for instance Caspar Schindler in Dresden and Jan Hess in Frankfurt. The technique of polishing parts of the matt-cut was one of Schwanhardt's innovations which greatly enhanced the reflective property of the glass surface.

Nuremberg goblets often show fine engraving, and it is during this period that the glass artist begins to add his signature to his work. Of Lehman, we have only one signed specimen, a conical beaker dated 1605 (Fig. 8), with shallow engraving and deeper undercutting, representing allegorical figures and coats of arms, although several engraved panels and glass vessels attributed to him have survived.

By about 1660–70, a robust colourless potash-lime glass had been perfected, and cutting and engraving became bolder with heavy wheel engraving in high relief and intaglio *(Hoch und Tiefschnitt)*. Enamelling was still popular, but became increasingly confined to domestic or household utility ware and of suitably less refined workmanship and character. Engraved and cut glass, however, joined the ranks of the aristocracy, and was favoured by the nobility and the wealthy *élite*. The finest work was produced in Silesia during the late seventeenth and early eighteenth centuries in the manner of rock-crystal engraving, which is also echoed in the form of the vessel, as for instance in the boat- or shell-shaped specimens reminiscent of the Italian Renaissance. The decorative treatment

17th century German and Bohemian Glass

and form of Silesian glass expresses a horizontal movement as opposed to the strictly vertical design concept in Bohemian cut glass of the period.

During the second half of the seventeenth century, the glass decorators emerge as a group of professional artists, removed from the influence and conditions of the glass-house. Guilds were formed for glass-painters, engravers and a number of allied sections, with the earliest guild established in 1661 by Count Johann Oktavian Kinsky, in Chřibská (Kreibitz).

Several German glass-houses such as Kassel, Potsdam and the Lauensteiner Hütte, were greatly influenced by the development of Ravenscroft's lead crystal. However, early attempts at applying the English formula were frequently affected by the glass disease of crizzling.

The Potsdam factory was founded in 1674 by the Elector Frederick William of Brandenburg. Here, Johann Kunckel, a man of great scientific and artistic talent, developed his famous *Gold-rubin* (gold-ruby) glass, obtained by the addition of gold and a complicated firing technique. Green and blue glass was also produced at Potsdam, and though plain facet cutting was preferred for coloured vessels, some of the finest glass engravers such as Gottfried Spiller and Martin Winter (d.1702) were employed by this factory (Fig. 1). Kunckel's book, *Ars Vitraria Experimentalis* (1678), forecasts a revival of the early Christian *fondi d'oro* glass, and Kunckel himself made use of gold-leaf in glass decoration.

The transition from a pure blown-glass style to a cut-crystal style swept aside the two hundred year old Venetian monopoly within a few decades. This was to a large extent due to the ability and inspiration of the seventeenth-century Bohemian and German glass-worker who emerges as an individual glass artist, quick to appreciate and interpret the infinite possibilities of his chosen material.

MUSEUMS AND COLLECTIONS

German and Bohemian glass of the sixteenth and seventeenth centuries may be seen at the following:

ENGLAND

Cambridge:	Fitzwilliam Museum
Edinburgh:	Royal Scottish Museum
Lincoln:	Usher Art Gallery
London:	British Museum
	Victoria and Albert Museum

CZECHOSLOVAKIA

Jablonc:	Museum of Glass
Prague:	Museum of Applied Art
	Museum of Decorative Art

GERMANY

Berlin:	Kunstgewerbemuseum
Cologne:	Kunstgewerbemuseum
Munich:	Bayerisches Nationalmuseum
Nuremberg:	Germanisches Nationalmuseum

U.S.A.

New York:	Corning Museum
Ohio:	Toledo Museum of Art

FURTHER READING

German Enamelled Glass by A. von Saldern, New York, 1965.

Der Nürnberger Glassschnitt des 17ten Jahrhunderts by E. Meyer-Heisig, Nuremberg, 1963.

Glass in Czechoslovakia by Karel Hettes, Prague, 1958.

Das Glass by Robert Schmidt, Vienna, 1922.

Fig. 10 ***Glass-blowing,*** *woodcut from* De Re Metallica *by Georgius Agricola, Basle, 1556.*

10

Mansell Collection

Fig. 11 ***Goblet*** *cut in facets and engraved with a portrait of Leopold I, Bohemia, c.1700. (Museum of Applied Art, Prague.)*

11

Museum Photo

12

Fig. 12 ***Reichsadler*** *(Imperial eagle) by Hans Burgkmair (1473–1531), 1510. Woodcut.*

Fig. 13 ***Reichsadler*** *glass showing the use of the Imperial Eagle motif. Enamelled. (Victoria and Albert Museum.)*

13

A. C. Cooper

Finery in the Field

Vesey Norman

1

Crown Copyright: Ministry of Public Building and Works

Fig. 1 **Open-faced parade helmet** *probably made at Augsburg, late sixteenth century. Made of embossed steel, the applied decoration is of gilt copper. (H. M. Tower of London Armouries.)*

Armour gradually became impractical as a defence against increasingly efficient firearms. The emphasis was placed on its rich and often finely wrought decoration, both etched and embossed, and also on the ornamental quality of the sword

The modern collecting of arms and armour dates from the Romantic Revival of the early nineteenth century. When Sir Walter Scott built his romantic, semi-medieval Abbotsford on the banks of the Tweed, he filled its dark gothic hall with arms and armour. They are still exactly as he arranged them, gleaming indistinctly in the romantic twilight which filters through the stained glass of his windows. He, and a few of his contemporaries such as Sir Samuel Meyrick, stimulated an interest that was to turn into a collecting craze by the middle of the century. As soon as Sir Richard Wallace inherited his father's legendary collection of Old Masters and works of art, he added to it a large and imposing armoury. Most of the great Rothschild collectors had some richly decorated parade armour in their houses. Collectors today usually have to confine themselves to more modest pieces, but even plain German field armour of the sixteenth and seventeenth centuries is usually well-made, with satisfying forms and lines.

Kings and princes had sets of matching armour for use in different kinds of combat

By about 1500, the fully enclosing armour had been developed and kings and princes had sets of matching armours for use in different kinds of combat – in the field or the tilt-yard, on horse or on foot. The less wealthy had a single armour with reinforces which could be worn over it and with alternative helmets, gauntlets and leg-armour to convert it for different occasions (Fig. 5). For instance, when serving on foot as an infantry commander the wearer might exchange the close-helmet for an open-faced helmet and discard the leg-armour altogether. The development of armour at this period was largely governed by fashion; the shape of the cuirass altered with the civilian doublet, while the thigh-defences (tassets) altered to accommodate differing fashions of breeches.

Improvements in firearms and the training of their users gradually forced armourers to increase the thickness and therefore the weight of their products and to provide additional breastplates (placates) to be worn over the normal breastplate. Early in the seventeenth century the armour for the lower legs was replaced by leather boots in order to lighten the burden carried by man and horse. By about 1630 complete armour began to be given up in favour of mobility; the best way of avoiding bullets was to close as rapidly as possible with the musketeers.

Although much seventeenth-century armour was crudely made, a few centres, particularly Augsburg, were able to produce well-made and well-designed suits. In 1622 Hieronymus Ringler, of Augsburg, made a complete armour for man and horse for the Elector Johann Georg I of Saxony, which is still at Dresden.

The normal method of decorating armour throughout the sixteenth century was by etching, that is, by eating away some of the surface of the metal by means of an acid. In the early part of the century, the metal was prepared by covering it with an acid-proof coating, part of which was scratched off with a fine point to allow the acid to reach the surface of the metal. This method was known as line etching. The effect of this type of etching, when seen at a slight distance, is not very sharp, but before 1520 a new method was introduced which produced sharper outlines and a

16th and 17th century German Armour

Fig. 2 ***Portrait of Henry, 5th Baron Windsor,*** *dated 1588. He is wearing an armour probably made at Augsburg, with a typical south German strap-work design. (By permission of the Earl of Plymouth.)*

Fig. 3 ***Hand and a half sword*** *with a single-edged blade bearing the mark of Melchior Diefstetter of Munich, c.1560–80. The blued-steel basket hilt is typically German. The grip is covered in ray skin. (Wallace Collection, London, by permission of the Trustees.)*

Fig. 4 ***Sword,*** *probably of the Munich town guard, c.1600. The blade bears the mark attributed to Wolfgang Stantler of Munich. (Wallace Collection.)*

greater contrast between the design and its background. In this method the design was painted on to the metal, the unprotected ground then being eaten away by the acid over quite broad areas. In either method the ground could be fire-gilt or blackened, usually leaving the design uncoloured in contrast. Fire-gilding is done by applying an amalgam of gold and mercury to the parts to be gilded, and then heating the metal until the mercury is driven off. The gold is left adhering firmly to the surface of the steel. In a special form of gilding called *Goldschmelz*, the design is carried out in gold flush with the fire-blued surface of the steel, and only the minimum of etching is used to sketch in the outline (Fig. 8). On most armours the decoration is confined to the edges of the plates and to accentuating the main lines of the armour, for instance the vertical centre line of legs, cuirass, and helmet. The main areas between were normally polished mirror-bright, but were occasionally blued or russeted. Alternatively these areas could be left rough from the hammer and then painted black. Additional colour came from the velvet and galloon-covered straps which held the parts together and of course from the plumes of the helmet.

2

Foliate scrolls, sometimes terminating in grotesque human forms or in monsters

Early sixteenth-century decoration usually consisted of bands of foliate scrolls, sometimes terminating in grotesque human forms or in monsters, with fruit and flowers, and often including birds or trophies of arms. During the 1530s, designs using strap-work and arabesques became fashionable in the decorative arts generally and so began to appear on armour. This was followed in about the middle of the century by a fashion for elaborate strap-work knots of various types based on textile designs and ultimately stemming, like the arabesques, from the East (Fig. 9). Each centre of production – Innsbruck, Nuremberg, Augsburg, Landshut and a so far unidentified north German area, had its own distinctive style, but identical designs were occasionally used in different towns, either because a published book of patterns had been used, or because one craftsman had deliberately copied another's work. In one case the design book of an etcher, Jörg Sorg of Augsburg, has survived and allows us to identify some of his work. The notes beside the drawings show that he worked for a number of different armourers and this helps us to distinguish between their work also. For instance, a shaffron (the defence for a horse's head) in the Wallace Collection was etched by Sorg for the armourer Hans Lutzenberger in 1550 for Don Andrés de Ribera. The decoration of this sort of armour is distinctive enough to allow us to identify the original pieces of a suit although now scattered in collections all over the world. The appearance of an armour in a portrait occasionally leads to the identification of the original owner. The famous Duke of Alba was painted by Antonio Moro wearing an armour, parts of which are still preserved at Vienna and which are recorded as his in a catalogue published in 1601.

An alternative form of decoration, used mainly for armours intended only for parades, was embossing (Fig. 1). The decoration is in relief, beaten up from the surface of the metal with the details finished by etching, chasing, gilding, or by damascening in gold or silver. It was always a good deal rarer in Germany than in Italy, but a few armours embossed all over with high quality decoration were produced in Augsburg.

During the early part of the seventeenth century it became fashionable to decorate armour with bands of incised foliage in place of etching. The design is usually rather sketchy, worked with chisels and a variety of punches.

A great many armours are marked, like silver, with a control mark, for instance the city arms of Nuremberg, and the craftsman's personal mark, such as the capital W of Michel Witz the Younger of Innsbruck. Unfortunately, the majority of armourers' marks are still unidentified and the north German armourers do not seem to have marked their work at all. Study of decoration and construction is only slowly distinguishing between the products of this important area and those of the southern German workshops.

Good-quality sword blades have probably been produced in the Rhineland since the Dark Ages. During the later Middle Ages and the Renaissance the two main blade-making centres were Passau and Solingen. The second of these, in particular, seems to have specialised in producing a wide variety of blades to suit different export markets. A document of 1628, for instance, gives the prices charged for blades of Spanish, Scottish and English types. Many different shapes of blades were made in Germany, both for the home market and for export; curved single-edged blades in the Eastern fashion; broad two-edged blades for infantry swords; long single-edged blades for infantry use, with a grip long enough to be grasped in both hands if the occasion demanded; purely thrusting blades (tucks) of triangular section with hollow ground faces; and numerous varieties of flattened diamond section, usually with a groove (fuller) running down the centre of each face for some distance from the hilt. As the sixteenth century progressed, long, light diamond-section blades designed primarily for thrusting but capable of giving a dangerous cut

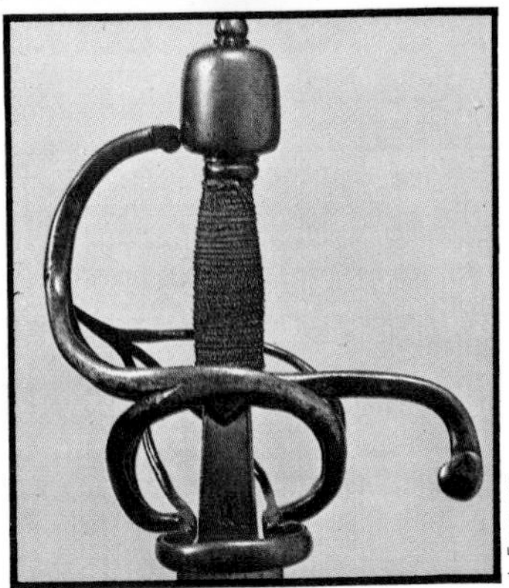

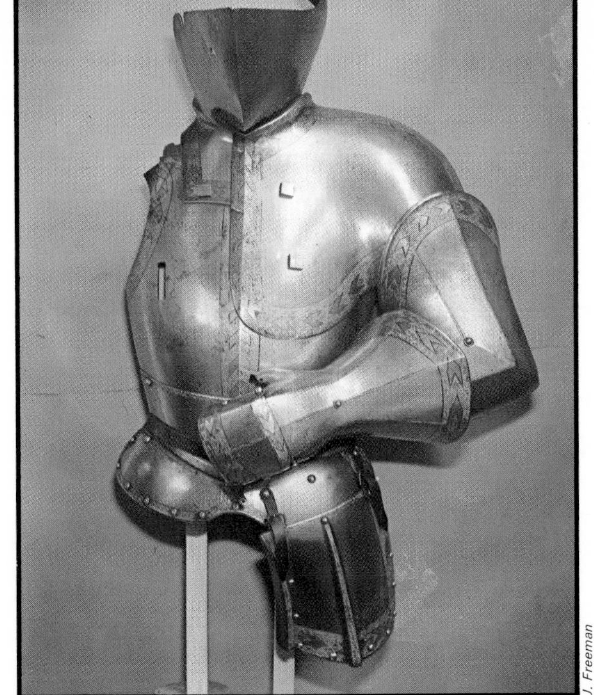

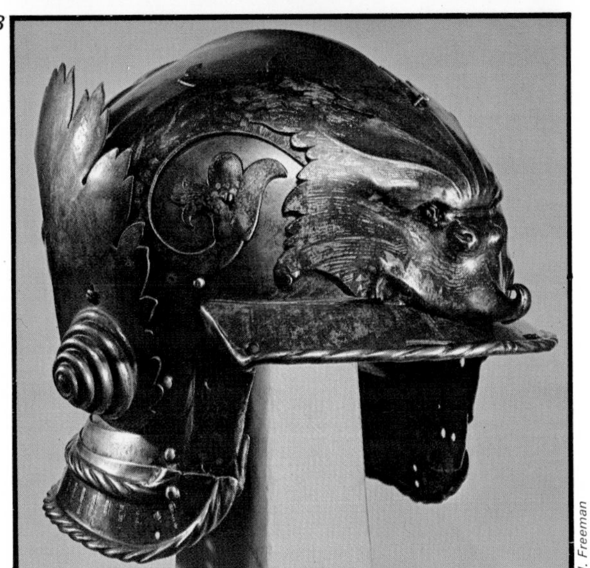

Fig. 5 ***Reinforcing pieces**, south German, c.1550. These were made for the tilt in the Italian fashion and are from a large garniture of armour made for a member of the Hirnheim family of Swabia.* (Wallace Collection.)

Fig. 6 ***Dress sword** with a chiselled steel hilt, probably the work of Caspar Spät of Munich, c.1640.* (Wallace Collection.)

Fig. 7 ***Morion**, a light open-faced helmet, Nuremberg, c.1590. Worn by one of the guard of the Elector of Saxony, this morion bears etched decoration including the figure of Mucius Scaevola, the Roman orator.* (Wallace Collection.)

Fig. 8 ***Open-faced parade helmet**, probably made by Koloman Helmschied of Augsburg, c.1520. Decorated with embossing and* Goldschmelz *– a special form of gilding. The wings and dolphin mask can be removed to make it into a fighting helmet.* (Wallace Collection.)

J. Freeman

became increasingly popular for the civilian sword – the rapier. By about 1630, blades of triangular section as long as forty-nine inches were not uncommon, and, when mounted in their original hilts, are not at all unwieldy. This type was gradually superseded for civilian wear by a shorter version as the French style of fencing triumphed over all others.

Unfortunately, although Solingen smiths used marks registered with their guild, they were allowed to leave their mark to their successors, or even to sell it, and thus unless a blade is dated, which is very rare, it is not always possible to identify its maker. Many blades were signed in full with individual letters punched in the fullers running down each face of the blade, but these names very often have no connection with the mark stamped near the hilt, presumably because the names of well-known makers were forged to enhance the price. The name of Andrea dei Ferari, a bladesmith working at Belluno at the edge of the mountains to the north of Venice, was certainly widely forged in Solingen, occasionally with the addition of a Toledo mark and the words IHN SOLINGEN, presumably to catch the tyro, whatever his taste. Although the maker's mark is usually stamped into the metal, in the seventeenth century it was sometimes etched on the blade within an oval circumscribed with the maker's name.

Scrolls and oval frames containing portraits of famous commanders

German blades were not usually decorated in the sixteenth century, but during the last quarter of the century it became fashionable to have the blade etched with a panel of foliage, strap-work or birds. In the following century, line etching again became popular. During the first quarter of the seventeenth century very fine blades were produced at Solingen, etched and gilt with the arms of their owners, and sometimes their titles,

16th and 17th century
German Armour

Fig. 9 **Tournament gauntlet** *by Wolfgang Grosschedel of Landshut, c.1560. The decoration of this gauntlet is Oriental in inspiration. (Wallace Collection.)*

9

J. Freeman

10

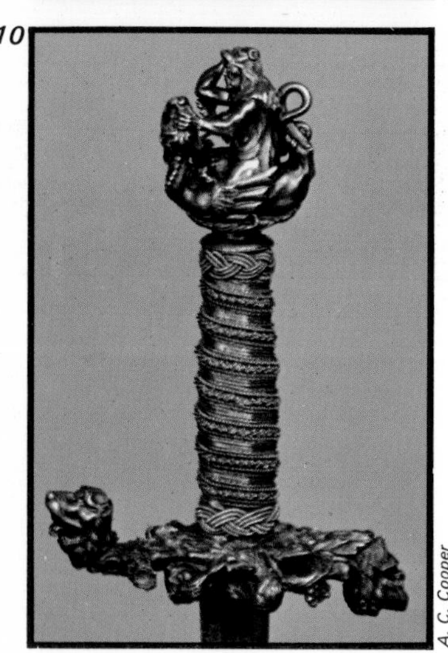

A. C. Cooper

Fig. 10 **Dress sword** *with chiselled steel hilt signed by Gottfried Leygabe, c.1650. The guards are formed of a figure of Hercules slaying the Nemean lion; the pommel presents the same figure slaying a dragon. (Victoria and Albert Museum, London.)*

and numerous mottoes, arranged symmetrically in rectangular panels. During the Thirty Years' War (1618–48) blades were often decorated with simple symmetrical bunches of scrolls and oval frames containing portraits of famous commanders such as Gustavus Adolphus and Bernhard of Saxe-Weimer, interspersed with mottoes and devices favoured by them. These are not usually gilt, the lines being simply filled with black composition. Later in the century the scrolls burst into flower and started to become less strictly symmetrical. Blades were also decorated with representations of the Emperor and the German electors, the twelve apostles, and the heroes of Antiquity.

Bladesmiths did not usually hilt swords; that was the job of the haft-maker who bought blades and mounted them in the fashion of his own area or to the choice of his patron. Occasionally specialist chisellers such as the Sadelers – Emanuel (died 1610) and Daniel (died 1632) – designed and decorated hilts to special order. Less often, jewellers such as Pery Juan Pockh made hilts of gold, enamelled and set with precious stones. The vast majority of swords, however, were hilted by anonymous haft-makers and signed hilts are exceptionally rare. It is therefore unusual to be able to identify the country of origin of a completed sword with any certainty. The work of a few haft-makers has been identified by the survival of a hilt and the bill for it in the same collection. As with armour, a few swords can be identified in portraits of their original owner. For a very large number of swords the only material for dating is the appearance of a similar hilt in a dated or datable portrait.

Since Germany was deeply influenced in its fashions by Italy, and later by France, probably all the types of hilt made in those countries were also made in Germany, and it is not normally possible to identify these imitations. However, the system of fencing used in Germany was different in that the fore-finger was not hooked over the forward bar of the cross-guard. Many German types of hilt are made so that it is quite impossible to place the finger in this position because of the form of the guards, while in order to give a firmer grip a thumb-ring is fitted on the inner side of the hilt. Even when Italian types of hilt were copied, the thumb-ring is usually present, and often an additional plate preventing the finger from passing over the cross-guard.

Forgeries have commanded better prices than original weapons

In the sixteenth century a great variety of basket-hilts were used by German infantry (Fig. 3), but the cavalry generally used more simple hilts with short grips, pyramidal or conical pommels, long spatulate cross-guards usually supporting a single side-ring filled with a shell, and a thumb-guard inside the hilt. Since these weapons were usually military, they were not normally decorated, but at Dresden, for instance, the ducal armoury contains many examples made for the aristocracy. Some have hilts chiselled all over with tiny figures, others have hilts partly encased in silver sheet, with characteristic engraving. This second style was produced throughout the latter half of the sixteenth century, and in a few cases the silver bears makers' marks. This style was widely copied in the years between the two World Wars, and in some cases the forgeries actually commanded better prices than original weapons offered at the same sale.

Little is known about specifically German types of hilts in the seventeenth century. Military fashions during the Thirty Years' War seem to have come largely from the Low Countries. The silver hilt of the Palatinate sword in the Treasury at Munich, which was made by Abraham Drentwett, the Augsburg goldsmith, in 1653, is in the form commonly seen in Dutch portraits of this date with the grip formed as a lion sejant supporting a shield with its fore-paws. By the end of the century, France had become the fashion centre of Europe. Books of engraved ornament carried the French style of decoration to every corner of the civilized world and it becomes increasingly difficult to identify the country of origin of an object. The small-sword hilt, which forms part of the garniture of arms made by Armand Bongard of Düsseldorf for the Elector Johann Wilhelm of Pfalz-Zweibrücken in about 1691, would pass for French both in form and in decoration, were it not still with the guns which bear the maker's signature.

Gottfried Leygabe, who was medallist to the Elector of Brandenburg from 1668 to 1683, is known to have made mounts for swords and pistols, but only one signed hilt by him seems to have survived. The guards are formed as a figure of Hercules slaying the Nemean lion, completely in the round, while the pommel is the hero slaying a dragon with his bare hands (Fig. 10).

CAUTIONS FOR THE COLLECTOR

1. Sword hilts have been widely forged and the more elaborate the decoration, the more cautious he should be.

2. He should examine any weapon he is offered with the greatest care, not only to ensure that the form of the guards is correct but to see that the decoration is original and that the pommel does actually match the guards.

3. Silver encrusting or gold damascening are often added to old hilts of poor quality to enhance their value. Since, in some cases, this was done as long ago as the 1860s, it can be very difficult to distinguish after a century of loving cleaning.

4. Fake blades are not very common, but over the years many hilts have been fitted with later blades to replace badly corroded or broken originals. Probably the only reliable test as to whether a blade actually belongs in a hilt is the presence of the original scabbard fitting the blade, with mounts matching the decoration of the hilt.

FURTHER READING

Blankwaffen, I and II by Heribert Seitz, Brunswick, 1965 and 1968.
European and American Arms, c.1100–c.1850 by Claude Blair, London, 1962.
European Armour, c.1066 to c.1700 by Claude Blair, London, 1958.

German Rococo
Interiors
Peter Cannon-Brookes

2

Edwin Smith

3

Author's Photo

4

Author's Photo

Breaking away from the French Rococo, the German court and rococo styles achieved a fantastic elaboration and exuberance

Broadly speaking, the rococo style of decoration flourished in Germany during the years spanned by the career of its greatest exponent, François Cuvilliés (1698–1767). Born in Hainault, Cuvilliés was sent to Paris by the Elector Maximilian Emanuel of Bavaria (1662–1726), to be trained under François Blondel the Younger (1705–44). On his return to Munich in 1725, he was appointed court architect alongside Joseph Effner (1687–1745). The Elector had been Stadtholder in the Netherlands from 1692 until 1699, and after the Battle of Blenheim he found himself back there as an exile, moving on later to live near Versailles (1704–7).

During this period of his career, Maximilian Emanuel cultivated a close personal interest in French architecture and decoration. These years saw the rejection by the more advanced patrons in Paris of the heavy splendour of the baroque style, favoured by Louis XIV and exemplified by Versailles, in favour of the much lighter and more delicate transitional style known as *Régence*. Joseph Effner built and decorated the Pagodenburg (1716) and Badenburg (1718) in the park of Schloss Nymphenburg on the outskirts of Munich for Maximilian Emanuel in this style, and in so doing laid the foundations for the flowering of German rococo decorations in Bavaria during the next reign.

In the decoration of the Amalienburg German designers broke away from French prototypes

Maximilian Emanuel died in 1726, to be succeeded by his son, Charles Albert (1697–1745), and by 1730 Effner had been entirely supplanted by Cuvilliés. The earliest decorations in Germany clearly inspired by French models were carried out shortly afterwards by Cuvilliés in the *Reichenzimmer* of the Munich Residenz (1729–37). Despite serious war damage and massive restoration, the surviving rooms in this suite are among the finest examples of the court style of Bavarian rococo decoration. Johann Baptist Zimmermann (1680–1758) from Wessobrunn, one of the greatest artists in stucco of the eighteenth century, executed the superb asymmetrical *rocaille* decorations on the ceilings, and these include naturalistic forms as well as the abstract scroll-work favoured by French designers. The decorations are brightly gilt and stand out against the plain white backgrounds, but no frescoes are included. Below, the panelling was carved by Joachim Dietrich and Wenzeslaus Mirofsky in the same style.

In Charles Albert's next important commission, the construction and decoration of the Amalienburg (1734–39) in the park of Schloss Nymphenburg, by the same team, the style of decoration breaks away entirely from French prototypes and the rooms mark the climax of the court style in Bavaria. Small in scale and essentially a pleasure house (pheasants used to be shot from the platform on the roof), the Amalienburg's decoration is of extra-

Fig. 1 (Frontispiece) ***Silvered stucco decoration*** *on the wall panels of the bedroom, Amalienburg. See Fig. 2.*

Fig. 2 ***View of the bedroom,*** *Amalienburg, Nymphenburg, near Munich, designed and decorated by F. Cuvilliés (1698–1767), 1734–39.*

Fig. 3 ***Detail of the ceiling and wall decoration*** *in the* Festsaal *of the Schloss Sünching, near Regensburg, by Ignaz Günther, 1761.*

Fig. 4 ***Corner of the Music Room*** *at Sans Souci, near Potsdam, decorated by J. M. Hoppenhaupt, 1745–53.*

Fig. 5 ***The Library*** *at Sans Souci, near Potsdam, decorated by J. A. Nahl (1710–81), 1745–47.*

ordinary delicacy and refinement. From the pale blue, pale grey, white and silver of the round Hall of Mirrors to the two tones of yellow with silver of the bedroom, there is an exquisite balance between the rich *rocaille* decorations and the highly imaginative colour schemes. In the small room set aside for the dogs, with little kennels built into the panelling, the *rocaille* decoration is freely painted on to the woodwork. Once again, there are no frescoes, but the wealth of naturalistic detail reaches a climax in the jets of water used as the central motifs on the ceiling of the Hall of Mirrors. The kitchen was clearly not intended for use by servants (food was probably passed in by servants through the windows as in the Pagodenburg), and is decorated throughout with Delft tiles, a precedent to be followed later by Charles Albert's younger brother, Clemens August, in the ground floor of Schloss Brühl.

Decorations in the Bavarian court style of the quality of the *Reichenzimmer* or Amalienburg were, by their nature, most exceptional, but from shortly after 1731 a series of rooms was decorated in the new wing of the Residenz at Ansbach for the Margrave of Brandenburg-Ansbach. Leopoldo Retti was responsible for the structure of the building and gathered together the artists who decorated the interior, but the identity of the designer of the superb Mirror Room of 1739–40 remains uncertain. The decorations at Ansbach are less exotic than those of the Amalienburg, and for many they are the quintessence of this phase of the German Rococo.

Parallel with the development of the Bavarian court style was the evolution of a native Bavarian/Swabian or Wessobrunn style of rococo decoration. In secular interiors this is best seen, at this early date, in the series of rooms in the Residenz at Kempten in the Allgäu. Decorated for the Prince Abbot Anselm I Reichlin Freiherr von Meldegg in about 1735–45, the elaborate stucco work by Johann Georg Übelherr is entirely different in character from that designed by Cuvilliés. Instead of large areas of gilding or silvering, the Wessobrunn style is characterised by the use of multicoloured stucco and *scagliola*, often combined with frescoes, and the relatively sparing use of gilding. In the Prince Abbot's Bedroom (*c.*1734) the walls are decorated with panels of delicate, moulded stucco formed of interlacing C- and S-scrolls enclosing small frescoes by Georg Hermann. Part of the stucco is gilt, but the gilding plays a relatively minor role in the total ensemble, while the illusionistic ceiling fresco also marks a complete break with French decorations.

An element of fantasy reaches a climax in the library of the Abbey Schussenried

The grandest room in the suite, the Throne Room, dates from 1742 and displays almost excessive richness. Here the windows are balanced by the large mirrors on the back wall, and the relatively small doors, decorated with geometrical patterns in marquetry, are crowned by *sopraporte* (above the door) paintings which have immensely elaborate *rocaille* frames. On the long axis of the room, the decoration of the walls is extended into the ceiling frescoes with large modelled stucco cartouches which are linked to smaller elements around the margin of the ceiling by short stretches of modelled stucco balustrade. This breaks down the division between the walls and ceiling, while the stretches of balustrade, a device evolved by Dominieus Zimmermann (1685–1766), creates a spatial ambiguity by rationally belonging to both the painted world of the fresco and the real world of the stucco. This element of fantasy is an essential characteristic of the Wessobrunn decorations. A climax is reached in the middle of the century in the library of the Abbey of Schussenried in Swabia, which was probably designed by Dominieus Zimmermann and completed in about 1757. Gentle, sinuous curves, lyrical sculpture and delicate colours culminate in the excellent rococo ceiling frescoes by Georg Hermann, and the gilding is confined to the occasional highlight only.

In 1740 Frederick the Great (1712–86) was crowned King of Prussia, and Maria Theresa succeeded the Emperor Charles VI (1685–1740) to the Habsburg domains. Frederick seized Silesia and the Elector Charles Albert was elected Emperor as Charles VII. But the Wittelsbach triumph was both expensive and short lived since, at the death of Charles Albert two years later, the tide of the War of Austrian Succession had turned and an Austrian army was occupying Bavaria. Not surprisingly, Southern Germany lost its dominating position in the field of secular rococo decorations. Instead, the lead passed to Prussia and those immensely rich ecclesiastical patrons in the Rhineland and Franconia who had succeeded in avoiding the worst troubles of the War.

The finest products of the Friederician Rococo are the result of the activity of Georg Wenzeslaus von Knobelsdorff (1699–1753) in the few years between 1740 and shortly after his withdrawal from court in 1746. It seems almost incredible that some of the finest interiors at Charlottenburg, Potsdam and Sans Souci were created during the difficult years of the First and Second Silesian Wars. To a certain extent, Knobelsdorff achieved a synthesis of the two styles evolved in Southern Germany and this is seen in the decoration of the *Goldene Galerie* of Schloss Charlottenburg in Berlin (1740–46), where the walls are decorated with elaborate, naturalistic, gilt *rocaille* motifs on a ground of pale green *scagliola* veined with red and violet. In contrast, the ceiling is decorated with much lighter, more wiry *rocaille* elements against a simple, white background, but, as in the more restrained dining-room (completed 1742), the independence of the ceiling from the walls was carefully maintained.

Fig. 6 ***Entrance Hall*** *of the Badenburg, Nymphenburg, near Munich, by Joseph Effner (1687–1745), 1718. The Badenburg was built solely as a bath-house for the Elector Max Emanuel. The design and decoration laid the foundations for the flowering of the German Rococo in Bavaria during the next reign.*

6

Edwin Smith

The sculpture of the brilliant and neurotic Nahl was of crucial importance in the Goldene Galerie

In the decoration of the music room in the Stadtschloss at Potsdam (1744–51), now destroyed, the lavish, gilt decoration was contrasted against two tones of green. Knobelsdorff filled the backgrounds of certain wall panels with a wavy pattern which picked up the basic forms of the *rocaille*, while the shape of the central field of the ceiling was repeated in the *sopraporte*. To carry out these schemes so successfully, Knobelsdorff leaned heavily upon the brilliant but neurotic sculptor, Johann August Nahl (1710–81), who fled from Berlin in 1746. Nahl's work was of crucial importance in the *Goldene Galerie* at Charlottenburg, as well as during the early stages in the decoration of the music room at Potsdam.

After 1746, his place was taken by Johann Michael Hoppenhaupt who, while tending towards greater naturalism, continued to work in Nahl's style and was responsible for much of the best decoration at Sans Souci (1745–53), including that of the music room there. After the departure of both Knobelsdorff and Nahl, the Friederician Rococo lost most of its strength, although as late as 1770 Frederick ordered his new apartments in the Neues Palais at Potsdam to be decorated in this style. Apart from the rooms in the Neue Schloss at Bayreuth, decorated for Frederick's sister Wilhelmine, Margravine of Brandenburg-Bayreuth, the Friederician Rococo made little impact outside Prussia.

Huge purple and white mottled marble columns carrying a vault decorated with gilt stucco and frescoes

Turning to the Rhineland and Franconia, German rococo interiors reached their climax in the long-drawn-out decorations of the vast palaces built by the Wittelsbach and Schönborn bishops. At Schloss Brühl, outside Bonn, the Elector Clemens August of Cologne called in Balthasar Neumann (1687–1753) who, from 1740, constructed the magnificent staircase and two principal rooms on the first floor. The small dining-room there, previously decorated by Cuvilliés in the Bavarian court style, provides a strong contrast to the gorgeous profusion of multicoloured *scagliola* and white stucco crowned by Carlo Innocenzo Carlone's brilliant fresco which decorates the adjacent staircase. Giuseppe Brilli, Giuseppe Artari and C. P. Morsegno were responsible with Carlone for the decoration of the music room and guard-room, as well as that of the staircase, work on which continued as late as 1765.

Also designed by Neumann is the suite of principal rooms in the Residenz at Würzburg constructed during the reign of the Prince Bishop Friedrich Karl von Schönborn (1729–46). The superb *rocaille* decorations of the *Weisser Saal*, executed by Antonio Bossi, were completed in 1744. As the room's name suggests, the stucco is white, and totally without gilding or other colour. These were intended to heighten the impact of the *Kaisersaal*, which is approached through it, and which is articulated with huge purple and white mottled marble columns carrying a heavy entablature of the same material and an elaborate vault decorated with frescoes and gilt *rocaille* stucco on a white ground. Prince Bishop Karl Philipp von Greiffenklau surpassed even his Schönborn predecessors in extravagance and called in Giambattista Tiepolo (1696–1770) to execute the frescoes in 1751–52.

Important rococo interiors in Germany created after the 1750s are few and far between. One of the most distinguished of these is the *Festsaal* of Schloss Sünching near Regensburg. The new eastern block of the Schloss was completed for Prince Bishop Adam Friedrich von Seinsheim in 1758, but the designer of the superb interior of the *Festsaal* is unknown. The importance of the ensemble is reflected in the team which decorated it, including the Wessobrunn stucco artists Franz Xaver Feichtmayr and Jakob Rauch, on whom fell the bulk of the commission. The delicate *rocaille* ornament painted in shades of pale blue is contrasted with a soft white background without any gilding; the brilliant wood-carvings by Ignaz Günther over the state portraits find a foil in the exuberant frescoes by Matthäus Günther.

Franz Xaver Feichtmayr also executed the stucco decoration in the last great rococo interior in Southern Germany, the *Festsaal* of the Schätzler-Palais in Augsburg, where the overall design was provided by the painter Gregorio Guglielmi who executed the ceiling fresco in 1767. Again, the colouring is very subdued indeed, and the almost overwhelming richness of the *rocaille* decorations is anachronistic. The room was not completed until 1770, and it was to prove the swansong of German rococo interiors.

7

Michael Holford Library

Fig. 7 ***The Spiegelsaal*** *(Hall of Mirrors), in the Amalienburg, by F. Cuvilliés, 1734–39. Glittering with icy blue and silver, the Hall of Mirrors is the focal point of the Amalienburg. The use of mirrors for lightening reception rooms had been quite common since Versailles, but rarely were they employed to such magnificent effect, and in such essentially intimate surroundings.*

WHERE TO SEE GERMAN ROCOCO PALACES

Ansbach:	Residenz
Augsburg:	Schätzler-Palais
Bayreuth:	Neue Schloss
Berlin:	Charlottenburg
Bonn:	Schloss Brühl
Munich:	Nymphenburg
Potsdam:	Neues Palais Sans Souci
Regensburg:	Schloss Sünching
Würzburg:	Residenz

FURTHER READING

German Rococo: The Zimmermann Brothers by Henry Russell Hitchcock, London, 1968.

Rococo Architecture in Southern Germany by Henry Russell Hitchcock, London, 1968.

Baroque Art and Architecture in Central Europe by Eberhard Hempel, Harmondsworth, 1965.

From Baroque to Rococo by Nicholas Powell, London, 1959.

Deutsches Rokoko by Hans Werner Hegemann, Königstein im Taunus, 1958.

Porcelain from Nymphenburg

Pietro Raffo

Figs. 1, 2 and 3 ***Columbina, Ottavio and Anselmo*** *from the* Commedia dell' Arte *series by Franz Anton Bustelli (1723–63), Nymphenburg, 1754–63. Hard-paste porcelain, painted and gilt.*
The artistic reputation of Nymphenburg in the eighteenth century rested almost exclusively on the chief modeller, Bustelli, who worked there from 1754 until his death in 1763. His favourite subjects were the characters of the Commedia dell' Arte, *the Italian troupes of actors who performed frequently in Bavaria. Many artists and modellers have tried to capture the liveliness and style of these travelling actors, but none has matched Bustelli's evocation of the gestures of their pantomime. (Victoria and Albert Museum, London.)*

Of the many minor porcelain works set up to rival Meissen, Nymphenburg produced some of the most beautiful and distinguished wares in the German rococo style

Germany in the eighteenth century was divided into many small states ruled by ambitious princes who took great delight in trying to outdo each other, not only on the battle-field but also in the building of palaces and in the encouragement of art and music. Following the spectacular financial and artistic success of Augustus the Strong's factory at Meissen, the lesser princes were not slow to start their own porcelain ventures.

During the second and third decades of the eighteenth century, numerous small factories sprang up in various parts of Germany and Austria. Many of them were set up with the help of workmen who had previously been employed at Meissen. The owners of the new factories had no scruples about luring away the workmen they needed with bribes and promises of larger salaries and easier working conditions. The arcanists, who had the secret of porcelain composition in their possession, were in the greatest demand. The Nymphenburg factory in Bavaria was no exception to this tradition of industrial piracy.

Bavaria, like the other German states, was for many years ruled by its own dukes and princes, and was particularly famous for its beautiful baroque palaces. For a short period it became equally famous for porcelain, rivalling even the great centre at Meissen. The earliest attempts at manufacturing porcelain in Bavaria were made in Munich in 1747 by Franz Niedermayer, a maker of tiled stoves. The project had the immediate interest and patronage of the Bavarian Elector, Prince Maximilian III Joseph, who was married to a grand-daughter of Augustus the Strong. He installed the undertaking in a nearby castle at Neudeck, and persuaded several workers from Vienna to move there. The most important of these was Jacob Helchis, a well-known porcelain painter, who became one of the first managers at Neudeck.

But the painter, however famous he may be, is not the most important person in deciding the success or failure of a porcelain factory. Neither

1

Museum Photo

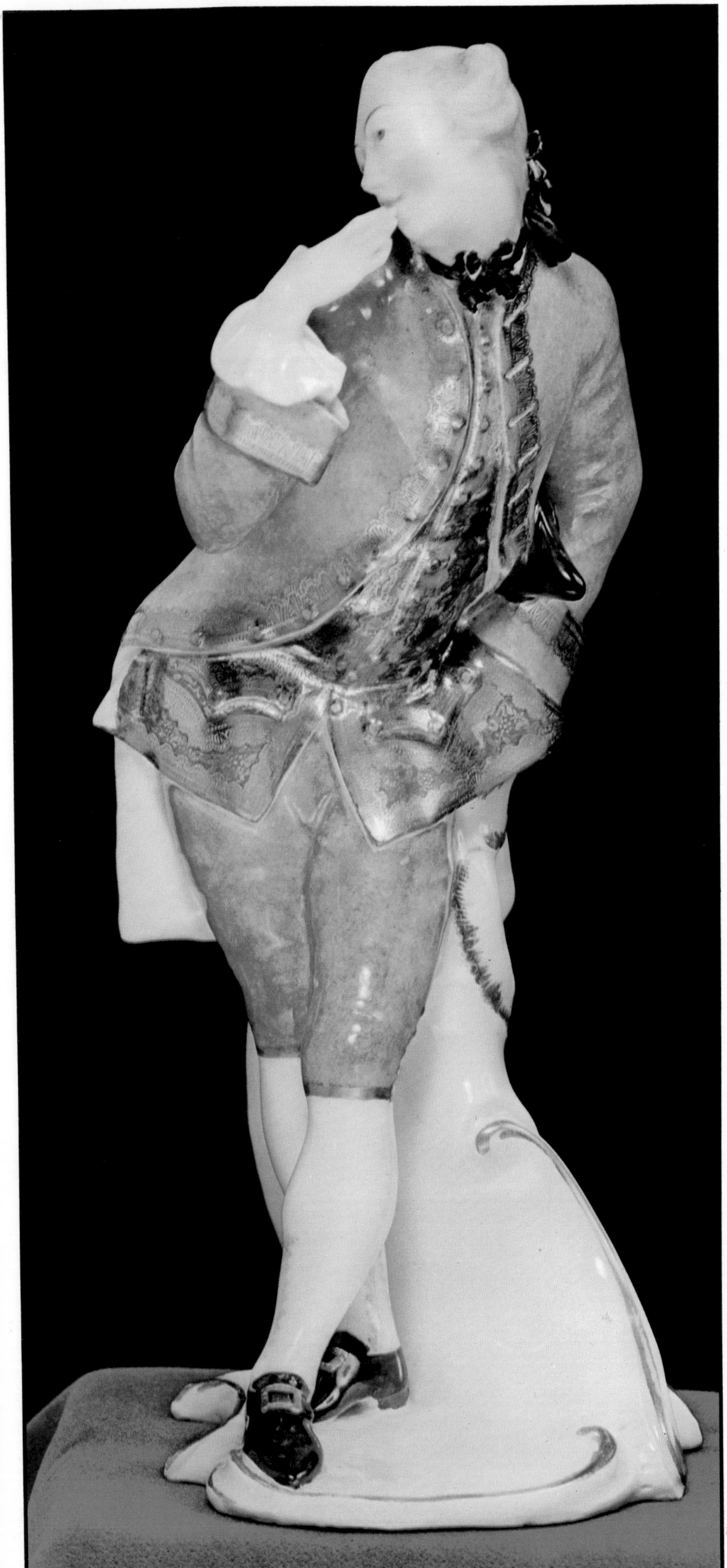

Niedermayer nor the workers from Vienna proved successful in their endeavours. The situation was saved by the arrival in 1753 of Joseph Jacob Ringler from Strasbourg. He was welcomed wholeheartedly by the Elector and by Count Sigismund von Haimhausen, who was director of the porcelain factory. Ringler was a great wanderer and had worked in Vienna and Höchst as well as Strasbourg. He remained at Neudeck for only a few years, being dismissed in January 1757. Nevertheless, he was successful in putting the concern on a sound basis, even in so short a time. He not only knew the recipe for the paste and the colours, but he also understood how to construct the necessary high-temperature kilns and wrote two books on these subjects.

Ringler was succeeded by the chemist Johann Paul Härtl, who had been working under him and who by this time had learned the whole process. He

3

Museum Photo

Museum Photo

Nymphenburg Porcelain

Fig. 4 ***Stand for a food-warmer**, Nymphenburg, mid-eighteenth century.*
In the wide range of tablewares made at Nymphenburg during the eighteenth century, food-warmers were a new addition. Note the delightfully asymmetrical scrolls with which the naturalistic decoration is combined.
(Victoria and Albert Museum.)

Fig. 5 ***Teapot**, Nymphenburg, mid-eighteenth century.*
Naturalistic flowers were a favourite decorative device at Nymphenburg, giving simple pieces such as this pot a delicate and naive charm.
(Victoria and Albert Museum.)

Fig. 6 ***Jardinière**, Nymphenburg, eighteenth century.*
The shape and the succulent flower decoration on this formal piece are both reminiscent of Vienna porcelain.
(Victoria and Albert Museum.)

Fig. 7 ***Box in the form of a shell**, inscribed 'C.H.Z. 1771' for the* Churfürstliche Hof Zohrgaden *(Bavarian Electoral Court Store Room) for which it was made, Nymphenburg, 1771.*
This unusual piece is made with the care and attention to quality seen on all Nymphenburg work.
(Victoria and Albert Museum.)

Fig. 8 ***Bust of a girl** from a model by F. A. Bustelli, marked with an impressed shield from the arms of Bavaria, Nymphenburg, c.1761.*
Bustelli's gift for lively, flowing expression is seen in his portrait busts as well as in the lively models of performers (Figs 1, 2 and 3).
(Victoria and Albert Museum.)

4

R. Todd-White

5

R. Todd-White

6

R. Todd-White

7

R. Todd-White

8

R. Todd-White

9

Fig. 9 ***Group** by F. A. Bustelli, marked with a shield with the arms of Bavaria, Nymphenburg, c.1760. (Victoria and Albert Museum.)*

Fig. 10 ***Group** by F. A. Bustelli, Nymphenburg, 1754–63. This elaborate group shows Bustelli's mastery of the difficult art of incorporating the flowing forms of his bases into the general design of the piece. This particular piece is intended for a table centre, and, like all Bustelli's work, is as attractive and lively from the back and sides as from the front. At the back of the pillar is a raised shield with the arms of Nymphenburg. (Victoria and Albert Museum.)*

Fig. 11 ***Animal group**, Nymphenburg, eighteenth century. (Victoria and Albert Museum.)*

Museum Photo

10

Museum Photo

11

Museum Photo

became manager, modeller and arcanist combined. At this time the chief painters were the Viennese Andreas Oettner, from 1756, and the Saxon Georg Christoph Lindemann, from 1758. By far the most important appointment, however, was that of the chief modeller, Franz Anton Bustelli, on 3 November, 1754. Of all the famous painters and modellers associated with Nymphenburg, he achieved the greatest renown, producing works comparable in artistic quality to those of Kaendler at Meissen.

Notwithstanding the galaxy of talent that was at hand, the factory did not run smoothly from a financial standpoint. Costs of production were high and some disagreements with a neighbouring monastery obliged the Elector to arrange for the removal of the factory to Nymphenburg, where premises were erected within the castle park. The transfer took place in May 1761, but the arcanist Härtl was not among those who set up at Nymphenburg. Apparently he declined to divulge to others his own particular formula and, having thus displeased both the Elector and von Haimhausen, he was dismissed.

Although the fame of Nymphenburg spread far beyond the frontiers of Bavaria, and showrooms were opened in Vienna, Turin, Venice and Brussels, profits lagged behind. The work force had increased from thirty-five in 1759 to one hundred and seventy-one in 1761 and, in spite of publicity campaigns and cuts in selling prices, unsold stock accumulated. Lotteries were held with porcelain pieces as prizes, but even this device failed to raise much money. From the foundation of the factory until 1767 there was, according to the books, a loss of 235,000

Fig. 12 ***Tankard**, Nymphenburg, eighteenth century. Painted porcelain with pewter mounts. Even such a humble object as a mug received the same skilful care and attention as the more magnificent products of Nymphenburg. (Victoria and Albert Museum.)*

12 

Museum Photo

13 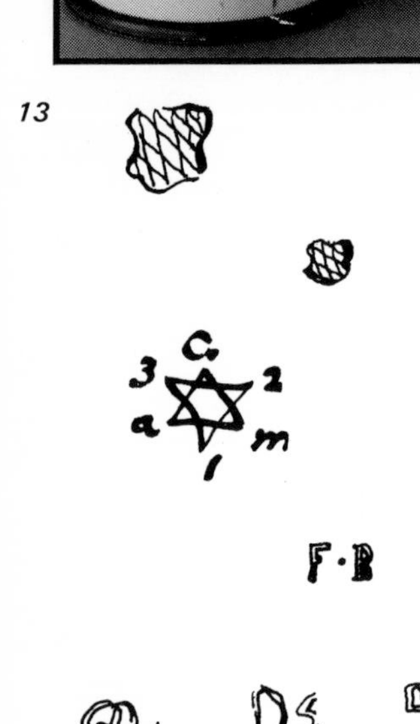

Fig. 13 ***Eighteenth-century marks from Nymphenburg,** from the top: Shield from the Bustelli period, 1754–63, impressed. Shield from the Auliczek period, c.1765–80, impressed. The hexagram mark, 1763–67, in blue. Initials of F. A. Bustelli, 1754–63, impressed. Initials of unknown workmen, incised.*

gulden, and it was possible to continue only by drastic reductions in staff. By 1769 the state subsidies were withdrawn, and so was the support of von Haimhausen. Linprun, the manager who had been at Nymphenburg since 1763, was now left to cope on his own with debts and a chronic problem of over-production. He did his best to remedy the state of affairs he had inherited, but competition from other factories aggravated the situation and he was compelled to cut down the work force to a mere twenty-eight men. This only made matters worse. Having clearly failed in his efforts, Linprun tendered his resignation in 1773 and was replaced by Dominicus Auliczek.

Auliczek had been employed at the factory since March 1762, and had been chief modeller since Bustelli's death in 1763. He remained in charge for an exceptionally long period until he was finally pensioned off against his will in 1797. Johann Peter Melchior, a former *Modellmeister* at Frankenthal and Höchst, then took over. He was artistically very gifted, but probably past his prime by the time he came to Nymphenburg.

As has already been said, the artistic reputation of eighteenth-century Nymphenburg rested effectively upon one man, the modeller Franz Anton Bustelli. His origins were humble and little is known about his early life. He was born in Locarno in April 1723, and probably received his early training in Italy, arriving at Neudeck in 1754. Although he became the artistic mainstay of the factory, he was never very well paid, his weekly wage starting at four florins and never rising above ten florins, only a quarter of the sum given to Auliczek.

Bustelli may be considered the greatest master of the rococo style in porcelain, as Kaendler had been the greatest master of the baroque. The liveliness and sense of movement in Bustelli's figures reveal him to be a true sculptor who did not look to two-dimensional prints for inspiration. Nevertheless, it is possible that he was influenced by some of the creations of the engraver Johannes Nielson, whom he knew personally. Nielson's engravings were widely copied by other porcelain-modellers, but Bustelli never made straightforward reproductions. His work was more closely related to the wood-carvings of the period.

Bustelli's elongated and delicate figures, which give so clear an impression of movement, could not be achieved in the medium of porcelain without supporting pillars and bases. In the work of previous porcelain-modellers the bases were often clumsy and conspicuous, but Bustelli mastered the art of incorporating the flowing forms of his bases into the general design. In this way he could make the base unobtrusive although it contributed to the total effect. A good example can be seen in the group illustrated in Figure 10, which is intended for a table centre. This perfect piece of rococo composition gives a remarkable feeling of space and landscaping. His gift for lively, flowing expression comes out in all Bustelli's work, in portrait busts (Fig. 8) as well as in his figures (Fig. 9). In comparison, the works of less gifted modellers seem like still, dead miniatures.

The real fame of Nymphenburg will rest for ever on the superb figures from the *Commedia dell' Arte* which were Bustelli's favourite subjects. His representations of Isabella, the Doctor, Harlequin and the rest are so lively that one seems to see them in reality, acting out their pantomimes before one's eyes (Figs. 1, 2 and 3).

During the time that Bustelli was chief modeller at Nymphenburg, little outstanding work was produced by the other modellers working there, with the possible exception of the figures made by J. P. Härtl. Although technically accomplished, however, Härtl's work never approaches the freshness of Bustelli's. Dominicus Auliczek produced some lively and inspired groups of fighting animals and other subjects, but for one who came to Nymphenburg with such a very good artistic reputation it is surprising that he did not produce many more exciting pieces.

The porcelain of Nymphenburg is of true hard-paste composition, fairly white in colour, and covered with a fine and brilliant glaze. Pieces of the early period are sometimes referred to as 'Neudeck-Nymphenburg', and most of the output was marked with an impressed *Rautenschild*, a diamond-paned shield from the arms of Bavaria. In about 1765 the so-called hexagram mark came into use in addition (Fig. 13). Following the practice at Meissen, defective pieces were often sold 'in the white' but with the factory mark cancelled by an engraved stroke.

Colour was used delicately and sparingly on the early pieces, and many groups and figures were left in the white (Fig. 11). Charming flat washes of red-blue, black and pink were used for the painting of dresses, together with a rich gold, all discreetly applied in a way that did not distract attention from the main design. Small pieces (*Galanterien*) such as snuff-boxes (Fig. 7), cane-handles and so forth, were made in large quantities in the early period, together with a good deal of tableware, but all were produced with the same care and attention to quality as in the case of the famous figures.

The Nymphenburg enterprise is a going concern to this day. Some of the old models bearing *Rautenschild* and hexagram marks are still reproduced, but many original pieces in modern styles are also being made.

MUSEUMS AND COLLECTIONS

Nymphenburg porcelain may be seen at the following:–

GERMANY

Berlin:	Schlossmuseum Kunstgewerbemuseum
Hamburg:	Museum für Kunst und Gewerbe
Nuremberg:	Germanisches Nationalmuseum

GREAT BRITAIN

Bedford:	Cecil Higgins Art Gallery
Cambridge:	Fitzwilliam Museum
London:	British Museum Victoria and Albert Museum

U.S.A.

New York:	Metropolitan Museum of Art
Washington:	Smithsonian Institution

FURTHER READING

The Commedia dell' Arte by G. Oreglia (trans.), London, 1970.

Porzellan aus der Sammlung-Blohm, Hamburg Museum für Kunst und Gewerbe, Hamburg, 1968.

German Porcelain and Faience by S. Ducret (trans.), London, 1962.

Early European Porcelain as collected by Otto Blohm by R. Schmidt, Munich, 1953.

German Porcelain by W. B. Honey, London, 1947.

STYLES IN GERMAN SILVER

Distinctive in both conception and design, German silver in the seventeenth and eighteenth centuries was among the most lavish and magnificent in Europe

Tom Milnes Gaskell

A period of intense hardship from which even the nobility were not immune followed the end of the Thirty Years' War in 1648. Not only were industry and commerce in a state of grave disrepair, but, in addition, intellectual life suffered. The old confidence in national strength had disappeared. The internal organisation of the country was chaotic; there were approximately eighteen hundred different states, some with populations of less than three hundred, all governed by an Emperor with limited powers who made laws only with the consent of the Reichstag, established at Regensburg. The picture of Germany in the middle of the century is certainly gloomy, with its crushing levies, nepotism and inefficient government. On the last score, Leopold I (1640–1705) saw his position solely as a means to promote the interests of the Catholic Church which, though arguably admirable in principle, did little to strengthen the internal structure of Germany or revive the earlier sense of optimism.

Fortunately there are always those who seek self-aggrandisement and one of the most obvious manifestations of this was in the spectacular rivalry of the lesser princes. Nothing was more suitable for ostentatious display than silver. Although the indigenous silver-mines were partly exhausted, a new source of supply was realised in America. Because obvious splendour was what mattered, the majority of the plate produced was partly or totally gilded. It was not a period that produced any startling new designs or techniques within the country; rather the designers stuck to what they knew, to the old traditions. Towards the end of the century, French influence became paramount, aided by the immigration of Huguenots who gave new life to the production of silver.

Exuberant ornamental detail was lavished on drinking-vessels

The standard of execution remained high throughout the seventeenth century and, while a preference was shown for repoussé and/or chased surfaces, the quality of engraving on occasion equalled the products of Friesland. As in contemporary architecture, there was an undoubted tendency to exuberance of ornamental detail, and this attention was lavished in particular on drinking-vessels, which form the majority of seventeenth-century German silver.

It was the custom to give a cup on any important occasion and the variety is legion. The *Riesenpokal* was unique to the German smiths; a large cup, sometimes forty inches high, it was intended solely for display. More familiar is the *Ananaspokal* (pineapple cup), the stem of which was often shaped as a tree trunk or a figure. Those with bowls decorated with large bosses *(bückeln)* continued to be produced until the end of the century, an example of the tenacity of tradition. The top cup of the *dop-*

1

K. Hoddle

Fig. 1 (Previous page) ***Salt-cellar*** *in the form of a monster, Augsburg, late seventeenth century. Height 7½ ins. (Victoria and Albert Museum, London.)*

Fig. 2 ***Beaker*** *by Christian Metz, Ohlau, late seventeenth century. Engraved with flowers and parcel-gilt, height 4½ ins. (Victoria and Albert Museum.)*

Fig. 3 ***Standing cup and cover,*** *German, eighteenth century. Mother of pearl and horn with silver-gilt mounts, height 15 ins. (Victoria and Albert Museum.)*

Fig. 4 ***Beaker and cover*** *by Johann Erhard Henglin, Augsburg, c.1720. Silver-gilt, height 6 ins. (Victoria and Albert Museum.)*

pelpokal (double cup) was reputed to be reserved for the exclusive use of the mistress of the house. A few terrestrial globe cups survive, the globe invariably supported by a figure of Atlas. Two fine examples are in the Staatliche Akademie für Werkkunst at Berlin; one is the work of a Magdeburg smith and was engraved by Wilhelm Jansson Blaeu in 1667. It was a gift from the Mayor to the Elector of Brandenburg. The other is probably by the Augsburg smith Lorenz Biller II, and was engraved by Christoph Schmidt in 1696. Another form of surface decoration was the imitation of faceted diamonds (*diamant-bückeln*) which owes its inspiration to the Venetian glassworks.

There was a long-standing popularity for cups modelled in the form of animals

A type of drinking-vessel indigenous to the country was that of cups modelled as animals. They may well have originated as three-dimensional representations of the owner's crest or part of his coat of arms. Each has a detachable head, and their forms included those of the chamois, griffin, panther, swan and pelican in her piety. They continued in popular use until the end of the seventeenth century. They were occasionally adapted to serve another purpose; the example in Figure 1 is a magnificent salt-cellar modelled as a monster holding in its claws a scallop shell.

2

K. Hoddle

The surfaces of tankards provided great opportunity for imaginative German goldsmiths. In the main, they chose to decorate them with chasing, the scenes represented often being of a mythological or biblical nature, and sometimes a combination of the two. Even in the last years of the century there were examples of typical high renaissance ornament, swags of fruit and flowers, garlands and strap-work. Nevertheless, these pieces remained expressions of distinct German individuality in conception and design.

In some cases a Netherlandish influence is apparent, which is hardly surprising in view of the predominance of Dutch merchants travelling in Europe. Pattern books were widely circulated and had some influence on design. The essence of the style created in Holland by the Van Vianens, and pursued to its logical conclusion by Johannes Lutma, was discretion. The style never engulfed a piece but on occasion became apparent, as for instance, on the scroll handle of a tankard or round the base of a standing cup. However, in the succeeding century the inspiration became increasingly eclectic.

There had long existed in Germany an interest in natural history; indeed, by the seventeenth century museums had been established devoted to this subject. A satisfactory manner of displaying natural objects to good advantage was mounting them in silver or silver-gilt. Cornelian, chalcedony, agate, mother of pearl, ivory, stoneware and faience were also used for this purpose. The silver-gilt cup in Figure 3 shows the unusual combination of horn and mother of pearl; the latter panels are finely engraved with hunting scenes. Equally, crystal, with its supposed property of divining the presence of poison, was popular.

Johann Melchior Dinglinger – a craftsman of extraordinary technical ability

The zenith of this art-form was reached by Johann Melchior Dinglinger; by 1708, with the assistance of his brothers Georg Friedrich as enameller and Georg Christoph as jeweller, he had completed his greatest work, a baroque creation called 'The Court at Delhi on the Birthday of the Great Mogul Aureng-Zeb'. Made for Augustus the Strong, it was housed in the Green Vaults at Dresden. Dinglinger, through his use of material and extraordinary technical ability, transcended the limitations of his craft. It is interesting but not surprising to note the influence on Dinglinger of some of the designs of the Frenchman Lepautre; the French influence was in the ascendant at this time. When in 1698 Augustus wished to have the Brandenburg rooms of his Dresden palace decorated, he summoned the French architect Raymond Leplat. The result was the latest Parisian style of restrained elegance, as exemplified by Jean Bérain.

The development of the Louis XIV style in Germany owed much to the publications of Abraham Drentwett (1647–1727) of Augsburg and Johann Jakob Priester, who worked in collaboration with Elias Adam. The latter specialised in mounts, as did Melchior Beyer. Several practising goldsmiths published designs, among them Johann Leonhard Eysler, Johann Erhard Henglin II and Johann

4

K. Hoddle

Ludwig Biller, who belonged to a well-known family of Augsburg smiths. Another from the same town was J. J. Baumgartner whose designs, published in 1727, included some *Chinoiseries*. The main centre for dissemination of the style was Augsburg, a city that remained pre-eminent in quality as well as in quantity of production throughout the eighteenth century.

It would, however, be wrong to assume that France was the only outside influence on taste. England admittedly was of far less consequence, but a ewer and basin now in the Lee of Fareham Collection, made by Daniel Schaeffler of Augsburg around 1710 and decorated simply with gadrooning, shows a strong stylistic similarity to some produced in England. In addition, when the Hanoverian Elector came to the English throne, this connection resulted in the direct copying of English designs by Hanoverian goldsmiths.

Frederick the Great was an enthusiastic patron of the arts

But by the middle of the eighteenth-century, Voltaire wrote from Potsdam: 'I am in France here. Only my own tongue is spoken. German is reserved for soldiers and horses'. Outposts of resistance against French domination were apparent, as in the behaviour of King Frederick William I of Prussia (1713–40), who loathed everything French. However, his successor, Frederick the Great (1740–86) showed antipathy to his father's views and became a great patron of the arts. He was a collector on a lavish scale and had a passion for snuff-boxes, mounted in gold or silver. An edict by Frederick in 1740 forbade the importation of any

K. Hoddle

French boxes and contributed to the eminence of Berlin silversmiths in this field. Two of the most outstanding exponents of this art were Johann Christian Neuber (1736–1808) and Heinrich Taddel, (active 1739–69), both at different times directors of the Green Vaults Museum. However, the leading exponent was the Parisian-trained goldsmith Jean Guillaume Georges Krüger, who also published designs.

Until the establishment of Augustus the Strong's factory at Meissen in 1710, the goldsmiths were unrivalled in their ability to produce an enormous range of luxury goods. If a gift was required, it invariably took the form of a piece of silver. This monopoly was terminated by the invention of true porcelain in Europe and accounts for the gradual decline in prestige of German silver during the eighteenth century. At times, the two crafts were advantageously combined in mounted wares, but the artistic emphasis in Germany was towards producing ever more magnificent examples of porcelain. The forms of decoration in the early eighteenth century, which included *Laub und Bandelwerk* (foliage and scroll-work), and stylised portrait busts, were well suited to both media (Fig. 4). Accordingly, the variety of silver produced was narrowed down; certainly it included drinking-vessels, such as goblets, beakers (often covered and sometimes inset with coins) and tankards, as well as candlesticks, *écuelles* and boxes, but the wine-cisterns, fountains, andirons (Fig. 5) and large dishes common in the late seventeenth century became increasingly rare. It was a time of consolidation for the goldsmith; the glory of the past two centuries allowed him to take stock of his position and to adapt to the new influences.

Another reason for a decline in the output of silver was the number of wars that beset the century, in particular the Seven Years' War (1756–63), in which Frederick the Great took on the combined forces of Austria, France, Russia, Saxony and Sweden, his sole help a small financial interest from England. Although victorious, this war was yet another indication that it was the time not for expansive display but for the retrenchment of artistic endeavour.

In technique the French designs laid emphasis on chasing and flat chasing. Engraving was usually restricted to an inscription or coat of arms.

The emergence of the rococo style *(Muschelwerk)* was hardly apparent before 1730, and it was during the following decade that it reached its peak. The German version of the Rococo is distinctive. It was frequently somewhat crude in conception and marred by over-elaboration of detail. There was a tendency for whimsical designs like those of

5

K. Hoddle

6

K. Hoddle

ig. 5 **Andiron** *by Philip Jacob* *rentwett, Augsburg, 1747–49.* *leight 17 ins.* *his is one of the rare fire-dogs* *ade after the late seventeenth* *entury.* *Victoria and Albert Museum.)*

ig. 6 **Beaker and cover,** *maker's* *ark $^{SB}_{F}$, Augsburg, late* *eventeenth century. Chased* *vith flower-heads and gilt,* *eight 6½ ins.* *Victoria and Albert Museum.)*

Meissonnier and Claude Ballin to be lost in the ungainly shapes used. A baptismal ewer and dish, now in the Bayerisches Nationalmuseum, Munich, made in Augsburg in about 1756, is, with its welter of florid extravagance, an example of this lack of restraint. This exuberance, however, is not always apparent. On occasion the chased detail is set off by plain surfaces; the *écuelle* in Figure 7 is a rare but happy example of a less riotous and more subdued interpretation of the Rococo.

The Rococo died slowly, continuing until about 1780; but the products of the later years are somewhat stiffly executed. They lacked the earlier exuberance, which was much assisted along its course by the designers Martin Engelbrecht and Caspar Gottlieb Eissler, both of Nuremberg.

By this date, England and France were under the artistic influence of neo-Classicism; Germany, however, remained almost untouched by it. Certainly, individual examples exist incorporating loosely draped figures, wreaths, urns and Arcadian landscapes, but they are few and far between; they remain examples of an international style as opposed to one fundamentally understood and transmuted into a means of nationalistic expression. This feeling lasted out the eighteenth century and explains the decline in quality and quantity associated with its last decades.

A. C. Cooper

Fig. 7 **Ecuelle, cover and stand** *by Emmanuel Drentwett, Augsburg, 1747–49. Silver-gilt, diameter of stand 9¼ ins. The German Rococo was far removed from the tasteful delicacy of the French. In Germany, shapes were often ungainly, and marred by over-elaboration of detail. This écuelle is a rare example of a more subdued interpretation. (Christie, Manson and Woods, Ltd., London.)*

WHERE TO SEE

German silver of the seventeenth and eighteenth centuries may be seen at the following:

GERMANY
Berlin: Kunstgewerbemuseum
Munich: Bayerisches Nationalmuseum
GREAT BRITAIN
London: British Museum; Victoria and Albert Museum
Oxford: Ashmolean Museum
U.S.A.
New York: Metropolitan Museum of Art

FURTHER READING

At the Court of the Great Mogul by Joachim Menzhausen (trans.), Leipzig, 1966.
Goldschmiedekunst in Dresden by Walter Holzhausen, Tübingen, 1966.
Augsburger Silbergeräte des Spätbarock by Sylvia Rathke-Koehl, Hamburg, 1965.
Deutsches Goldschmiedekunst by Heinz Leitermann, Stuttgart, 1954.
Johann Melchior Dinglinger by Walter Holzhausen, Berlin, 1946.

William Allan

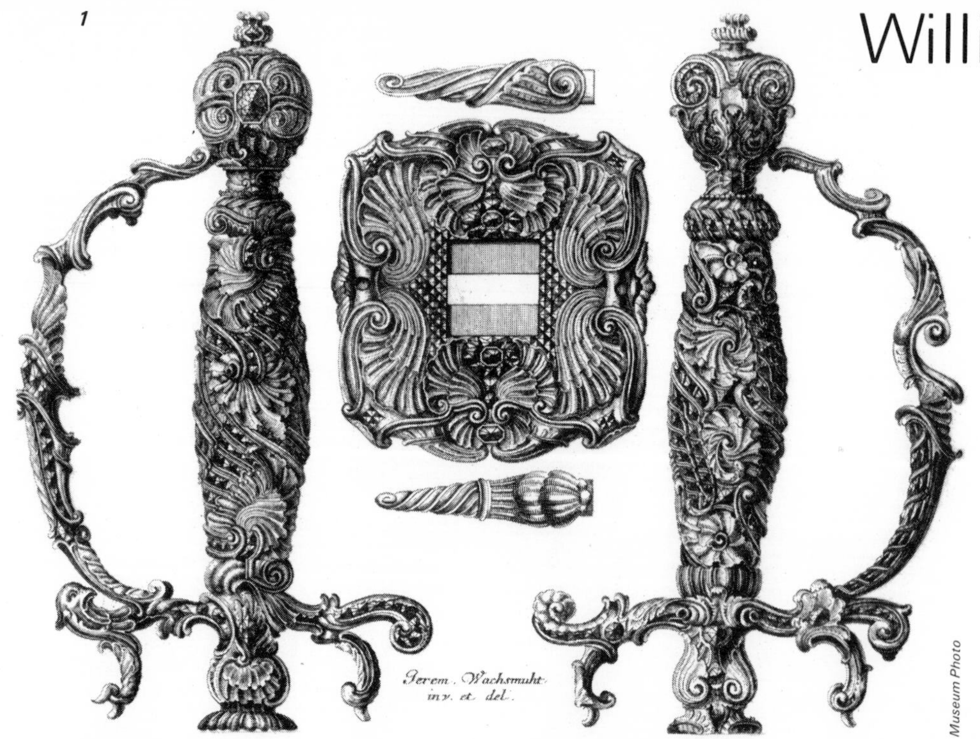

Museum Photo

The Panoply of War

Fig. 1 ***Designs for small-sword hilts*** *by Jeremias Wachsmuht (1712–79), published in Augsburg, third quarter of the eighteenth century. Sword hilts became increasingly elaborate as the eighteenth century wore on.* *(Victoria and Albert Museum, London.)*

Fig. 2 ***Officer of the Esterhazy Regiment,*** *drawing, 1774. During the Seven Years' War, the Hungarian regiments with their colourful partly Magyar and partly Turkish uniforms were the most feared in the Austrian army.* *(Heeresgeschichtliches Museum, Vienna.)*

Fig. 3 ***Partisan*** *made for Augustus the Strong, Elector of Saxony, King of Poland. Dresden, early eighteenth century. Engraved steel. Highly decorated weapons of this sort were carried by household troops in all the German states.* *(Wallace Collection, London.)*

In eighteenth-century Germany, elegance of design was not confined to the arts of peace. Not only swords and pistols, but the whole panoply of war was influenced by a desire for symmetry and visual beauty

During the Thirty Years' War (1618–1648), the horrors that were an inevitable part of campaigns conducted by untrained or mercenary soldiers were amplified by religious zeal and an ardent sense of moral rectitude. By contrast, there was a decorous and restrained quality about warfare in the eighteenth century. There was a complete revulsion from the 'blood purging' of the *Landsknechte*; instead, there were Frederick the Great's *'fröhlichen Krieges'*. Such wars were fought for a definite political objective, in which ingenuity of manoeuvre, in both the diplomatic and the military chess game, counted for more than the weight of any individual blow.

This contrast was manifest in every department of war. In the 1630s, commanders wore body armour and broadswords into the fight, and their soldiers tramped after them to the sombre and menacing sound of kettledrums and fifes joined in the *Seckenheimer Marsch*, or *Der Pappenheimer*. A hundred years later, body armour was for portraits only, and regimental officers, small-sword in hand, led their soldiers to the delicate sound of oboes and clarinets.

Considerations of civilian life and property played at least a part in the strategy of eighteenth-century generals. It was Frederick the Great's fond hope that the civil population of Prussia should remain in utter ignorance that a war was in progress, and the Bohemian Chancellor Kinsky, charged with the defence against Frederick, successfully urged the appointment of the inept Count Neipperg in place of the energetic Khevenhüller because 'the Count will be less busy in his war-making, and bring less suffering on the province'. One result of this fastidious approach to the business of war was that uniforms and appointments came to reflect the changed attitude to a remarkable degree.

For example, the white uniforms of the German heavy cavalry regiments, which aroused much adverse comment amongst British soldiers, had their origin in the leather coats worn in the preceding century. These coats became worn and dirty quite quickly, and it was customary to restore their appearance by painting them with a white substance. By the 1730s, these leather coats were discarded as being too cumbersome and inhibiting, and were replaced by white cloth tunics, stitched along the seams in the regimental colour. Prussian cuirassiers continued to wear white until 1914, despite British comments that it was 'showy, boastful and horribly modern-looking'!

Every item of military costume became more refined and more decorative. Heavy boots gave way to shoes and gaiters, wide-brimmed hats to the neater tricorn, and the long pike to the decorated partisan or spontoon. Alongside this ruthless trimming of the rough edges, there was a corresponding increase in the variety and scope of colours to be seen on the battlefield. There were more than three hundred separate states in Germany, each one of which raised and maintained a military force, if

Regt: d'Esterhazy.

Museum Photo

3

J. Freeman

4

5

6

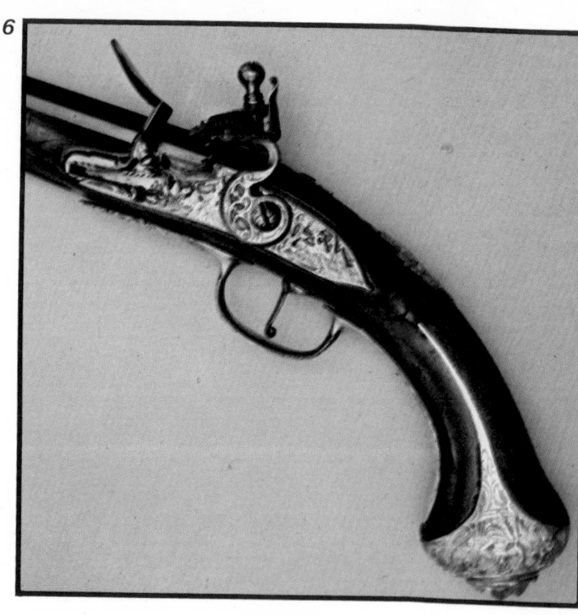

Figs. 4 and 5 ***Plates from Preussische Armee Uniformen unter Friedrich Wilhelm II,*** *Potsdam, 1789. Figure 4 shows two officers of the infantry Regiment von Schwerin. The Prussian army was noted for the simplicity and elegance of its uniforms and equipment. Figure 5 shows how older traditions found a place within the conventions of eighteenth-century uniforms. The* Garde du Corps *carried the Prussian eagle on their cuirasses in imitation of the armorial breast-plates of an earlier age, and retained their white coats from the seventeenth century down to 1914.* *(Victoria and Albert Museum.)*

Fig. 6 ***Butt of a flint-lock holster pistol,*** *Bohemian, the barrel signed by Lazaro Lazarino, first quarter of the eighteenth century. Length 18 ins. Although there were few technical improvements in pistol-making in the eighteenth century, these weapons became lighter and easier to handle. Decoration remained simple, in order not to affect the balance of the pistol.* *(Victoria and Albert Museum.)*

only to escort the Prince Bishop from carriage to cathedral. The largest and most heterogeneous army was the Austrian, drawing as it did on the resources of such diverse places as Timisoara and County Tyrone. A glance at the army list for 1769 shows the astonishing diversity of the Imperial infantry alone. Regiments twelve to sixteen were those of Los Rios, O'Wallis, von Moltke, Salm-Salm, Pallavicini and Livingstone. The Imperial infantry wore white or cornflower-blue coats, with white breeches and black or brown gaiters.

The cavalry were far less regular in appearance; the most famous and feared units were the Hungarian hussars, who wore their national costume until 1755, when a more standardised uniform became compulsory. These regiments, Esterhazy, Batthany and Bethlen, to name the three most celebrated, wore a remarkable panoply of partly Slav, partly Turkish derivation. They carried intricately carved and inlaid matchlocks, lacquered and ornamented pistols and long Turkish scimitars, mounted with silver and semi-precious stones (Fig. 2).

One further remove towards the oriental and barbaric were the *Grenztruppen*, or Borderers. These units were recruited in the Slav lands close to the Turkish frontier, among dispossessed hill farmers who were willing to fight in the Imperial army in exchange for land and the right to live within the frontiers of the Empire. The appearance of these 'Pandours', as they were called, was extraordinary. Baggy purple or red trousers, green vests, and a profusion of belts and sashes were the only common features; for the rest, they wore jerkins of coloured leather, gigantic yellow turbans or hats, and fur cloaks. Their chosen weapon was the dagger, although most carried a long matchlock or pistol as well.

In addition to these elements, the Austrian army included the famous old Bohemian Dragoon regiments of Kallowrath and Stampach and highland companies complete with bagpipes. Towards the end of the century, regiments of Tyrolean *Jägers* were raised, and in 1772, the first of the famous Polish lancer regiments was incorporated into the Imperial Guard corps. The equipment for all these troops was fairly standard; the Vienna Guild of Gunsmiths, founded by Leopold I in 1661, supplied patterns for the various muskets and carbines, and the Salzburg armourers produced swords that were of simple but elegant design.

The smaller German states were divided in their sartorial as in their political allegiance between Catholic Austria and Protestant Prussia. Brunswick and the different Hessian and Saxon states followed the Prussian model, while Bavaria, Württemberg and Baden looked southward to Austria. Some states obeyed neither imperative; the Grenadiers of Greiz-Lobenstein, and the Regiment of Schwarzburg-Sonderhausen, wore a remarkable uniform of white and red, while the cavalry of Schaumburg-Lippe-Bückeburg refused to move away from the seventeenth century, riding to battle in full armour, topped with steel helmets and fur hoods.

Another remarkable regiment was the Bavarian *Leibgarde der Hartschiere*, dating from the fourteenth century. They wore a hauberk of blue and silver, a bright metal helmet topped with a golden lion, and rode black chargers with scarlet horse-cloths. In 1789, Count Rumford reorganised the Bavarian army into 'the prettiest array in all Europe', pale blue and white with silver buttons and ornaments. In Württemberg, Duke Karl Alexander re-equipped his army in 1733 with a uniform of dark blue and yellow, and his northern neighbour, the Grand Duke of Baden-Durlach, promptly countered with a uniform of red and gold for his tiny army.

The Prussians presented a more severe picture in the line of battle. Dark blue and red were the colours for the infantry (Figs. 4 and 5), white for the cavalry and a lighter blue for the Dragoons after 1745. The hussar regiments, raised in 1721, were the only exceptions, appearing in variegated uniforms of green, brown and black. The regiment of Joachim von Zeithen, Frederick II's great cavalry leader, wore red and white with fur-edged pelisses. In this way, the battlefields of the eighteenth century came to present a spectacle which, for symmetry and colour, has never been equalled.

The traditional care in the design and manufacture of small arms still obtained, despite the move away from brutally offensive weapons. The heavy pistols and long, straight swords typical of seventeenth-century warriors were replaced by weapons which were scarcely heavier than duelling pieces. Pistols became lighter and longer, of smaller calibre, with finely engraved barrels and guards (Fig. 6). As far as swords were concerned, the heavy cavalry of all armies still carried a long-sword or

7

8

9

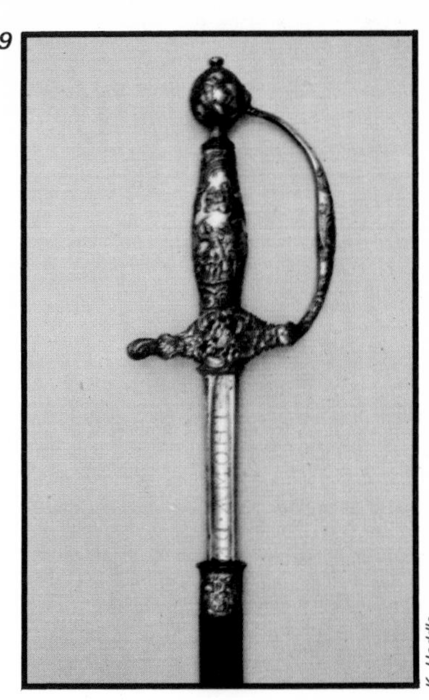

Fig. 7 ***Small-sword hilt,*** *German, late eighteenth century. Gilt bronze with painted enamel grip, length of sword 3 ft.*
In Germany, far more than in France or England, porcelain and enamelled hilts were widely manufactured. In Saxony, above all, fine examples of this type were much sought after.
(Victoria and Albert Museum.)

Fig. 8 ***Hunting knife hilt,*** *German, mid-eighteenth century. Carved ivory, length of knife 2 ft. 4 ins.*
Carved ivory was the usual material for hunting knife hilts because of its associations with the chase. The same designs, with brutal scenes from hunting lore, were used from the sixteenth century and are seen even up to the present day. The finest examples in the eighteenth century came from southern Germany.
(Victoria and Albert Museum.)

Fig. 9 ***Small-sword and sheath,*** *German, c.1750. Chiselled and gilt steel, length of sword 2 ft. 10 ins.*
Chiselled steel swords were much used, as they combined high quality decoration with great practicality. Despite their apparent delicacy they were frequently carried into battle.
(Victoria and Albert Museum.)

sabre of a pronouncedly seventeenth-century pattern, with a rather square knuckle-guard and heavy pommel. Light cavalry in imitation of the Poles and Hungarians carried a Turkish scimitar, either without a knuckle-guard at all, or with a curve quite typical of the previous century. Infantry officers, and all gentlemen of worth, carried a small-sword, a refinement of the earlier rapier without its length or elasticity (Figs. 7 and 9).

Despite the revulsion from the murderous weapons of the past, German swords in the eighteenth century were generally reckoned to be slightly longer and heavier than those of other lands. Intense care was taken over the design and embellishment of the hilts. In south Germany, the great armourers and engravers of Augsburg, Johann Baumgartner and Jeremias Wachsmuht, produced rococo sword hilts of unexceptional shape but magnificently decorated with warlike trophies, vines, scrolls and armorial bearings (Fig. 1). An indication of the growing importance of this purely decorative aspect of sword-making is that some of the finest swords in the Bavarian National Museum are the work of Franz Mazenkopf, who was court medallist from 1738 to 1776. Equally well-known engravers such as Georg Daniell Heumann thought it worthwhile to publish collections of designs for sword-hilts, often of remarkable intricacy.

The old established pike, too, ceased to be the care of the village armourer, and was accorded as much care in its design as the sword. Shortened to the old form of partisan, those highly decorated weapons carried by household troops and serjeants were more reminiscent of the medieval halberd than the seventeenth-century pike (Fig. 3).

Apart from war, hunting was the other major occupation of the nobility and gentry. There was a long-standing tradition that swords were not carried in the hunting field, and in the eighteenth century a fresh outlet was found for the swordsmith's skill in the adaptation and elaboration of the hunting knife (Fig. 8). Blades were etched with scenes of the chase, and were divided from the ornamented hilt by a plain, curved guard. Some of these hunting knives are of exquisite workmanship, particularly those made in Munich and Dresden. The Saxon smiths worked in collaboration with the porcelain manufacturers of Meissen and Dresden to produce swords and knives with hilts decorated with porcelain panels. This was a uniquely German device, and some of the swords decorated in this way were among the most beautiful made in that century.

The weight of German swords led to the development, or rather refinement, of the sword belt as a work of art. The Poles, Hungarians and Croats all wore elaborately worked belts. The Turks excelled in making fine belts, stirrups and harness of leather-work and precious metal and their enemies copied this style; it persisted into the eighteenth century.

Officers of all the German armies wore gorgets, the last survivor of the plate armour of the later Middle Ages. In common with the other metallic details, gorgets were beautifully designed and engraved either with the national arms or those of the Colonel proprietor of the regiment. Belt plates and cap plates, which are the most frequently found relics of eighteenth-century warfare, were also fine pieces of workmanship. These items were usually made of brass but there was a high rate of wastage on campaign and units often returned to their winter quarters with pouch caps and belt plates of pewter or even wood, with the regimental insignia carved crudely on them. ℛ𝒮

MUSEUMS AND COLLECTIONS

German arms and armour may be seen at the following:

AUSTRIA

Vienna:	Heeresgeschichtliches Museum

GERMANY

Baden:	Schloss Rastadt
Brunswick:	Staatliches-Herzog-Anton Ulrich-Museum
Munich:	Bayerisches Nationalmuseum
Solingen-Gräfrath:	Deutsches Klingenmuseum

GREAT BRITAIN

London:	H.M. Tower of London Armouries

SWITZERLAND

Berne:	Bernisches Historisches Museum

FURTHER READING

The Ancient Art of Warfare by Jacques Boudet, two volumes, London, 1966.
Blankwaffen by Herbert Seitz, Brunswick, 1965.
Die Handwaffen des Brandenburgisch-Preussisch-Deutschen Heeres by Werner Eckhardt, Hamburg, 1957.

William Collier

Rococo Furniture in Germany

1

Walter Steinkopf

In central Europe, as elsewhere, the elegant new rococo style became fashionable in the sophisticated courts of the mid-eighteenth century

In mid-eighteenth-century Germany, princes were still the chief patrons of the applied arts. Court life, with its formalities and splendours, was well suited to the baroque style, and the change to rococo lightness and elegance was gradual. This was partly due to the older generation's continued patronage of the style which had been fashionable in its youth. As soon as a young prince succeeded his father, the court style was apt to change, as in fact happened in several of the main centres for the spread of the rococo style in furniture.

One of the earliest and most brilliant designers in this style, François Cuvilliés, was given his major commissions at Munich and Nymphenburg not long after the accession of the Electoral Prince Charles Albert of Bavaria (1726–1745). Though Charles Albert deserves most of the credit for patronising so talented an artist, some is due to his father, Maximilian Emanuel, for recognising the potential abilities of Cuvilliés and sending him to be trained in Paris. On his return to Munich, Cuvilliés worked at first with the old court designer Joseph Effner. Charles Albert gave him sole responsibility for designing and furnishing a suite of rooms in the Munich Residenz and for creating the Amalienburg pavilion in the grounds of the Nymphenburg palace. Cuvilliés himself superintended every detail of the furniture and decoration, relying for the execution of his designs on a team of skilled craftsmen, among whom were the wood-carvers Wenzeslaus Mirofsky and Joachim Dietrich.

The resulting harmony between this furniture and its setting was a remarkable achievement. Many makers of baroque furniture had been concerned that each piece should be a work of art in itself. The advent of court workshops and the subordination of different crafts to the direction of one co-ordinating artist had enabled some designers of the early eighteenth century to relate furniture and setting. But even late baroque furniture is still

3

Verlag Gundermann Würzburg

2

Museum Photo

Fig. 1 **Corner cupboard** *by J. A. Nahl (1710–81), Berlin, c.1745. A designer in the royal workshops under Frederick the Great, Nahl produced many superb pieces intended for specific locations; note how the level of the central division coincides exactly with the moulding on the wall. (Schloss Charlottenburg, Berlin.)*

Fig. 2 **Chair,** *south German, c.1745. Carved walnut. The rococo style flourished earlier in the south than in the north of Germany, and was characterised by the exaggerated and fantastic forms and carving seen here. (Victoria and Albert Museum, London.)*

Fig. 3 **Sofa** *made by Johann Köhler of Würzburg for the Residenz, 1764. Carved and gilt wood. This virtuoso piece of carving was intended more as a showpiece of Köhler's skill than as a practical piece of furniture. (Residenz, Würzburg.)*

too strongly sculptural to avoid contrasts with flat wall-surfaces. Cuvilliés softened this implied discord by covering the walls of his rooms with lightly curved mouldings. These made a gold or silver filigree which was taken up again over the backs of settees and the fronts of commodes. Wall-mouldings were echoed in the curving supports of tables, chairs and stools. Abandoning heavy architectural motifs and sculptural scenes taken from classical mythology, he created a fresh world of elegant fantasy out of plants and flowers, trellis-work, birds, animals and cupids (Fig. 7).

Cuvilliés' accomplished work owes its elegance to a balance of straight and curved lines

There is a taut, resilient quality about Cuvilliés' furniture. It is achieved partly by sensitive carving and partly by designs which provide for decorative enrichment of salient curves, so that they are given greater emphasis. Birds perch on scroll-work as though on branches, and lattice-work repeated from walls and ceilings helps to suggest an arbour. Where furniture is intended to stand against a particular part of a wall, it is designed to harmonise with its position, so that the curved back of a settee in the drawing-room of the Munich Residenz follows the curved border of the looking-glass on the wall above it, and a pierced metal fire-guard grille in the bedroom fits exactly below the chimney-piece. In the Amalienburg's Hall of Mirrors the shallow arched recesses of the curving walls are neatly filled by console tables.

Cuvilliés reached maturity as a craftsman in the mid-1720s, and worked actively for over forty years. Knowledge of his designs was further circulated by his three books of engravings, the last two produced in conjunction with his son. In his designs for wall-decorations, the furniture appears as an adjunct, the lightly carved designs seeming to flow from the walls over the surfaces of the furniture, paying no attention to functional divisions such as the edges of drawers. It would appear that Cuvilliés thought of furniture in terms of decoration first and utility second.

The engravings illustrate another interesting characteristic of his work. Although the rococo style is often defined in terms of curving lines, these compositions of furniture and wall-panelling in fact rely not simply on curves and flourishes but on these forms alternating with vertical lines and horizontal surfaces. The resulting sense of balance between straight and curved lines contributes to the general impression of elegance in Cuvilliés' wonderfully accomplished work, all the more surprising when it is remembered that he started his career as the court dwarf. Such perfection from so misshapen a form must have seemed to contemporaries an astonishing triumph.

The Rococo did not begin to flower in the North until a decade later. While splendid display was everywhere regarded as a prince's duty – one which he was seldom reluctant to perform – there could be no guarantee of his taste. That of Frederick William I of Prussia ran to massive silver furniture, after the outdated example of Louis XIV's earlier years, and his palaces in Berlin and Potsdam were filled with a profusion of silver-framed pictures, silver-coated sideboards and tables, and even armchairs with arms and legs heavily embossed with silver. He calculated that they could be melted down for ready cash in time of need. This did in fact happen not long afterwards, in the reign of his son Frederick the Great.

A visit to Augustus the Strong helped to form the taste of Frederick the Great

Already, as Crown Prince, Frederick had furnished his castle at Rheinsberg in the rococo style. In place of the rich colours of the Baroque, Frederick insisted on softer, muted shades of grey, rose and blue to complement the lighter mode of carving in the woodwork. The panache and taste for exaggeration in his character also had to find expression, and this trait appears in the *chinoiserie* room which he had made for his wife, the Crown Princess Elisabeth, as well as in his own bedroom with its bed canopy on Corinthian columns and its walls lined with green silk ornamented with white and yellow parrots.

Frederick's taste for *Chinoiserie* may have started in Dresden. He had been there with his father to visit Augustus the Strong, King of Poland and Elector of Saxony, whose sixteen palaces included many rooms furnished in keeping with his remark-

4

5

Fig. 4 ***Design for an interior*** *with sofa, console tables and chairs, by F. X. Habermann, Augsburg, mid-eighteenth century. Engraving. Changes of style spread throughout Germany by means of engraved books of designs. Habermann's work, with its lightness worthy of Chippendale, was very popular at this time.* *(Victoria and Albert Museum.)*

Fig. 5 ***Commode*** *by Heinrich Wilhelm Spindler, Potsdam, c.1765, the mounts probably by Johann Melchior Kambli. Tortoise-shell veneer with gilt-bronze mounts. Brought from Bayreuth to Berlin in 1764 by Frederick the Great, the brothers Spindler collaborated with the Swiss craftsman, Kambli, to produce magnificent furnishings for the Neues Palais at Potsdam.* *(Sans Souci, Potsdam.)*

able collection of oriental and Meissen porcelain. Much of the fine lacquer furniture was by Martin Schnell, who turned aside from the sombre heaviness of his earlier style to brightly coloured backgrounds which are inlaid with isolated individual plants, birds and animals. This picturesque naturalism must have appealed to Frederick for, besides the *chinoiserie* work at Rheinsberg, he ordered a Chinese tea-house to be built at Sans Souci when he became King.

Frederick's accession to the Prussian throne in 1740 brought a flood of orders to the court workshops. The architect G. W. von Knobelsdorff (1699–1753), whom he had employed at Rheinsberg, was appointed General Director under close royal supervision. He assembled a talented team of artists under the direction of the sculptor and designer J. A. Nahl (Fig. 1); the brothers Hoppenhaupt were given charge of the furniture making. Frederick was a taskmaster as exacting in matters of art as in war, and this soon drove both Von Knobelsdorff and Nahl to leave his service. Johann Michael Hoppenhaupt and his brother Johann Christian remained to furnish and decorate Sans Souci and other palaces in their own version of the Rococo. As a wood-carver, trained in Vienna and Dresden, Johann Michael was more concerned with detail than with general proportions. His furniture is characterised by curiously spindly, turned-in feet which were copied by other Berlin cabinet-makers; but he provided the inventiveness and fantasy which appealed to Frederick.

The feeling for nature characterised by Watteau and Lancret and akin to that present in *Chinoiserie* was also expressed by J. M. Hoppenhaupt. Little knots of flowers and leaves sprout from his tables and chairs, while climbing plants twine around the borders of panels. His designs, engraved and published in the 1750s after he had left Frederick's employment, were often imitated and copied (Fig. 6). Similar pieces by his brother Johann Christian helped to furnish the King's new palace where the royal desk is lacquered and has silver decoration in relief. This decoration accords with the French fashion of the 1740s for silvered furniture mounts, and also with Frederick's liking for lavish display – a taste which increased with age.

The opulent appearance of gilt bronze particularly appealed to him. It was often used on the royal furniture and the King had an entire room, the *Bronzezimmer*, decorated with it in his Berlin palace. The principal craftsman responsible was the Swiss J. M. Kambli who established a workshop which turned out products as fine as those of Paris. Elaborate marquetry, also after the French manner, was made for Frederick by the brothers Spindler, who achieved light but sumptuous effects by the use of mother of pearl, silver, ivory and tortoise-shell (Fig. 5). This striking use of materials was matched in most of the royal furniture by bold designs of asymmetrical flourishes and lines curving strongly back and forth.

'Nothing in the world pleases me so much as that which comes from the Indies'

A less vigorous rococo style developed in Vienna. A change of ruler in the same year as Berlin produced a change of fashion in art; the accession of Maria Theresa in 1740 led before long to orders for renewal of work on the great imperial palace of Schönbrunn. Its furniture and decoration were both commissioned in the new style, for which the Queen Empress had a decided preference. She liked sofas, a rococo innovation, and she adored *Chinoiserie*. 'Nothing in the world', she wrote, 'pleases me so much as that which comes from the Indies', referring in this case to a lacquer cabinet presented to her by one of her subjects.

Like many of her contemporaries, Maria Theresa was none too precise as to where lacquer cabinets originated, but this is immaterial as they represented not a particular country but two strands of rococo taste: the exotic and the naturalistic. Most Viennese court furniture, relying on scrolls and flowing curves, lacks the ingenuity which characterised the work of Cuvilliés and the Hoppenhaupts. For naturalistic motifs at Schönbrunn one must turn to the chandeliers, those in gilt bronze portraying flowers and the crystal ones formalised stalactites.

The courts of minor princes were less influential in setting fashions in art but they often employed fine craftsmen trained in the larger centres. Cuvilliés worked for a time in the Rhineland for Clemens August of Cologne, younger brother of the Elector of Bavaria, and Nahl, after leaving the service of Frederick the Great, was employed by the Elector of Hesse at Wilhelmsthal near Kassel. Where a small court could not offer enough scope, the process was reversed, as when the brothers Spindler came to work for Frederick from his sister

Fig. 6 ***Design for a console table and looking-glass*** *by J. M. Hoppenhaupt, c.1750.*
A feeling for nature, seen here in the twining, climbing plants and sprigs of flowers, is often apparent in Hoppenhaupt's work. (Victoria and Albert Museum.)

Fig. 7 **Commode** *designed by François Cuvilliés (1698–1767) and carved by Johann Adam Pichler for the* Kurfürstenzimmer *in the Residenz, Munich, 1761. Carved and gilt wood against a white painted ground.*
Cuvilliés was one of the most influential of the German rococo designers, achieving a new harmony between furniture and interior decoration. (Residenzmuseum, Munich.)

Fig. 8 ***Writing-table*** *by Abraham and David Roentgen, Neuwied, c.1765. Height 52½ ins.*
This father and son team specialised in pictorial marquetry. (Rijksmuseum, Amsterdam.)

7

Museum Photo

6

K. Hoddle

8

Museum Photo

Fig. 9 ***Detail of a marquetry figure*** *from the table in Figure 10, showing the fine quality and great detail of the marquetry work. (Victoria and Albert Museum.)*

Fig. 10 ***Writing and games table*** *attributed to Abraham Roentgen, Neuwied, mid-eighteenth century.*
Apart from great skill in woodwork, the Roentgens were noted for the complex mechanical devices built into their desks and tables, which often enabled the pieces to be used for more than one purpose. The elaborate top-structure of this writing desk disappears, allowing a games table to unfold above it.
(Victoria and Albert Museum.)

Wilhelmina's court at Bayreuth. There was even a valuable interchange of craftsmen between Germany and France, so that one finds a Frenchman, Hulot, as the principal furniture-maker in Dresden and many German names – Riesener, Oeben, Weissweiler, Beneman – among the famous *menuisiers-ébénistes* of Paris. French influence was strong at the courts of Mannheim and Ludwigsburg, as well as at Ansbach where the court employed P. A. Biarelle of Liège.

Side by side with this work went that of the guilds. Particularly strong in the free towns, the home of traditional craftsmanship, the guild workers continued to produce pieces of high technical quality with an emphasis on fine inlay and marquetry. The Viennese, who maintained particularly high standards, made tables and bureaux veneered with ingenious abstract patterns. Styles changed gradually as craftsmen modified their designs over the years, the guild in each town forming a close community which discouraged abrupt innovations.

Engraved books of designs played an important part in bringing about the evolution of style. Some of the most popular of these designs were by F. X. Habermann of Augsburg. His bureaux with their vigorous serpentine curves are recognisably Continental, not unlike those in which the guild workers of Mainz specialised. His settees and chairs, however, are light enough in construction to have been designed by Thomas Chippendale (Fig. 4).

The Roentgens' workshop at Neuwied was internationally famous

English rococo taste was brought to Germany by Abraham Roentgen. He had worked in London in the 1730s and returned to the Rhineland to found a flourishing workshop at Neuwied which, with the aid of his son David, became internationally famous. It specialised in mechanical devices built into desks which allowed them to be used in different ways (Fig. 10), as well as in pictorial marquetry of excellent quality (Fig. 8). Free from restrictions of both guilds and courts, the Roentgen father and son were the first of the modern furniture manufacturers, supplying examples of the latest designs to clients all over Europe.

MUSEUMS AND COLLECTIONS

Austrian and German rococo furniture may be seen at the following:

AUSTRIA

Vienna:	Schönbrunn Palace Österreichisches Museum für Angewandte Kunst.

GERMANY

Frankfurt am Main:	Museum für Kunsthandwerk Ludwigsburg Schloss
Munich:	Residenz Nymphenburg, Amalienburg pavilion
Potsdam:	Sans Souci Neues Palais
Würzburg:	Residenz

HOLLAND

Amsterdam:	Rijksmuseum

FURTHER READING

Bauernmöbel aus Süddeutschland, Österreich und der Schweiz by Leopold Schmidt, Vienna, 1967.

World Furniture ed. by Helena Hayward, London, 1965.

Le meuble baroque et rococo By F. Windisch-Graetz, Paris, 1959.

Fränkische Rokokomöbel by H. Kreisel, Darmstadt, 1956.

Meisterrisse und Möbel der Mainzer Schreiner by F. Arens, Mainz, 1955.

L'oeuvre de De Cuvilliés, Paris, *c.*1930.

Abraham und David Roentgen by H. Huth, Berlin, 1928.

THE AGE OF METTERNICH

Peter Carson

Martin Colour

Fig. 1 ***Biedermeier Interior*** *by Johann Erdmann Hummel (1769–1852), c.1820–25. Water-colour. The sparse furnishing of this room characterises the regard for usefulness and the lack of ostentation of the Biedermeier period. (Museum für Kunsthandwerk, Frankfurt-am-Main.)*

2

3

Museum Photo

The Biedermeier style

Fig. 2 **Elizabeth of Bavaria's Bedchamber, Tegernsee Castle** *by F. X. Nachtmann (1799–1846), c.1840. Water-colour. Elizabeth was married to Frederick William IV of Prussia. (Sanssouci, Potsdam.)*

Fig. 3 **Study of Queen Teresa of Bavaria,** *possibly later used by Princess Elizabeth, by F. X. Nachtmann, c.1843. Water-colour. (Sanssouci.)*

Fig. 4 **Karl Friedrich Schinkel** *(1781–1841) by Franz Krüger, 1828. Lithograph. (Kunsthalle, Bremen.)*

Museum Photo

Biedermeier – a bourgeois style of decoration, the expression of polite, smug virtues and, in retrospect, a time of some charm

Throughout the Viennese autumn and winter of 1814–15, night after night, there trooped into dinner at the Imperial Hofburg two Emperors, an Empress, four Kings, one Queen, two Hereditary Princes, three Grand Duchesses and three Princes of the Blood. Over two hundred heads of princely families were present in the capital of the Austrian Empire which played host to a formidable assortment of European statesmen and diplomatic delegations, visiting monarchs, courtiers and lackeys and members of the international fashionable society attracted by the festivities.

These potentates had assembled in Vienna for the Congress that was to reconstruct Europe after the defeat of Napoleon, and, as many thought, to bring back the old order of before the Revolution. A casual visitor, attending the tedious imperial galas, the receptions of Princess Trautmansdorff, Countess Zichy or Prince Talleyrand, might well assume that the old order of dynastic politics and aristocratic cosmopolitanism was restored.

In spite of the distractions, those seriously involved with the Congress worked hard, and by the summer of 1815 the problems of Europe were dealt with. The Corsican monster had escaped in the meantime but had been defeated at Waterloo, thanks to Wellington's tactics, the timely arrival of the Prussians or the state of Napoleon's health.

Foto Marburg

6

Museum Photo

Fig. 5 **Design for the Raphael Room** *for the Pavilion at Charlottenburg by K. F. Schinkel. (Sanssouci.)*

Fig. 6 **Design for a colonnaded wall** *by K. F. Schinkel. (Kunsthalle, Bremen.)*

The political frontiers of Europe, then, were settled, and her heartland returned to the leadership of the ramshackle Habsburg Empire, embracing Germans, Austrians, Czechs, Poles, Magyars and Italians. Austria headed a new German Confederation, made up of thirty-nine states, rather than the three hundred existing in 1789, and including an increasingly powerful and ambitious Prussia.

The master political mind of the Empire was that of the Imperial Chancellor, Prince Metternich. At the Congress of Vienna, and at the international congresses at Troppau, Leibach and Verona, he devoted his diplomatic skills to securing the continuity of legitimacy and of established authority. Whether this was a policy of out-and-out reaction, or whether Metternich realised that time was needed for Europe to absorb the shock of the French Revolution and Napoleon, is beside the point. Europe was no longer the same. The Chancellor was too intelligent a man not to perceive it even if he was too sceptical to sympathise with the new social tensions of a continent where the old notion of monarchy, nobility and armies was giving way to 'Great Powers', parties and peoples, whose most articulate section, the bourgeoisie, was talking of nationalism, constitutionalism and reform.

Biedermeier: the style of the middle classes, 1815–48

Austria continued to preside somewhat shakily in central Europe until 1848. In that year there was a revolution in Paris which sparked off riots in all the major German states, in Lombardy and Venetia, in Budapest, Prague and Vienna. Metternich fled to Brighton. The Concert of Europe as the monarchs had programmed it in 1815 was really over – even though the liberal aims of the bourgeois revolutions were subsequently defeated.

In social, political and intellectual terms the period in Austrian and German history between the Congress of Vienna and the 1848 Revolutions forms some sort of unity. While one cannot say that the visual and applied arts flourished greatly during that time, one style (if it is that) did bloom in that climate which vanished at the blast of revolution and which anyway could hardly have survived the growth of the 'industrial arts' in the economic boom of the second half of the century. This style is called 'Biedermeier'.

7

8

Fig. 7 ***Bedchamber with Blue Walls, Tegernsee Castle,*** *German, nineteenth century. Water-colour, 10 ins x 13½ ins. The florid plasterwork on the ceiling contrasts with the strictness of the floor design and the comparative simplicity of the furniture. The continuing influence of the Empire style can be seen in the upholstery on chairs and sofa, in the wall-covering made to suggest a tent. The work-table, foot-stool and shape of the chairs are all, however, redolent of Biedermeier. (Sanssouci.)*

Fig. 8 ***Drawing-Room of the Princess Elizabeth in the Palace at Berlin*** *by Eduard Biermann, 1829. Water-colour. Large vases of flowers and festoons of greenery were much admired in the Biedermeier period. (Sanssouci.)*

The term is derived from the names of two characters in a Berlin journal, Biedermann and Bummelmeier. It is perpetrated in the title of a book published in 1850 at the end of the period, Ludwig Eichrodt's *Poems of the Swabian Schoolteacher Gottlieb Biedermaier*, a figure who embodies all the virtues of a gentle, smug, poorly educated middle class in a pre-industrial age. The term has subsequently come to be used to denote all that was most petty, philistine and narrow minded in the bourgeois. But the painting, literature, furniture, porcelain and music that have come, with a reversal of taste and an increasing nostalgia, to be discussed under the name of Biedermeier do have positive, uncomplicated, if unexciting, virtues, and very considerable charm.

Biedermeier is essentially a style of the middle classes. An excellent example of its mood – and of the change that had come over the arts within the century – is provided by a portrait of 1840 by the Viennese genre painter, Peter Fondi, of two little Princesses von und zu Liechtenstein reading at a table. Though a rather grand garden glimpsed through the window gives a clue to their rank, the cosiness of the scene could belong otherwise to any burgher's ideal of childhood. A hundred years before the girls would have been portrayed as brocaded dummies; fifty years before they might have been poised with artificial informality in a sylvan landscape. One of the most obvious points about Beidermeier, and indeed all art in the nineteenth century, is the disappearance, as the market altered, of the aristocratic as an element of key importance in style and patronage.

Genre scenes were the essence of Biedermeier paintings

One can go on defining the Biedermeier mood in terms of the subjects of its paintings: another by Fondi of a middle-aged officer and his stout and very plain lady promenading and being saluted; a girl sharing her breakfast with a dog; the elderly Goethe writing in a simply furnished study; Schubert playing charades with friends; soldiers lighting their pipes; family evening prayers; countless views of Switzerland and the market squares of quaint old towns; slightly naive portraits of Freiherr von —— and Frau Professor ——, confident in their stiff best clothes that Progress was coming their way.

Another essential point about Biedermeier is that, allowing for local qualities and quirks, it was an international style. One can recognise the Biedermeier spirit all over Europe, anywhere far from metropolitan academies and cabinet-makers and the nascent arts of industry. It is present in a manor house in Wales or the Urals, in a merchant's house in Augsburg or in a Milanese apartment.

Neat, foursquare houses, filled with solid furniture

As we have seen, Biedermeier painting was a naive mixture of genre, sentimental and romantic traditions. Its furniture and bric-a-brac were what one would expect from local craftsmen – plain and sturdy, sometimes clumsy, sometimes endearingly fanciful. Its porcelain, simply shaped and brightly coloured, was the product of factories still working in the neo-classical taste but moving away from the concept of colossal presentation dinner-services and the like, into a mass market.

At the top of the pyramid of the arts in central Europe the classical and the romantic were working out their complex relationship. The most notable monuments of the period are the ponderous but undoubtedly handsome Grecian public buildings erected in Berlin and Munich. Particularly noteworthy is the Parthenon-like 'Valhalla' built near Regensburg in Bavaria. But the great body of buyers in the cities of Germany and the Habsburg Empire had neither the taste nor the funds for an academic art that was majestically chilly. They preferred neat, foursquare houses, classical only in their proportions and lack of fuss. They bought solid settees and secretaires, often in fruitwood, derived at some removes from the Empire style. They bought engraved ruby glass from Bohemia or souvenir mugs painted with Cologne Cathedral or the sheep-like face of the Emperor Francis. They filled their houses with porcelain from the still flourishing Berlin and Dresden factories decorated in harsh colours and gaudy with gilding and luxuriant flowers or views of the becastled Rhine-

Fig. 9 **Prince Metternich** (*detail*) (*1773–1859*) *by Sir Thomas Lawrence* (*1769–1830*). *Oil on canvas. Metternich, Imperial Chancellor from 1809 to 1848, dominated European politics between the Fall of Napoleon and the Revolutions of 1848.* (*By gracious permission of H.M. the Queen.*)

Fig. 10 **Francis I** (*detail*) (*1768–1835*) *by Sir Thomas Lawrence. Oil on canvas. Emperor of Austria, called by his subjects 'Franz der Gute', he was respected for his simple mode of living and devotion to duty.* (*By gracious permission of H.M. the Queen.*)

Fig. 11 **Professor Classen and his family** by Carl Julius Milde (*1803–75*). *Water-colour. The quiet, unpretentious domestic life, described by writers of the Biedermeier period, is seen to perfection in this painting.* (*Hamburger Kunsthalle, Hamburg.*)

Fig. 12 **In front of the Mirror,** *by Georg Friedrich Kersting* (*1783–1847*), *first half of the nineteenth century. Oil on canvas.* (*Kunsthalle, Kiel.*)

11

Ralph Kleinhempel

Copyright reserved

Copyright reserved

12

Museum Photo

land. They prized ornaments like a Vienna group of 1848 showing a mother in cap and shawl holding a baby brandishing an ice-cream cornet, accompanied by a boy reading a book, a cat chasing a ball, a doll and a rocking-horse.

Perhaps the most evocative works of the period are the numerous little paintings of interiors, usually in water-colour, which became popular in the years just before the invention of photography. They minutely record every detail, every drape and wallpaper stripe, each potted plant, and the arrangement of objects on a table. The rooms are nearly always empty of people and look like nothing so much as the scene just after the curtain has risen on a nice, old-fashioned play.

One cannot say that Biedermeier art demands a very high level of appreciation or analysis. Its undoubted charm lies in what we can read back into it, and what we see is the secure innocence of the bourgeoisie before the Fall, happily reading aloud *en famille*, playing the piano and doing needlework, looking forward to the millennium which would dawn when His Apostolic Majesty would grant a constitution, when coal would be found under the meadows of Silesia and the Ruhr and the railway would link all good Germans.

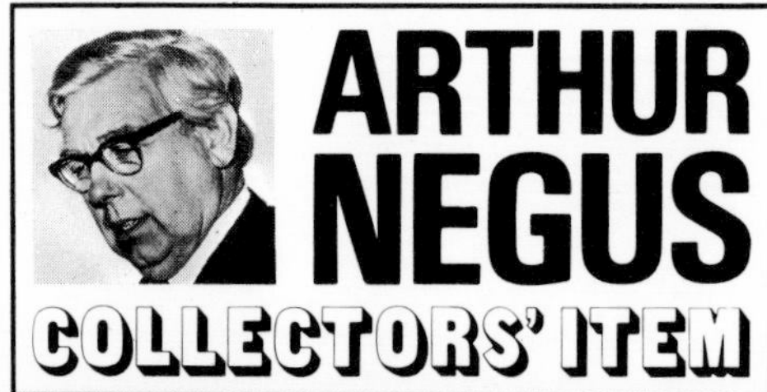

Bassett-Lowke Ltd.: A. Hornak

Steam Age, London S.W.1: A. Hornak

TOY TRAINS

Collecting toy, or more accurately model, trains is a most fascinating hobby because there is such a variety of types from which to choose. Many collectors prefer the very early type of toy which was mainly produced in Bavaria by such firms as Marklin, established in 1859, and Bing, established in 1865. Most of these early examples were crudely made, although they were substantially constructed, a fact suggested by the surprising numbers that have survived to the present day. They also have a great appeal as they are in no way scale models.

In Britain, too, there were manufacturers of model locomotives, notably the firm of Bassett-Lowke. They commenced production at the end of the last century and many of the firms are still in business today. Apart from dealing with early toy trains they also offer superb scale models from 'O' gauge, which is $1\frac{1}{4}$ ins. between the rails, right up to magnificent $7\frac{1}{4}$ in. models capable of hauling trains carrying about thirty adults.

Model and 'toy' trains are powered by clockwork, electricity or steam, and to the collector of early types the method of propulsion is not as important as whether or not the train is in its original condition. Certain manufacturers had their marks; Bing was GBN, Marklin GMC, Carrette G.C. & Co., although many models can only be identified by such small items as couplings between the locomotive and the coaches and similar small clues. Apart from this, the collector must spend time on research as many firms made parts for their apparent rivals and it is probably this fact that creates a great part of their interest today.

Passenger coaches are an enthralling extension of this interest. Some of the early German toy coaches contain miniature seats, kitchens and even lavatories. Occasionally it is still possible to find them complete with their complement of fragile Elastolin passengers.

Prices

Individual coaches and locomotives can be bought for under twenty pounds, but sets of coaches and locomotive may be expected to cost anything up to £75, or more if they are of exceptional interest.

Top left: ***Gauge 1 clockwork train*** *and a section of a bridge made* c.*1905 by Bing of Nuremberg, about £75.*

Top right: ***Brass locomotive and tender,*** *steam-driven with angled wheels, last quarter of the nineteenth century. £150 the set.*

Below: ***Great Northern Atlantic*** by Carette, c.*1910. Clockwork, about £95.*

Opposite: ***Railway station and coach by Bing of Nuremberg,*** c.*1900. The station, lit by candlelight, would cost about £20, and the coach about £8.*

Bassett-Lowke (Rlys.) Ltd.: A. Hornak

Bassett-Lowke (Rlys.) Ltd.: Angelo Hornak

1

Author's Photo

Anne Clifford

Berlin

2

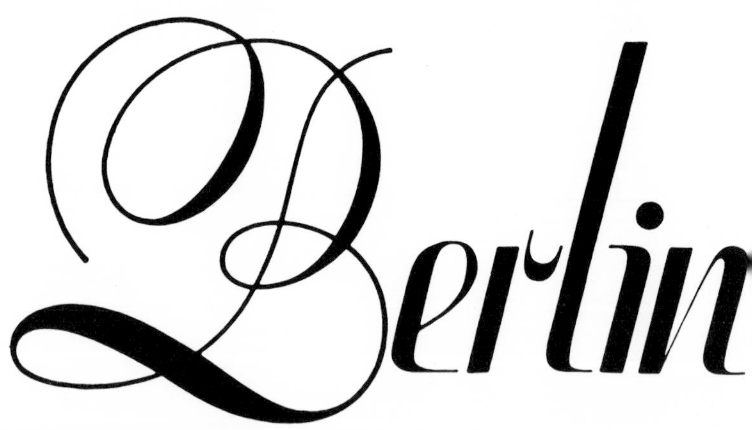

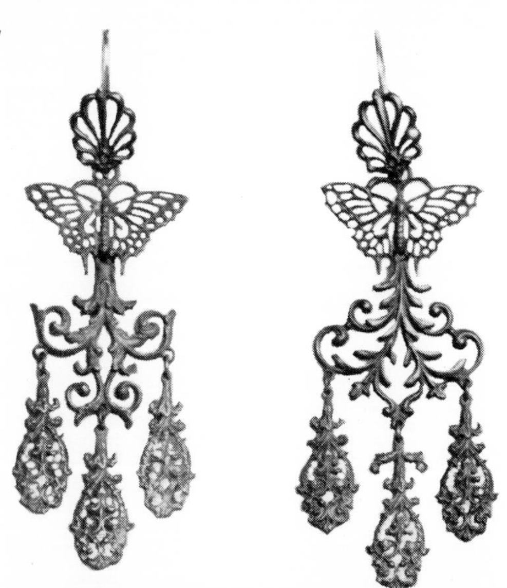

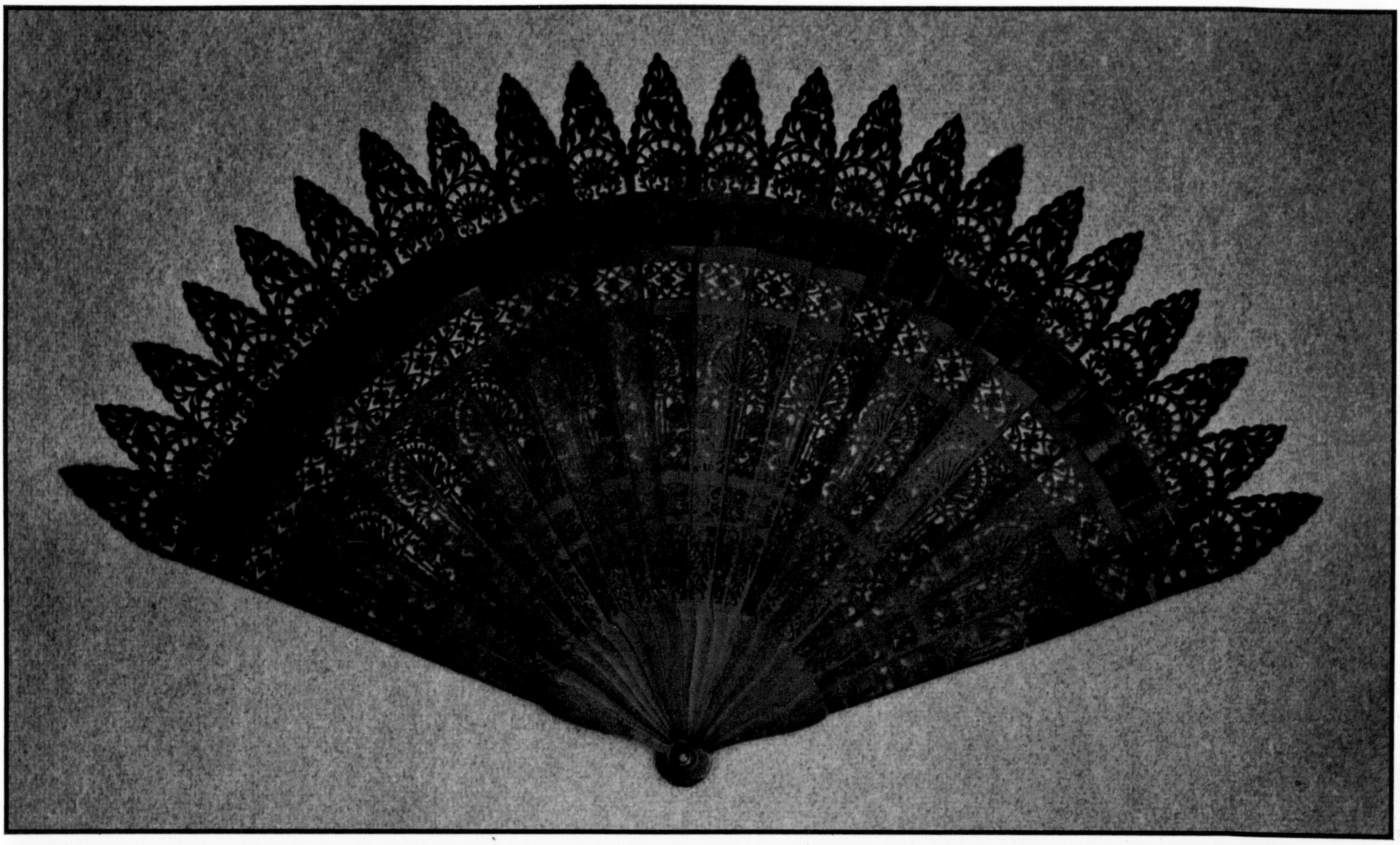

3

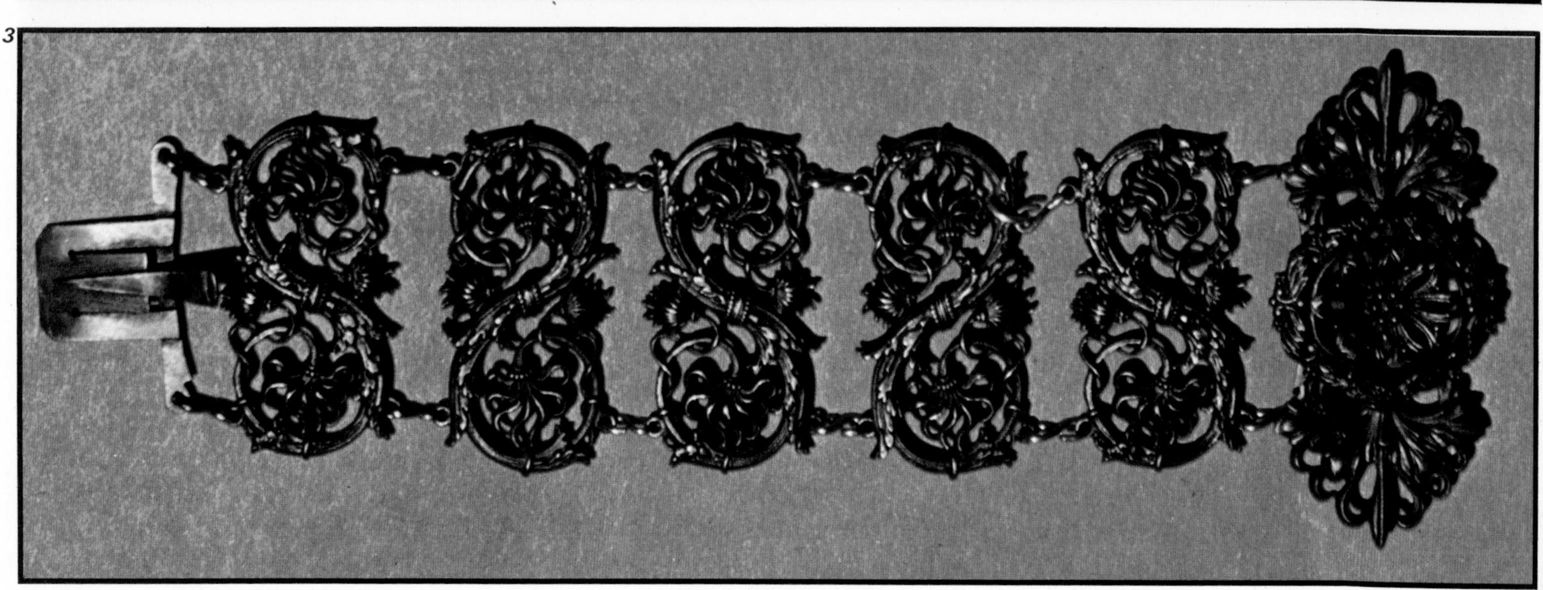

Iron Jewellery

Fig. 1 ***Butterfly ear-rings,*** *said to have been designed by Karl Friedrich Schinkel (1781–1841), the Biedermeier architect and designer.* *(Private Collection.)*

Fig. 2 ***Fan*** *by Edward Schott, Ilsenburg-am-Hartz. This was shown at the Great Exhibition of 1851.* *(Victoria and Albert Museum, London.)*

Fig. 3 ***Bracelet*** *by Geiss, mid-nineteenth century.* *(Private Collection.)*

Fig. 4 ***Fire-dog in the form of a greyhound,*** *probably late nineteenth century.* *(Private Collection.)*

Fig. 5 ***Hair-comb.*** *Iron wire-work with a relief of a classical head. The iron was cast in moulds, beaten in plates, woven into steel mesh or drawn into a wire.* *(Victoria and Albert Museum.)*

Given fresh impetus by the events of the Napoleonic wars, Berlin ironwork became an important artefact of the jeweller as well as the blacksmith

Iron as a useful material has been known from ancient times. It was worked by the Assyrians and ancient Egyptians and was used to make statues in India and China over a thousand years ago. In the European Middle Ages its ease of working and comparative cheapness made it the chosen material for everyday articles which needed to be strong and hard. As times became more peaceful, useful objects such as shields, helmets, hinges of doors and chests, gates, and even keys became increasingly and often needlessly elaborate.

Ornamental ironwork became much more widespread during the Industrial Revolution. Minor arts, which had existed for the pleasure of only a few, were taken over by keen men of business who saw that by the new methods of mass production they might be made available to the many. In England William Duesbury gathered a large part of the porcelain-making trade into his hands in Derby; Josiah Wedgwood in Staffordshire commercialised a refined pottery on a scale greater than ever before; and Matthew Boulton, first in London and later in Birmingham, made ornamental objects of silver, Sheffield plate, gold, ormolu and steel, on so large a scale that he exported his candelabra, buttons, shoe-buckles and cut-steel jewellery all over the world. The Germans, with their long tradition of skilled work in iron, explored the commercial possibilities of decorative ironwork.

The largest iron-foundries in Germany were originally in Silesia, where the ore was mined. During the War of the Austrian Succession, Frederick the Great invaded Silesia and the foundries were moved to Berlin, the capital of Prussia, partly because it was centrally placed on the canals which were necessary for transport and partly for reasons of military security. Apart from heavy engineering works ambitious iron-masters looked for new ways of using their material. Two interesting and profitable developments were the making of iron plaques and jewellery.

Iron bas-relief plaques had been made in one form or another for many centuries throughout Europe. They appeared generally in the form of firebacks, but much finer work had been used on the faces of door-locks and box-lids. This work was developed for a wider public, and commemorative reliefs were made with designs representing an historic occasion or a conspicuous achievement, such as the building of the Charlottenburg Bridge or the erection of the Monument to the Liberation on the Calvary of Berlin in 1821.

These *eisen plakketen* caught the popular imagination; they were given as Easter presents and

4

R. Todd-White

5

Karin Haddle

6

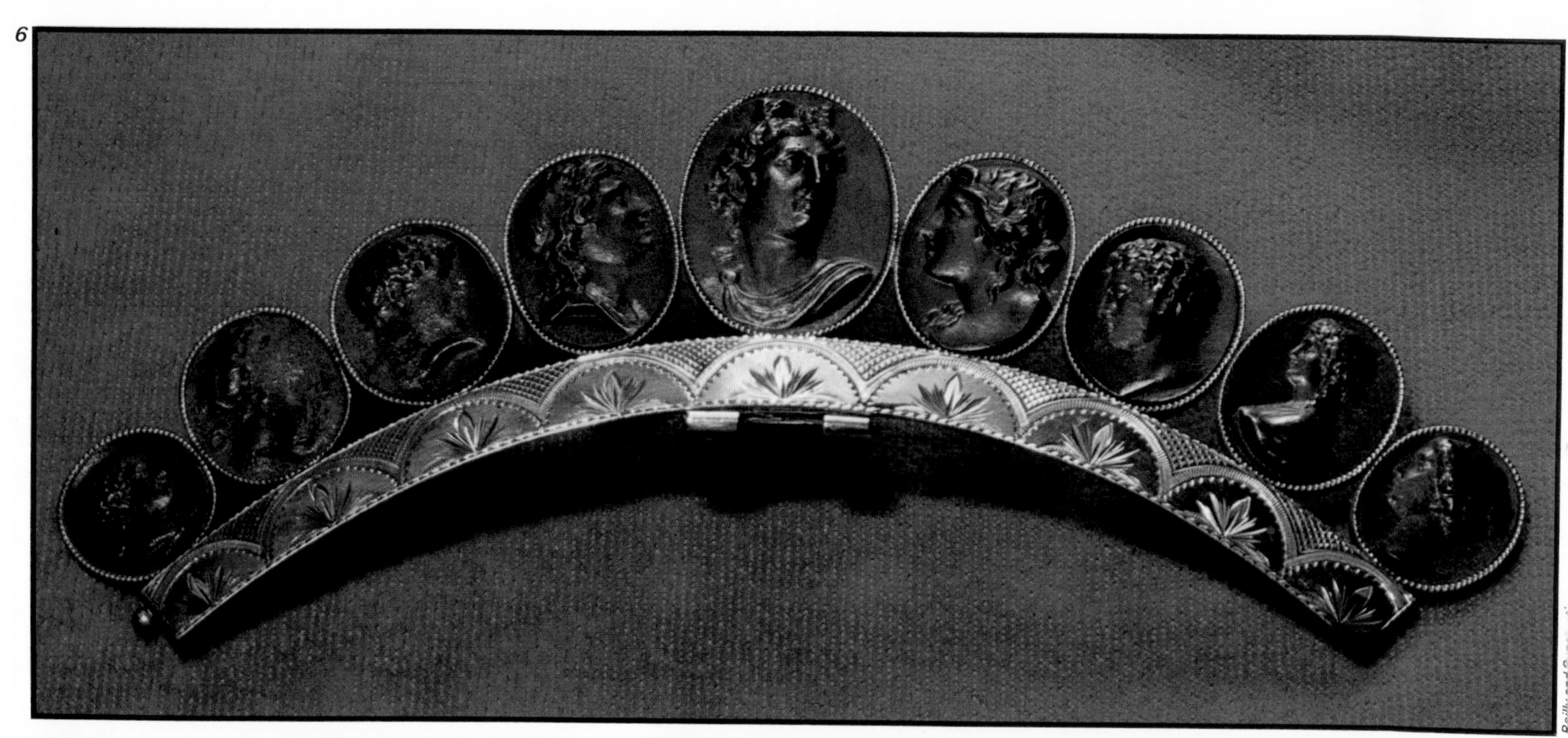

7

R. Todd-White

8

R. Todd-White

9

R. Todd-White

Fig. 6 ***Hair-ornament.*** *Early Berlin ironwork jewellery was worn as a visible receipt for silver, gold and precious stones sacrificed to the Prussian war effort.*
(City Museum and Art Gallery, Birmingham.)

Fig. 7 ***Bracelet,*** *probably by A. F. Lehmann, mid-nineteenth century.*
Probably one of a pair, this bracelet is remarkable for its lightness.
(Private Collection.)

Fig. 8 ***Parure,*** *probably by Geiss, consisting of two necklaces, one with a cross pendant, and a pair of bracelets which can be joined and worn as a collar.*
(Private Collection.)

collected rather as postage stamps are today. New examples were eagerly awaited. Because of the local appeal of their subjects the plaques were not often seen outside Germany and are not easily found, even in their homeland.

There was nothing new in the making of these iron plaques; the novelty lay in their development as a popular art and their use of contemporary motifs. The production of iron jewellery was a very different matter. Jewellery had long been made from rare and costly materials: gold, silver, enamels and precious stones; but it had also been notable for the high quality of its workmanship.

In England, where the art of making jewellery out of faceted steel-heads had already been developed, the base metal was used in imitation of the glitter and shine of diamonds and as a competitor of the popular paste jewellery. English cut-steel jewellery was a natural extension of the jeweller's art into a cheap material. German ironwork, however, reached back to the intricacies of the goldsmiths' art as it had been practised before the new methods of cutting gem-stones led to the dominance of the diamond. Earlier jewellery does not seem to have had much to do with iron jewellery design, the originality of which grew naturally from the way the material was used; the bracelets and necklaces were not typical of a conventional jeweller's work but were rather a natural extension of the work of a man used to making iron gates and keys.

It is unlikely that fashionable Prussian ladies would have taken to iron jewellery without some powerful inducement. Prussia had suffered military defeat and political dismemberment at the hands of Napoleon. The Prussian government demanded that privately owned articles of silver, gold and precious stones should be sacrificed for the good of the nation. Those who complied were given iron rings, hair-ornaments (Fig. 6), or seals as a visible token of their patriotism. At the same time encouragement was given to the Berlin iron-founders by making these receipts take the form of the already developed, but not yet popular, iron jewellery. It is from this time that ornaments date bearing the words '*Gold gab ich für Eisen 1813*' ('I gave gold for iron 1813') or '*Eingetauscht zum Wohl des Vaterlands*' ('Exchanged for the welfare of the Fatherland') and '*Unvergesslich 1813*' ('Lest we forget 1813').

Although it was necessary to show patriotism by wearing the new iron jewellery, it is reasonably certain that the fashionable ladies of Prussian society would not have worn these base-metal replacements if they had not recognised in them a new sort of chic. These strange, new, contemporary designs in a material which in spite of its vulgarity had always been revered in Germany as a symbol of strength, had all the qualities that make an instant vogue. The sharp contrast of the black metal against the whiteness of bared neck, shoulders and wrists was instantly conspicuous. The intricacy and variety of the patterns gave an admirable opportunity for exclusiveness. One could be in fashion and be different, and, because the material was cheap, one could buy a fresh parure whenever a slight shift in taste produced a new design.

Iron may be worked in several ways. It may be cast in moulds, beaten in plates, drawn into the form of wire or woven into steel mesh. All these methods were used, and sometimes several of them were combined in the same object. There were two main styles, the first of which was neo-Classicism. In iron jewellery, the neo-classical style took the form of oval or circular medals with famous classical profile heads in low relief. Sometimes these medals were made entirely of iron, but more often the black iron profile appeared in cameo on a polished steel plate. The medals were linked together to make necklaces and bracelets (Fig. 8). Pericles, Alexander, Neptune and Medusa were typical subjects with, curiously, Antinous perhaps more popular. These little profile portraits were framed either with a moulded iron rim or with coiled iron wire. The repertoire of medals was not very large but variety was achieved by the different ways in which they were combined, linked and mounted. The medal form cropped up throughout the time iron jewellery was made; the reliefs were varied with open-work silhouettes within the oval frames, and later the subject-matter became less severely classical. Cupid sharpening his arrows, sprays of naturalistic flowers, and even the *putto* that peers over the frame of Raphael's *Sistine Madonna*, took over from the helmeted head of Pericles.

The second popular style in which iron jewellery was made was the neo-Gothic. Gothic designs had

10

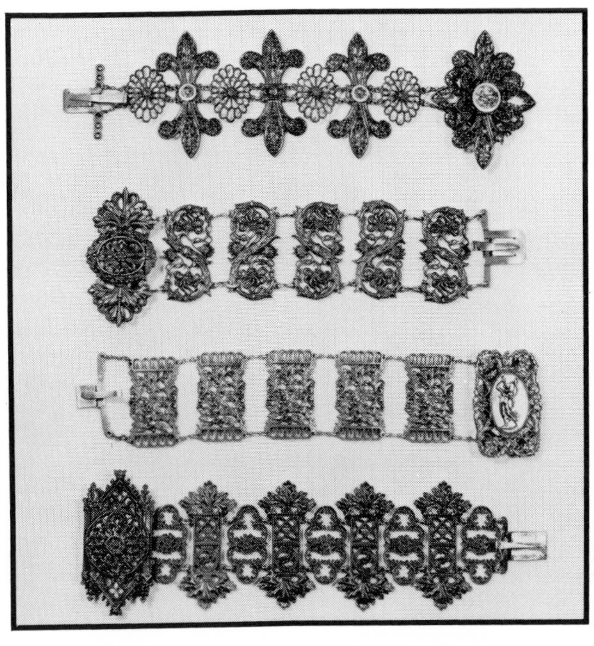

Author's Photo

11

Museum Photo

Fig. 9 ***Necklace*** *by Geiss, c.1820.*
The medallions have polished-steel backings. The entwined stems and leaves diminish in size on the inside edge of the necklace to form a curve.
(Private Collection.)

Fig. 10 ***Bracelets,*** *mid-nineteenth century.*
The bracelet second from the top is marked 'Geiss' on the clasp; the lowest one is unmarked but known to be a Geiss model. The other two are probably French, made by stamping the pattern on sheets of iron.
(Private Collection.)

Fig. 11 ***Parure.***
(Nordiska Museet, Stockholm.)

12

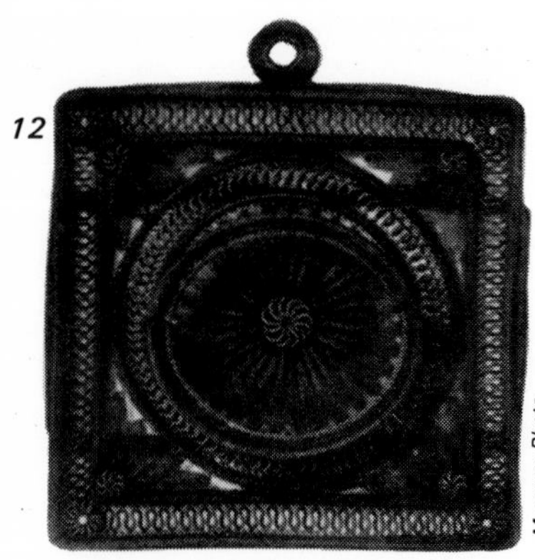

Museum Photo

Figs. 12 and 13 ***Purses** in iron filigree with steel sequins. (Musée de Ferronnerie Le Secq des Tournelles, Rouen.)*

13

Museum Photo

been produced since Horace Walpole's villa Strawberry Hill had attracted Europe; it continued to be popular until the late nineteenth century.

Dating the specimens is particularly difficult. The neo-classical style became less fashionable after Napoleon's downfall, but nineteenth-century taste drew so heavily on the past that it is not certain, for example, that all bracelets with medallion heads were made in 1812–14 when they were at the height of fashion; some were probably made later.

There is little variation in quality. The poorest types are made of rather thin metal, which looks as though it were stamped out of thin sheets of iron. The better ones are crisply moulded, and the best examples often incorporate an edging of gold. These luxury pieces give the impression of being early work, which suggests that the sacrifice of gold for iron was being made with restraint by some wearers. Just as the way of working it was not always the same, nor was the way that it was blackened. Those made in carbon-coated moulds received a matt black finish, but the stamped and drawn examples could not be coloured in this way and seem to have been lacquered rather in the same manner as early bronze statuettes. They usually have a harder, glossier, more painty surface than the moulded ones. Some of the most interesting specimens were the ear-rings, where the opportunity for three-dimensional design led to some extremely delicate and attractive cage effects. Technically the height of skill was reached at the Great Exhibition of 1851, where an exquisite fan, now in the Victoria and Albert Museum, was shown (Fig. 2). The middle of the century, however, seems to have been the turning-point, and when bare shoulders and necks became unfashionable, iron jewellery also disappeared.

Just as Berlin iron is not easy to date, so it is not always easy to say where it was made. Some of the work was done in Silesia before the foundries moved to Berlin, and again, when the French captured the city in 1806, they were so attracted by the beauty of the work that moulds were taken back to Paris, so that identical pieces were made in the two cities. A certain amount, perhaps a good deal, of Berlin ironwork is French, and some was probably made in the Low Countries, while a little experimental work was possibly done in England. It seems probable that wherever the iron industry was successful someone would have tried to start up this profitable trade.

Signed pieces are not uncommon. The names of Lehmann (Fig. 7), Geiss (Figs. 8, 9 and 10), Schott (Fig. 2), Deveranne and Schinkel (Fig. 1) have all been recorded.

Jewellery, although it is the most remarkable of the Berlin iron products, is by no means the only one. Other objects of the same material such as tinder-boxes, fire-dogs, watch-keys, combs, seals, buckles and even clavichord keys, were made and often decorated with similar motifs. There can have been few objects which the ambitious and energetic iron-masters did not at one time or another try to manufacture commercially, all of them having a distinctive charm and fascination for collectors.

MUSEUMS AND COLLECTIONS

Berlin Iron Jewellery and other decorative objects may be seen at the following:

GREAT BRITAIN

Birmingham: City Museum and Art Gallery
Brighton: Art Gallery and Museum
London: Victoria and Albert Museum
Nottingham: City Art Gallery and Museum

FRANCE

Rouen: Musée des Beaux-Arts et de Céramique

GERMANY

East Berlin: Kunstgewerbemuseum
Märkisches Museum

FURTHER READING

Cut-Steel and Berlin Iron Jewellery by Anne Clifford, Bath, 1971.
Decorative Antique Iron-Work by H. R. D'Allemagne, New York, 1968.
History of Jewellery by J. Evans, London, 1953.

Barrie and Jenkins: from Meissen by H. Morley-Fletcher

Fig. 1 ***Jay***, *mid-nineteenth century. Hand-painted porcelain, height 15 ins.*
This is a version of Kaendler's figure of a jay of 1739–40, though the surface is shinier and the decoration bolder and, in the original, more of the porcelain was left unpainted. A number of old moulds were re-used at this period and, indeed, so much of the Meissen output was reproduction that in 1846 the Minister of Finance pronounced that a new and 'pure and noble style' should be sought after. (Private Collection.)

MEISSEN IN TRANSITION AND DECLINE

Pietro Raffo

Although in severe financial difficulties throughout the nineteenth century, the Meissen factory perfected some interesting and attractive new techniques

The history of Meissen is a good example of the influence of political upheavals on the development of the decorative arts. Until 1756, under the patronage first of Augustus the Strong and then of his son Augustus III, Meissen had no serious rivals. Then came the disastrous Seven Years' War, when Meissen was occupied by Frederick the Great of Prussia, who had started a factory of his own in Berlin.

Some of Meissen's most talented artists were induced to move to Berlin, and those left behind, including the great Kaendler, were put under pressure to produce the kind of objects Frederick needed: the dinner-services, and also the snuff-boxes and other small *objets d'art* which the victorious King liked to present to his friends. Indeed, in 1762 he explained very frankly: '*J'ai commandé ici de la porcelaine pour tout le monde: en un mot je ne suis riche à présent qu'en cette fragile matière.*' ('Here I have ordered porcelain for everybody: briefly, I am rich at the moment only in this fragile material.').

Despite these large orders from the King, Meissen gradually lost its lead to the factories at Berlin and Sèvres. After peace was declared in 1763, Augustus III returned and tried to revitalise the factory. The

2

R. Todd-White

3

A. C. Cooper

court painter, C. W. E. Dietrich, was made consultant, and with him the so-called 'academic period' began, characterised by a sentimental, neoclassical style. The aging Kaendler was ill at ease with this new style and his later work hardly lived up to his great reputation.

In 1774 Dietrich died and a new Director, Count Camillo Marcolini, eagerly set about proposing improvements and rectifying inefficiencies. His efforts were only temporarily successful, and the combined effects of foreign competition and protectionist policies finally defeated him. Austria, Prussia, Denmark, Sweden and Portugal all forbade the importation of Meissen wares, while Russia, France and England applied crippling import duties. The markets for Meissen luxury pieces were almost totally lost, while those for the cheaper wares were seriously diminished by competition from the small Thuringian factories. An influx of creamware from England and an infiltration of foreign imitations of Meissen, some bearing copies of Meissen marks, added to Marcolini's troubles.

Marcolini resorted to a variety of expedients: auctions, lotteries with prizes half in money and half in porcelain, laying off workers and reduction of wages. At the turn of the century the situation became so bad that he asked to be released from his post; but he was persuaded to remain and given a court appointment. For a brief period affairs improved. Between 1804 and 1806 a profit of 40,000 talers was made, a taler being the equivalent of the English crown. But then the effects of the Napoleonic Wars began to be felt. It became more and more difficult to transport porcelain across Europe. In 1807 Marcolini reported that business was at a standstill and unpaid bills were piling up. He was compelled to ask for a subsidy and received 5,000 talers per month. By 1810 the financial position had deteriorated still further, and only fear of a serious workers' rebellion kept the factory going. Prices had to be lowered and permission given to sell porcelain in an unpainted state. In September 1813, part of the factory had to be given over for soldiers' billets, and there was talk of reconverting the whole Albrechtsburg into a fortress. On 1 January, 1814, weary and sad, Marcolini departed for Prague, where he died on 10 July that same year.

Kühn, who succeeded as manager at Meissen, apparently blamed Marcolini for failure to exploit the Russian market. In reality the difficulty lay with the Prussians. The Meissen export depot was at Warsaw, and when the Prussians occupied that city it was forced to close, since only dealers in exclusively Prussian wares could get the necessary permits. Kühn was able to introduce some helpful changes. He refused to tolerate a system in which the arcanist could conceal the secrets of the paste even from the management. An able administrative council was appointed. This included the merchant Martini, from 1816 till his death in 1824, when he was succeeded by Märtens. The same year the arcanist Köttig joined the council.

In spite of all this effort the factory could not be made to thrive. Napoleon's devastating invasions had brought poverty to the Germans, and there was little money for luxurious porcelain. Although the war had cut off English supplies, some German potters had learned to imitate Wedgwood creamware and Jasper ware and were in a position to sell

Fig. 2 **The Happy Parents** *after a model by M. Acier (died 1799), marked with incised crossed swords in a triangle and 'E3' and '183', mid-nineteenth century. Biscuit porcelain, height 9 ins. Acier was the author of severe neo-classical groups which were often allegorical. (Victoria and Albert Museum, London.)*

Fig. 3 **Comport** *by G. F. Kersting (1783–1847), from the grand table-service presented to the Duke of Wellington by King Frederick Augustus II of Saxony, c.1818. Hand-painted and gilt porcelain. Kersting was a pupil of Kühn, who had discovered a way of applying gilding cheaply in liquid form, fixing it at the same firing as the ordinary enamel colours. (Wellington Museum, London.)*

Fig. 4 **Vase of Flowers.** *Porcelain. The rococo model for this piece is found very rarely in its eighteenth-century form, but this nineteenth-century reproduction is quite common. Pink and turquoise combined with gilding is characteristic of Meissen porcelain of the mid-nineteenth century. (Private Collection.)*

4

5

R. Todd-White

6

R. Todd-White

7

A. C. Cooper

attractive substitutes for porcelain at lower prices (Fig. 5). No sooner was Napoleon driven back across the Rhine than the real English creamware reappeared and the Meissen factory found itself unable to keep pace with the elegant new designs from England.

At this critical juncture, when it was essential to reduce costs, Kühn found a method of cheap gilding. This was really a lustre, applied in liquid form and fixed at the same firing as the ordinary enamel colours. Other inventions followed. In 1828 the *Lithophanien* were introduced. This decoration was produced by pressing a die, or stamp, on to very thin slices of porcelain. When viewed in front of a light the impressed decoration gave the illusion of a three-dimensional design.

As the demand for Wedgwood creamware and Jasper continued to grow, Meissen resorted to making imitations, both of the designs and of the materials used by Wedgwood, but these attempts were not very successful. In 1831 some tea- and coffee-sets were made from casts of pressed glass, but the method was not very practicable and was soon discontinued. In 1824 gilt lithography was introduced by the painter and gem-cutter C. G. Böttger. In 1827 the same artist succeeded in decorating porcelain by transfer-printing under the glaze. About 1830, chrome was introduced for green decoration. This was the culmination of experiments that had been going on for some thirteen years. The new system was an improvement on the use of copper because chrome would stand a much higher firing temperature and could be applied under the glaze. The most gifted of the artists under Kühn was probably G. F. Kersting (1783–1847), who is said to have designed and devised the decoration for the grand table-service presented by the King to Wellington (Figs. 3 and 7).

In spite of all its technical innovations and its famous artists, Meissen could not be classed as one of the foremost porcelain factories of the nineteenth century. In the mid-nineteenth century Meissen was producing large numbers of groups and busts in biscuit, but the material never achieved the beauty of French or English biscuit. The Empire style was still very popular at Meissen long after it had been given up by other factories. Old moulds were brought out and used quite indiscriminately (Fig. 1). *Ozier* (basketwork pattern), *mosaik* and Watteau services were all copied shamelessly and without even troubling to use the original colours. Articles in a rococo style were also reproduced in quantity by the prolific modeller Leuteritz. Indeed so much was reproduced of old styles that at the Dresden Exhibition of 1845 the Meissen wares attracted much unfavourable comment.

In 1846 the Minister of Finance advised the Meissen administration not to keep exclusively to the rococo mood, but to look for 'a pure and noble style'. He also felt that new modellers and designers should be sought and trained. Anton Seelig, the Dresden sculptor, was called in to advise. He suggested consulting the professors of the Dresden Academy of Fine Arts.

In 1850 the Finance Minister again criticised the Meissen painters and modellers for lack of originality. It was his ambition to bring in new blood and new ideas and to employ artists who had not previously been involved with the medium of porcelain. Unfortunately nothing came of these

Fig. 5 ***Cup and saucer** in imitation Wedgwood, marked with crossed swords and a star in blue. Porcelain. At a time when Wedgwood creamware and Jasper ware were popular, Meissen made a number of imitations, copying both the design and the materials.*
(Victoria and Albert Museum.)

Fig. 6 ***Cup and cover and saucer,** marked with crossed swords and a star in under-glaze blue. Hand-painted porcelain. The cup is decorated with a miniature portrait of the painter Angelica Kauffmann, probably from the engraving by F. Bartolozzi after Reynolds. On the saucer Ariadne is deserted by Theseus on the Island of Naxos with Cupid weeping at her feet, probably from the engraving by E. G. Krüger after the painting by Angelica Kauffmann in the Dresden Gallery.*
(Victoria and Albert Museum.)

Fig. 7 ***Two plates** from the set given to the Duke of Wellington by King Frederick Augustus II of Saxony (see also Figure 3). Hand-painted and gilt porcelain. Work on the service, designed and with decoration devised by G. F. Kersting, began in 1818. The decoration shows Apsley House in the background.*
(Wellington Museum.)

schemes. The Meissen factory won first prize at the Munich Exhibition of 1854. Another important event was the London Exhibition in 1862 at which Meissen produced a good and varied collection. Among the objects which received particular notice were two vases painted in maiolica style by Schnorr (1794–1872) after the seventeenth-century Bolognese artist Albani, and a set of the four seasons painted by Nicolai and Braundorf. A candelabra nearly six feet high and a fountain four and a half feet high were also exhibited with great success, together with a collection of sixty-nine animals, probably after Kaendler. These exhibits seem to have had more success with the English public than with the then Finance Minister, Von Friesen. He called a meeting at which the director Kühn and members of the administrative and artistic departments were present. He told them that he thought Meissen could now stand competition from other centres, but he thought that English ceramic art had progressed so much that it continued to threaten the Saxon production. A decision was taken to buy some English models in order to copy them. It was also resolved to produce porcelain painted with views of Italy and the Rhine country. The Minister wanted his directives to be put into operation at once. It seems that this was done. The *pâte-sur-pâte* style was soon being imitated, as well as the styles of enamel painting used at Worcester and Limoges.

Imitations of oriental porcelain were developed on a grand scale

Kühn contributed a great deal to the achievement of some financial success at Meissen after the disasters of the Napoleonic Wars. As a result, the old premises were found to be too small and antiquated and new ones were constructed outside the Albrechtsburg. Kühn died in 1870 and was succeeded by Reithel, who kept the factory going in good shape. From 1878 onwards America became one of the main outlets for Meissen exports. The need to sell luxury goods by auction was no longer felt. In 1873 the new building was enlarged, and still further extended in 1884–85, when machinery was installed to make production more industrial. During Reithel's management, imitations of oriental porcelain were developed on a grand scale. These included imitations of eggshell, of crackleware and of Chinese coloured glazes, such as *sang de boeuf*. However, towards the end of the nineteenth century Meissen came in for much criticism from contemporary artists who disliked the continual emphasis on imitations and reproductions.

The artistic decadence of Meissen can be traced right back to the disasters of the Seven Years' War, when the factory first ceased to be the leader and creator of ceramic design and began instead to follow the dictates of political and financial expediency. Considering the output of the whole period of the nineteenth century, one can see that the worst and most persistent artistic fault was an excessive dependence upon old styles. The efforts of successive ministers and artistic directors to encourage a change of policy seems to have had little effect on the activities of the factory workshop.

When the Meissen workers did try to produce articles in contemporary style, they were not particularly successful. At the end of the eighteenth century they had failed to master the neo-classical forms. Admittedly these were difficult to adapt to porcelain, even hard-paste porcelain. The stern lines and rigid symmetry are apt to give an impression of stiffness, but the problems could have been surmounted. There is, after all, the example of neo-classical Wedgwood designs which proved successful and well-loved all over the world.

Another mistake of the Meissen artists, when making porcelain figurines and groups, was to abandon Kaendler's superb sculptural techniques. In place of the beautifully individualised crinolines on Kaendler's female figures, the nineteenth-century Meissen workers produced stiff reproductions by a semi-mechanical process. Real lace was dipped in slip and then fired. The fabric burned away, leaving behind the lace pattern imprinted in ceramic.

The economic difficulties which forced the management to sell undecorated china gave rise to a form of competition which was very deleterious to the factory's reputation. In the nineteenth century various independent and unscrupulous decorators from the city of Dresden embarked upon the decoration and sale of Meissen pieces on a grand scale. They copied the marks as well as the styles of old Meissen, but the standards of these pirates were very inferior to those of similar home decorators of the previous century. Among these nineteenth-century imitators was Madame Wolfsohn, who exploited the famous AR (*Augustus Rex*) mark to give the impression of genuine early Meissen. Eventually, after a successful legal action against her, she was made to desist and to substitute the word 'Dresden' on her products. Other imitators used a variety of marks, often incorporating crossed swords and crowns to give a spurious suggestion of Meissen origin.

Marks on Meissen pieces are of limited value for identification purposes, owing to the abundance of imitations. During the Marcolini period, from about 1775 to 1814, the standard mark was a pair of crossed swords with a star between the hilts. Later the swords appeared alone. Since the marks on eighteenth- and nineteenth-century wares are similar, and the pieces often come from the same moulds, the date of a piece is not immediately obvious. Generally, the nineteenth-century pieces can be distinguished by the large incised or impressed numbers which appear on the inside surface of open bases. Furthermore, the nineteenth-century factory employed colours, such as chrome green, which had not been available in the previous century.

MUSEUMS AND COLLECTIONS

Nineteenth-century Meissen porcelain may be seen at the following:

GERMANY
Dresden: Staatliche Kunstsammlung
Hamburg: Museum für Kunst und Gewerbe
GREAT BRITAIN
London: Victoria and Albert Museum
Wellington Museum

FURTHER READING

Pottery and Porcelain 1700–1914 by B. Hillier, London, 1968.
Dresden China by W. B. Honey, London, 1947.
Königlich-Sächsische Porzellanmanufaktur Meissen: 1710–1910, Meissen, 1910.

Biedermeier Furniture

William Allan

1

Fig. 1 ***Bed,*** *designed by the architect Karl Friedrich Schinkel (1781–1841) for Queen Louise of Prussia. Pearwood veneer. (Charlottenburg, Berlin.)*

Fig. 2 ***Sofa,*** *German, c.1835. Typical of much south German furniture, this sofa is severe in ornament and imposing in its scale. (Münchner Stadtmuseum, Munich.)*

Fig. 3 ***Sofa,*** *Austrian, c.1820. Fruitwood with ebony and gilt decoration. The use of light-coloured wood was a characteristic of Biedermeier, but here the inspiration came from France. (Bethnal Green Museum, London.)*

The Biedermeier period saw a return to a simpler style of furniture, more in tune with current conditions and epitomising the relaxed, easy atmosphere following the Napoleonic Wars

Biedermeier furniture faithfully reflects the needs and tastes of the generation that came after the Napoleonic Wars. Self-consciously modest, it acts as a conductor between the severe classicism of the Empire style and the tasteless exuberance and technical virtuosity of the later nineteenth century. The name itself is an amalgam of the names of Biedermann and Bummelmeier, two comic characters who epitomised the cheerful philistinism of middle-class Germans in the 1830s. Biedermeier has become linked with the word *bourgeois* for more than alliterative reasons. The patriotic fervour which accompanied the War of Liberation gave rise to the hope that the German states, fusing their political differences in a common sense of nationhood, would come together to form a united Germany. It is not too far fetched to link the collapse of this ideal, with its heroic and classical overtones, with the emergence of an almost anti-heroic style. This style reflected the self-confidence and sentimentality of a class protected politically by Metternich and the Holy Alliance, and economically by stringent controls after 1815.

In the Austrian Empire the financial reforms of Count Stadion were especially important for the development of a new style. His deflationary policy resulted in an acute shortage of money at a time when private credit hardly existed in Austria. In the German lands merchants had to contend with renewed competition from English manufactured goods, and in Hungary and Galicia landowners faced the threat of imported Russian wheat. There simply was not enough money for new building projects or lavish schemes of decoration.

The Emperor himself gave the lead in cultivating a simpler style in tune with the changed conditions. Franz der Gute was scarcely a heroic character.

Museum Photo

A. C. Cooper

Museum Photo

Angelo Hornak

Fig. 4 **Work-table.**
Although the lyre-shape is strongly neo-classical, the round form is a prominent feature of the Biedermeier style. (Schleswig-Holsteinisches Landesmuseum, Schleswig.)

Fig. 5 ***A pair of chairs,*** *German or Austrian, c.1830. Oak. The shape of the chairs is based on a style popular throughout Europe during the first three or four decades of the nineteenth century. Many such chairs survive in mahogany or light-coloured wood, often decorated with metal mounts. These are of oak and are very solidly made, which may suggest that they were made by a provincial chair-maker. (Private Collection.)*

The virtuous, narrow figure hurrying along the corridors of Schönbrunn was hardly the man to inspire a return to the baroque splendours and financial extravagances of the eighteenth century. Practical, inexpensive furniture was all that was needed and all that the bad state of Austrian finances allowed. Derived from classical example, Biedermeier furniture 'suited the modest size and unostentatious needs of comfortable bourgeois houses'. Workshops such as Danhauser, which flourished between 1804 and 1838, produced furniture in which the severity and tension of Empire design was softened into a more relaxed style, where comfort took precedence over appearance. One of the most popular innovations was the sofa (Fig. 2). Rectangular, with high back and sides, sofas looked deceptively hard: in fact their depth and solidity made them very comfortable. Armchairs, too, became more comfortable as changing fashions permitted men to sit back and take their ease; upholstery was brightly coloured.

The neo-classical *torchère* was transformed into a massive pedestal, surmounted either by a piece of statuary or by a flambeau whose proportions presaged the monstrous light-fittings of the 1860s and '70s. One new and omnipresent feature was the piano, the polished surface of which became a resting place for clocks, pieces of porcelain and the inevitable basket of flowers. There was also a vogue for cabinets (Fig. 10), to house collections of any objects which might proclaim the artistic sensibility of the household.

The less severe appearance of furniture led to a less formal arrangement of the rooms as a whole. Flowers, screens, work-tables and knick-knacks of all sorts helped to give a sense of humdrum family life. Paintings by Georg Kersting (1783–1847) and Franz Heinrich (1802–90) amply demonstrate what is often called 'the quiet happiness of Biedermeier'.

Although Biedermeier was essentially a product of south Germany, its greatest exponent was the Prussian architect and designer Karl Friedrich Schinkel (1781–1841) (Fig. 1). Despite the proverbial dreariness and meanness of the Prussian Court, Schinkel was encouraged to produce furniture and

Fig. 6 **Cupboard,** north German, *c.1820. Mahogany with gilt plaster decoration. The use of gilt plaster and mahogany together derives from late Empire forms. (Bethnal Green Museum.)*

Fig. 7 **Writing-desk,** German, *c.1835. This is an unusual piece, the nationality of which was in doubt for some time. The rich use of veneers as surface decoration gives it a much less severe appearance than many German pieces of this date. (Bethnal Green Museum.)*

Fig. 8 **Work-table,** German or *Austrian, c.1835. Veneered with very light-coloured wood and retaining its interior fittings. (Victoria and Albert Museum, London.)*

Fig. 9 **A living-room,** Lübeck. *Though this room, as arranged, looks typical of the decade 1860–70, much of the furniture is earlier. The sofa is in the style of the 1850s, but pieces in this style were being made into the 1860s. Note that the cupboard is very similar to that in Figure 6. The mirror over the cupboard dates from the '30s and is hung at the correct angle. The chairs date from the '40s, and the arrangement of the curtains and the pattern of the wallpaper from the same decade.*

6

A. C. Cooper

even jewellery for the Prussian Royal Family. His style combines the aesthetic delicacy of neo-Classicism with the functional and restrained qualities of Biedermeier. Schinkel's reward for being the most original of all German designers was a commission to design the new school of artillery.

Despite Schinkel, the Biedermeier style in south Germany was certainly more attractive than its northern counterpart. In Austria, light-coloured fruitwoods were popular (Figs. 3 and 8) and there was less use of heavy veneering or inlay. The Viennese sat on cherrywood sofas to read the comedies of the Austrian playwright and poet Grillparzer while, in the vast barrack of Berlin, Prussians sat forward on mahogany chairs upholstered in black horsehair to listen to the dynamic logic of Hegel.

In the 1840s Biedermeier gradually gave way to the curves and flourishes of the neo-rococo revival in Vienna. In the north, the romantic movement led to the dramatic rediscovery of medieval Germany and the long night of the Gothic Revival.

7

A. C. Cooper

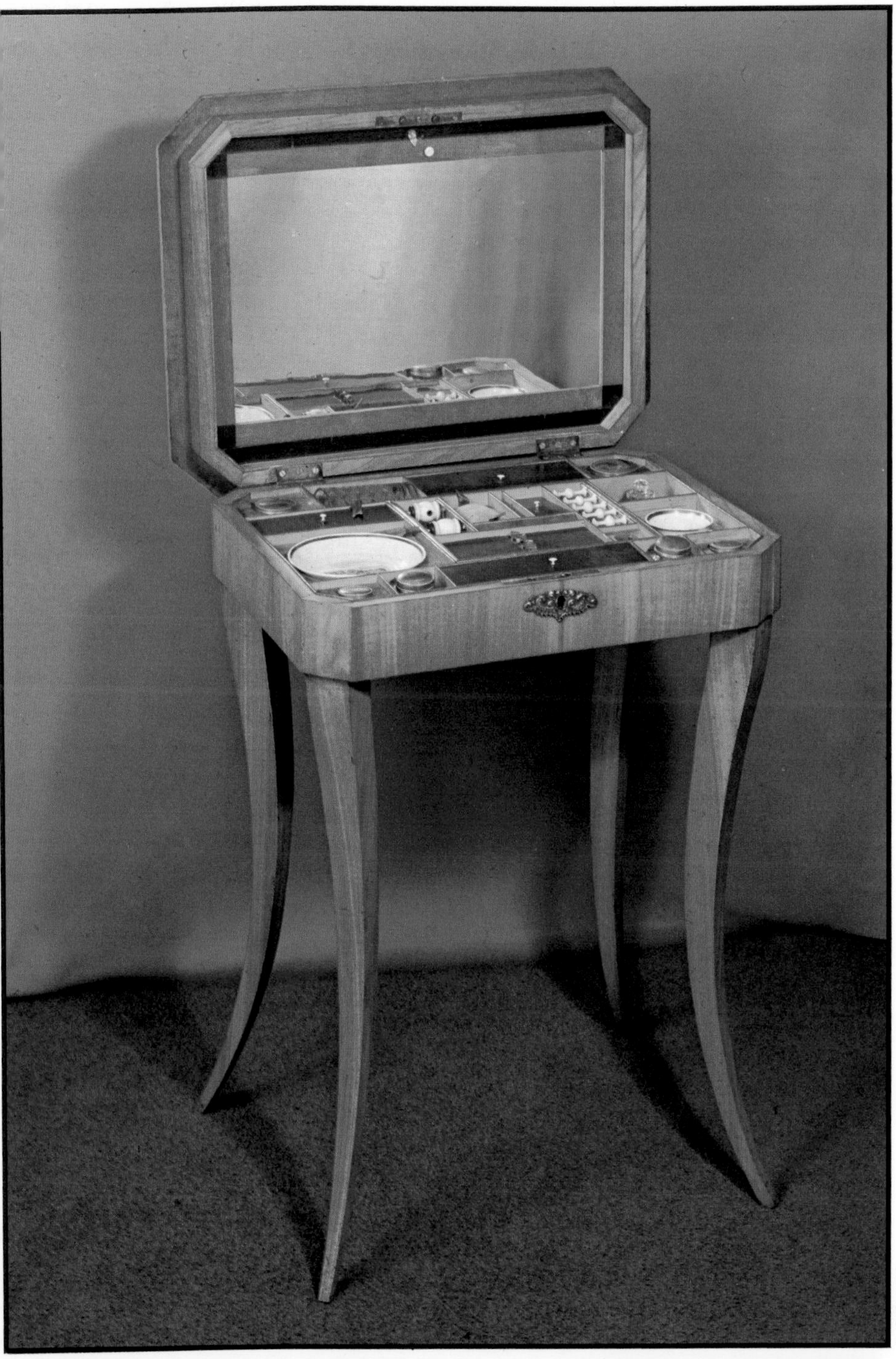

A. C. Cooper

Fig. 10 **Collector's cabinet on stand**, *German*, c.1835. *The cabinet is veneered in bird's-eye maple and decorated with transfers in the form of mezzotints of German scenes. Inside is a number of shallow drawers. The stand is very much in the rococo revival style and has pronounced cabriole legs. Cabinets of this sort were often made as master works by craftsmen who had completed their apprenticeship, for they readily lent themselves to elaborate veneering and delicate carving and were therefore ideal tests of a craftsman's skills.* (*Bethnal Green Museum.*)

10

A. C. Cooper

Foto Marburg

MUSEUMS AND COLLECTIONS

Biedermeier furniture may be seen at the following:

AUSTRIA

Vienna: Schloss Schönbrunn

GERMANY

Munich: Münchner Stadtmuseum

Schleswig: Schleswig-Holsteinisches Landesmuseum

GREAT BRITAIN

London: Bethnal Green Museum
Victoria and Albert Museum

FURTHER READING

World Furniture ed. by Helena Hayward, London, 1965.

Das Möbelwerk by Hermann Schnitz, Berlin, 1926.

Biedermeier: Deutschland von 1815 – 1847 by Max von Boehn, Berlin, 1923.

Deutsche Möbel des Klassizismus by Hermann Schnitz, Stuttgart, 1923.

Fig. 1 ***Beaker,*** *Bohemian,* c.*1830–40.* Lithyalin *glass, height* $4\frac{1}{4}$ *ins.*
Lithyalin *is a marbled glass invented in 1823 by Friedrich Egermann (1777–1864), who had a glasshouse at Blottendorf in Bohemia. This beaker illustrates the wide variety of marbled colours that could be produced by this method.*
(Victoria and Albert Museum, London.)

Fig. 2 ***Mug,*** *Egermann factory,* c.*1830.* Hyalith *glass, height* $4\frac{1}{2}$ *ins.*
Hyalith *was invented in 1822 by Count George Buquoy in imitation of Wedgwood's black basalt. To compete with the porcelain so popular at the time, eighteenth-century Bohemian glass-workers introduced an opaque, white glass;* hyalith *glass was a later experiment towards the same end.*
(Richard Dennis Antiques, London.)

1

R. Todd-White

2

R. Todd-White

3

Glass from Bohemia

Keith Middlemas

Museum Photo

Fig. 3 **Vase,** *Bohemian, c.1830–40. Glass, cut and engraved on the wheel, with yellow and pink stains and silvering, height 8 ins. The Biedermeier period in glass manufacture was characterised by elaborate surface decoration in various forms, either in a repeating pattern or applied irregularly, and a chunkiness of the glass itself. (Victoria and Albert Museum.)*

Fig. 4 **Decanter,** *Bohemian, c.1840. Ruby glass, cut on the wheel, height 12¾ ins. Much Bohemian coloured glass had engraved portraits or topographical views in the panels. This, however, is an undecorated piece, impressive on account of the heavy, flawless texture of the glass and the bold shape. (Victoria and Albert Museum.)*

Bohemian glass-workers resumed their former supremacy by adopting vivid colours and bold, often faceted, forms

The Napoleonic Wars brought disaster to the glass-houses of Bohemia. For the better part of twenty years, the markets in Spain and the Americas were closed and trade with Britain, the Low Countries and Holland disrupted. But the eighteenth-century supremacy of Bohemian cut and engraved glass had been threatened even before the French Revolution, as the fashion for English and Irish lead glass – simple, facet-cut, lustrous and relatively cheap – became popular throughout Europe.

When Napoleon was exiled to St. Helena in 1815 (a scene frequently depicted on glass by Bohemian artists), and the Congress of Vienna restored the old royal families, the glass-houses faced an uncertain future. The British had undercut their traditional markets and the decorative coloured and opaque glass of Clichy, St. Louis and Vonêche (later Baccarat) had established the fashionable French Empire style.

Just as Bohemia had met the challenge of porcelain by the introduction of opaque white glass in the eighteenth century, so her glassworkers in the nineteenth developed an entirely new style and composition of glass and recaptured, during the Biedermeier period, their former supremacy.

The romantic revolution was under way, the most fruitful and original era of change in European cultural history since the Renaissance. At the same time a profound economic transformation took place: the Industrial Revolution spread outwards across the Continent, creating new wealth in different hands and bringing railways, even to remote Bohemia, by the 1860s. Speed of movement as much as the new liberalism freed art from its predominantly aristocratic patronage. The triumph of the middle classes was reflected, through their demands for luxury, in all the domestic arts, and glass followed suit. While the nobility still ordered imposing tableware and ornate chandeliers, there grew up a far more diverse requirement for decorative objects in glass for both display and use. Above all, in the first enthusiasm of the rediscovery of landscape, the German public bought souvenirs – delicate and expensive, perhaps, but essentially no different from the 'trifle from Brighton' and the glass toys of Stourbridge.

Surprisingly, considering their enormous production in the nineteenth century, Bohemian and Silesian glasshouses remained backward in adopting modern technology: as late as 1870, only twelve of the hundred and sixty-nine largest furnaces were burning coal. In the early part of the century, most glassworks were still strictly controlled by the families who owned them, and their sons were apprenticed to the business as agents in foreign markets.

During the period which may be called Empire (1795–1815), a reversion took place from formal magnificence; glass-blowers concentrated on simple, plain shapes, producing cylindrical tumblers or decanters, bowls and vases very similar to contemporary English patterns. Even the English style of facet and diamond cutting was followed closely. Later, in the Biedermeier period, the classic design was a trumpet-shaped beaker with a heavy foot, often facet-cut, called the *Ranftbecher.* The diversity of forms became so great as to defy classification, and almost every object of domestic use, from snuff-boxes to candlesticks, was made in decorative glass. It is this exuberance that marks the second great age of Bohemian glass.

Portraits in the form of medallions, silhouettes or painted parchment were used as decoration

Older traditions survived, of course. The first great artist in the neo-classical mode belongs almost wholly to the eighteenth century. Johann Josef Mildner (1763–1808), of Gutenbrunn in Lower Austria, used the *zwischengoldglas* technique to decorate glasses with portrait medallions. This involved setting a sheet of gold leaf, often on a red ground, into circular recesses in the side and base of the glass and etching the portrait or design, then laying another disc of glass over it, so that the surfaces fitted exactly. Silhouettes or portraits painted on parchment served equally well, and Mildner's work on clear and opaque white tumblers was usually given fire-gilt borders of a very high standard.

Another artist in the eighteenth-century mode whose signed pieces are extremely valuable is the engraver Dominik Biemann (1800–57), whose workshop engraved ornamental glass. Biemann was one of the first artists to follow the tourist trade; he spent

5

Museum Photo

6

Fig. 5 **Tumbler,** *Bohemian, 1830. Clear glass with engraving cut through a ruby flash, height* $4\frac{5}{8}$ ins.
This highly decorated glass illustrates the combined use of several of the techniques practised by Bohemian glass-workers at this period. The flash is a layer of surface colour applied to clear glass. (Victoria and Albert Museum.)

Fig. 6 **Footed beaker,** *Bohemian, c.1830–40. Faceted on the wheel, the foot stained yellow, the bowl painted in transparent enamel colours, height 5 ins.*
A vivid yellow was one of the most popular colours in Bohemian stained-surface glass. (Victoria and Albert Museum.)

Fig. 7 Left: ***Covered goblet,*** *Bohemian,* c.*1850. Engraved clear glass with coloured coating, height 11 ins.*
The engraving, in the manner of Karl Pfohl, is of a startled horse. Pfohl was one of the finest nineteenth-century Bohemian glass-engravers. Seven panels on the opposite surface of the goblet reflect the horse in miniature. These reflecting panels are found only on the highest quality engraved glass. (Richard Dennis Antiques.)

Right: ***Beaker,*** *Bohemian,* c.*1825. Engraved clear glass, height* $6\frac{1}{2}$ *ins.*
The beaker has five panels, four with views of Baden and the fifth bearing the name of its original owner. Souvenir glass was very popular in the spas of Europe, supplying the tourist trade with engraved portraits and landscapes. (Richard Dennis Antiques.)

Fig. 8 **Cup and cover,** *Bohemian,* c.*1840. Opaque white glass, height 8 ins. (Bethnal Green Museum, London.)*

Fig. 9 ***Tankard,*** *Bohemian, early nineteenth century. Glass, cut and engraved on the wheel, height 7 ins. (Victoria and Albert Museum.)*

each season at the fashionable spa of Franzensbad, undertaking commissions and working on special orders – exquisite portraits and landscapes.

The names of the finest engravers include Karl Pfohl, Mattoni of Carlsbad and the families of Moser, Pelikan of Meistersdorf and Simms of Gablonz. They often signed their work, but a host of unknown craftsmen depicted small masterpieces – horses, mountaineers with ropes, children at play, or public buildings, palaces and views of towns.

The great wealth of the souvenir market was opened up with the invention of painting in transparent enamel colours. Immediately it became possible to paint in far greater detail and with more sensitivity than earlier artists using opaque colours. From about 1810 a series of major artists gave vent to their feeling for landscape in its wild and romantic aspects. Mountain scenes, ruined castles and gothic fantasies appealed to the sense of awe, while genre scenes of children and animals satisfied the sentimental. Expensive mementos recalled picnic suppers by the banks of the Rhine or vistas of Prague or Charlottenburg. The highest standards of painting were achieved by the Mohn family: Samuel Mohn (1762–1815), who settled in Dresden in 1809, and his son Gottlöb (1789–1825), who worked chiefly in Vienna. Signed pieces by either are rare and expensive. The father painted simple naturalistic landscapes, views of cities and churches, and the son indulged in romantic pastorals and sentimental allegories.

Followers of the Mohns worked in Berlin and Bohemia as well as Vienna, and in all the spas and watering-places – such as Carlsbad, Marienbad, Teplitz and Baden (Fig. 7, r.) views of which appear on tumblers and goblets with increasing regularity after 1815. Anton Kothgasser (1769–1851) of Vienna carried the fashion to its peak; his portraits, genre scenes, moonlit views and illustrations of proverbs, usually set in elegant gilt borders, are technically superb, if rather stylised, works of art. There was no lack of imitators, given an eager public, and the fashion remained vital until the 1850s although the standard, especially on glasses designed for export, had begun to decline.

Engraved and cut clear glass was produced in great quantity throughout the nineteenth century mostly for the export market. Designed for a mass market, it reflected commoner tastes and is generally heavy and repetitive. In Germany and the Austro-Hungarian Empire, the tables of less wealthy city-dwellers and country farmers would have been decorated with cheap machine-made pressed glass or clear and coloured glass with crude enamel designs. These, with sprays of flowers, birds, or more modern emblems, such as railway trains, hark back to the seventeenth century and may be compared with English souvenir glass from Stourbridge and Nailsea with which they are often confused.

Innovation was for the wealthy new patrons, whose taste dictated the use of new colours and materials. Bohemia's response to this demand in the 1830s and '40s was the most colourful in the long history of glassmaking – colour in the glass metal itself or superimposed by painting, staining and overlay.

Just as white opaque glass (*milchglas*) had been made in imitation of porcelain, nineteenth-century inventors strove to match the black basalts of Wedgwood. In 1822 Count George Buquoy succeeded in creating a dense black glass which he called *hyalith* (Fig. 2), and also a red glass, curiously like sealing-wax. Enhanced with formal designs of *chinoiserie* scenes in fire-gilding, the effect of his tall vases and tea- or coffee-sets is monumental. A year later, in 1823, Friedrich Egermann (1777–1864) introduced similar wares at his glassworks at Blottendorf in northern Bohemia. Later he developed what he called *lithyalin*, a marbled glass of astonishing variety, like jasper or agate, whose colours ranged from brick red streaked with green, to deep blues and purples (Figs. 1 and 10). These, too, were gilded and

R. Todd-White

9

R. Todd-White

8

A. C. Cooper

painted, sometimes with simple mottoes like '*Erinnerung*' (Remembrance). *Hyalith* and *lithyalin* were used prolifically for vases, beakers, table-sets, scent-bottles, inkwells and candlesticks, and a wide range of designs can be found in trade catalogues of the 1840s.

Egermann was a notable inventor; he discovered the gold stain, made with silver, which Kothgasser often used as a background colour, and he made possible the cheap manufacture of ruby glass, by replacing the gold with copper. A wave of striking colours characterised the 1830s, as new substances like antimony and uranium were added to the metal. Turquoise, topaz, chrysoprase, and the shades of uranium green called *Annagrün* and *Annagelb* came from the factory of Joseph Riedel. But new colour in glass was only one of many innovations bringing the finest glassware within range of the middle-class market. Stained glass (clear glass given a surface colour) was widely popular and to the eighteenth-century purple stains were added vivid reds, greens, yellows and sometimes a layer of gold or silver arabesques in high relief (Figs. 3 and 6).

Cased glass was a much prized and highly secret process

The most noted technique, however, was that of overlay, or cased, glass, in which the glass vessel was encased in opaque glass or glass of another colour; these surfaces were then cut away in broad facets to reveal the contrasting layers beneath. The panels would be shaped and then finely gilded, painted or engraved as the designer's fancy chose. Until the 1850s, the process remained a secret in Bohemia. Decanters and sets of glasses, lustres and tall vases were for sale for high prices in London, Paris and New York until imitators caught up and repeated the technique.

The variety of decoration, even on the basic tumbler, beggars description, and a collector could spend a lifetime without exhausting the richness of Biedermeier glass. One should mention the *Perlbecher*, a beaker with a closely woven net of multi-coloured glass beads round the base of the bowl, and the many goblets bearing portraits of monarchs or notables in sulphide cameos, similar to those produced by Desprez in France and Apsley Pellatt in England. At both ends of the market, Bohemian supremacy lasted until the 1848 Revolution shook the whole of Europe. The uneasy amalgam of placid prosperity and liberal intellectual aspirations dissolved, to be succeeded in central Europe by a decade and more of reaction and repression.

Even without that check to artistic confidence, Bohemian glassworks could hardly have fought off, for the whole nineteenth century, the competition from Britain and America. Cutting costs was the answer; and for every fine example of an engraved goblet or a painted overlay tumbler, a dozen factory-made lifeless copies were sent out in the 1850s and '60s. Modern methods of production helped to emphasise the trend. Design deteriorated; form became heavy. The restless search for novelty produced pearl satin glass and imitations of Venetian *latticinio, millefiori* and aventurine glass – yet the results were not inspiring. Vast quantities crossed the Atlantic, and the firm of Lazarus and Rosenfeld of New York distributed what they called 'Bohemian art glass ware' – lamps and vases in 'Rose de Bohème' and 'Green de Bohème' – cheap things from Altrohlau and Steinschönau which had an equally depressing effect on better English and American equivalents.

The originality of Bohemian glassware was saved by a few enterprising industrialists and the deliberate policy of the Austro-Hungarian authorities of stimulating trade schools of design and decoration – the first at Kamenicky Senov in 1839 and another at Novy Bor in 1870. The intense mood of pan-Germanism prevalent at the time of German

10

R. Todd-White

11

R. Todd-White

Fig. 10 ***Jug,*** *Egermann factory, c.1820.* Lithyalin *glass, height 8¾ ins. (Victoria and Albert Museum.)*

Fig. 11 ***Goblet,*** *Bohemian, c.1840. Glass, cut and engraved through a layer of yellow stain, height 7 ins. (Victoria and Albert Museum.)*

unification encouraged revivals of the Teutonic tradition of glass decoration. The Viennese glass designer Louis Lobmeyr strove to coordinate these factors in a single centre and, with the help of Viennese and Bohemian craftsmen, he produced on the one hand excellent glassware in the seventeenth- and eighteenth-century tradition (including enamelled and *schwarzlot* drinking-glasses and engraved and gilded goblets) and on the other hand a series of modern designs in clear, thin-walled glass, not unlike those of his contemporary, James Powell, of the Whitefriars glasshouse in London.

Others followed: the Moser glassworks at Carlsbad, and Meyers Neffe at Adolfov. While it was true that in 1890 the factory of W. Hirschmann at Munich could issue a trade catalogue of standard replicas of antique glass, and many Bohemian factories were flooding the world market with cheap imitations of Stourbridge cameo carving made rapidly, in very low relief, with the use of hydrofluoric acid, the last quarter of the century was a period of experimentation, rather than archaism, and it led, as happened with French Art Nouveau, towards the blossoming of its German equivalent, Jugendstil.

The iridescent glass which Lobmeyr first exhibited in 1873 became a speciality of the Neuwelt factory, and in 1879 Henrichs and Company, distributors of Bohemian glass in New York, announced the arrival of 'the finest selection of iridescent glass and bronze glass ever assembled under one roof'. J. Lötz of Klostersmühle in Austria produced a new method of obtaining iridescence in 1898 and achieved a *succès d'estime* at the famous Paris Exhibition of 1900.

MUSEUMS AND COLLECTIONS

Nineteenth-century German and Bohemian glass may be seen at the following:

AUSTRIA
Vienna: Kunsthistorisches Museum
CZECHOSLOVAKIA
Prague: Museum of Applied Art
Museum of Decorative Art
GERMANY
Berlin: Kunstgewerbemuseum
Cologne: Kunstgewerbemuseum
Munich: Bayerisches Nationalmuseum
Nuremberg: Germanisches Nationalmuseum
GREAT BRITAIN
Cambridge: Fitzwilliam Museum
Edinburgh: Royal Scottish Museum
Lincoln: Usher Gallery
London: British Museum
Victoria and Albert Museum
U.S.A.
Corning, N.Y: Corning Museum of Glass
Toledo, Ohio: Toledo Museum of Art

FURTHER READING

Continental Coloured Glass by Keith Middlemas, London, 1971.

Bohemian Glass, a Victoria and Albert Museum handbook, HMSO, 1965.

Glass in Czechoslovakia by K. Hettes, Prague, 1958.

Europaische Glas by R. Schmidt, Berlin, 1927.

Gläser der Biedermeier Zeit by G. Pazaurek, Leipzig, 1923.

Das Glas by R. Schmidt, Vienna, 1922.

VIENNA IN THE 1890's

Peter Hart

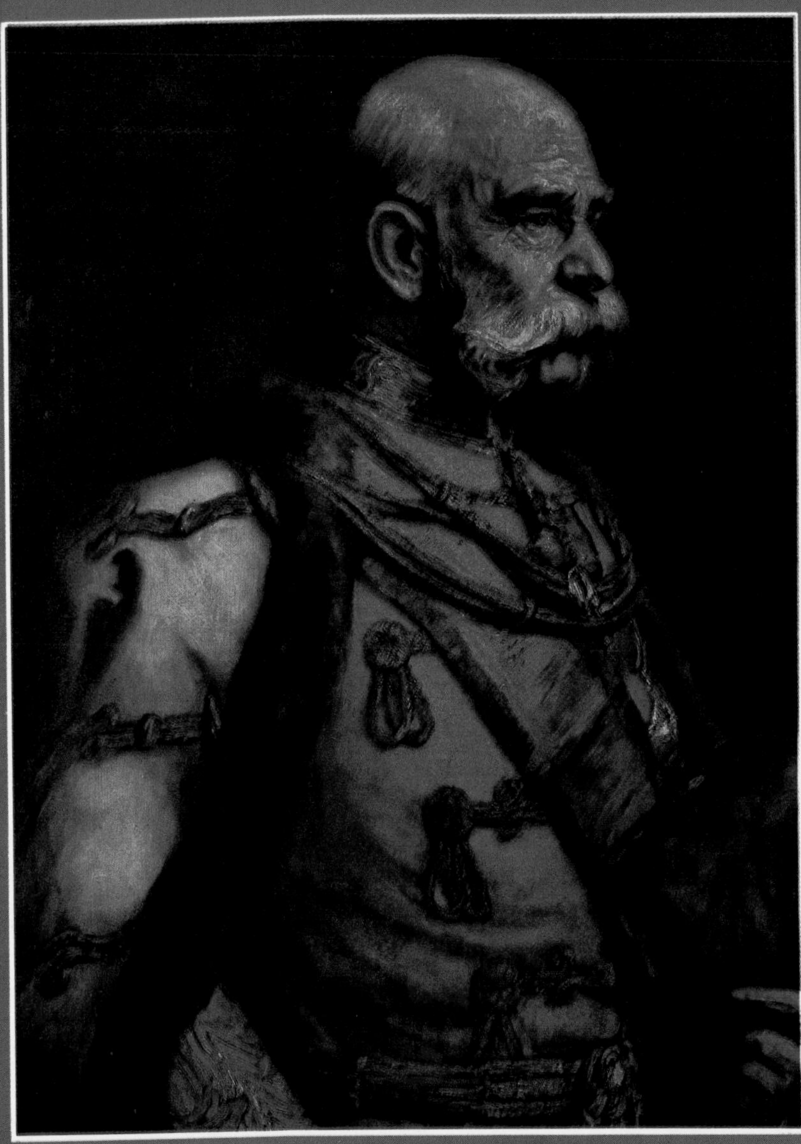
Photo Meyer

2

Mansell Collection

3

Mansell Collection

4

Mansell Collection

5

Mansell Collection

Fig. 1 ***Kaiser Franz Josef I*** *(reigned 1848–1916) by Munkacsy, in the uniform of a Hungarian Field Marshal (Kunsthistorisches Museum, Vienna.)*

Fig. 2 ***The Reichsrath*** *(Parliament House).*

Figs. 3 and 4 *Representatives of two conflicting cultures:* Left, ***Gustav Mahler*** *(1860–1911), director of the Imperial Opera from 1897 to 1907;* right, ***Katharina Schratt****, an actress with a conservative mind who became the friend and companion of the ageing Kaiser, and arbiter of official taste.*

Fig. 5 ***The Opera House.***

6

EINE NACHT IN „VENEDIG" IN WIEN

Museum Photo

Socially rigid and artistically dormant, Vienna at the turn of the century became a European centre of culture, fashion and gaiety

Vienna in the 1890s was the fourth largest capital in Europe. It had one of the most advanced systems of water-supply on the Continent, but few baths. It was also an imperial city.

Situated at the frontier separating the German, Slavonic and Magyar races, it was the hub of a vast cosmopolitan empire of forty-five million souls which the Archduke Rudolf had called a 'mighty ruin'. This ethnic diversity was reflected in the city of Vienna itself. The principal nationalities were Germans, Hungarians, Bohemians and Slovaks; but there were also Poles, Ruthenes, Serbo-Croats, Italians, Russians, French and Swiss; there was a parallel religious diversity. However, the aged Emperor, Franz Josef, resident in Vienna, spoke German and was Roman Catholic.

As at other periods in its long history, the face of Vienna was changing fast in the second half of the nineteenth century. What Louis Napoleon did for Paris, Franz Josef, albeit unwillingly, did for Vienna. His Letter Patent of 20 December, 1857, put in hand the demolition of the old city walls and paved the way for the construction of the Ringstrasse, which followed the same line, encompassing the old city, the Innere Stadt, like a horseshoe. At the same time, the Glacis, the open space in front of the city walls which had been used for military parades, became available as building land.

Together, these two developments triggered off a spectacular construction programme and the neo-renaissance palaces of the *nouveaux riches* shot up almost overnight. Even so, only the very wealthy such as Baron Todesco or Friedrich Schey could afford to maintain whole establishments, and the new temples to Mammon were to a large degree tenement palaces (*zinspaläste*) divided into apartments.

However impressive superficially, it cannot be said that the architecture of the Ringstrasse is beautiful. It is eclectic and derivative, and no new style emerged from the activity of these years. The *penchant* for grand façades belying what lay

7

Museum Photo

8

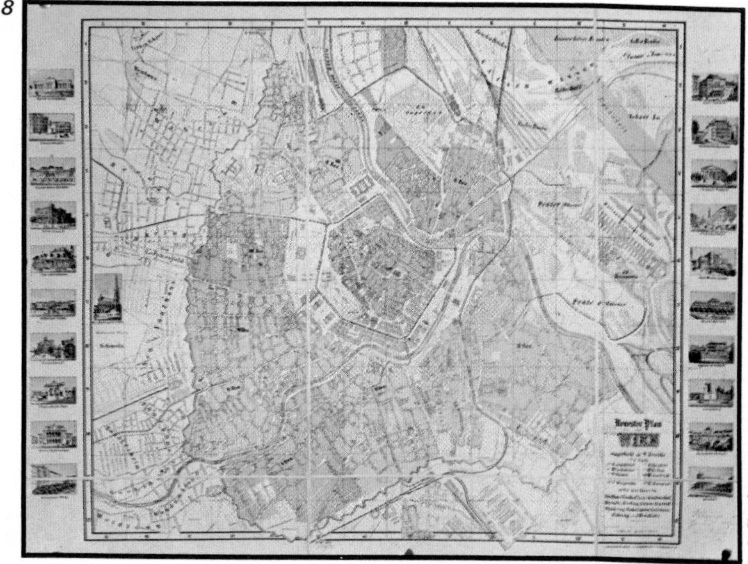

R. B. Fleming

Vienna in the 1890s

Fig. 6 ***A Night in 'Venice in Vienna'*** *by F. Witt, 1900. Watercolour. These gay boating parties took place in the Prater. In the background is the Big Wheel, and just to its right, the Imperial and the Royal Hungarian crowns in lights. Also to be found at this fabulous playground just outside Vienna were innumerable other diversions, including the famous Constantin Hügel Café. (Städtische Museen, Vienna.)*

Fig. 7 ***The Washermaids' Ball*** *by Wilhelm Ganse, 1898. Oil on canvas. These balls were given as Mardi Gras celebrations. To them came the middle classes, the women dressed as washerwomen, for a night of riotous dancing and drinking. (Städtische Museen.)*

Fig. 8 ***New Plan of Vienna*** *by Klimsch and Co., Frankfurt am Main, 1873. Clearly to be seen in the centre is the Ringstrasse, built on the old line of the city walls when they were demolished in 1857; at the right is the Prater. Round the margins are twenty-one coloured views of the principal buildings of Vienna. (British Museum, London.)*

Figs. 9 and 10 ***Plans*** *for the apartment-palaces* (zinspaläste) *off the Ringstrasse in Vienna. These magnificent neo-renaissance palaces were built for the* nouveaux riches *of Vienna who could not, however, afford to maintain large establishments. (Magistrat der Stadt Wien, Vienna.)*

behind continued, and the young architect Adolf Loos (1870–1933) characterised Vienna as a 'Potemkin city' after the style of Potemkin's villages. The architecture of the Ringstrasse style represented the second great building boom that Vienna experienced in the modern age, the prosperous reign of the Empress Maria Theresa having produced the first.

At the same time almost every Viennese institution, imperial and municipal, was rebuilt in a staggering variety of 'neo' styles between 1860 and 1890. The new Opera House of Van der Nüll and Siccardsburg, the Imperial Museums of Art and Natural History, as well as Ferstel's new University building, were built in the neo-renaissance style; Hansen's House of Parliament was neo-Grecian; Friedrich Schmidt's Town Hall was in the Flemish style and Ferstel's graceful Votifkirch neo-Gothic.

By most accounts, the Vienna of the 1890s was an agreeable city in which to live. Typhoid had virtually disappeared as a result of the impressive waterworks construction of 1873 although the changeable climate drew unfavourable comment from foreign visitors: Walburga, Lady Paget, remarked: 'The climate of Vienna is neither healthy nor agreeable . . . and rather exhausting'.

Vienna was a city pre-eminent for the facilities it afforded for spending money, whether it was on sweetmeats at Demmel's, on coffee and liqueurs at the fashionable Constantin Hügel Café in the Prater, or on luxury goods in the smart Graben thoroughfare. In clothes, furniture and carriages, Vienna, with Paris, set the fashion.

The medieval centre of the city, the Innere Stadt, was still the centre in 1890. The Emperor lived there in the Hofburg; the aristocracy had its palaces there, around the Herrengasse; and in the same district were the imperial and municipal offices, the embassies and legations and the principal hotels.

These years saw an increase in migration to Vienna of Slavs from Bohemia and Moravia to satisfy the demands of quickening industrial activity. By 1890 suburbs such as Favorita were solidly Czech. As elsewhere, this movement of population had a debasing effect on the living standards of the working class. The hours were long and one industrialist estimated the useful working life of his labourers at ten years.

However, more was done for the poor in Vienna than in most capital cities of Europe. By the last decade of the century some relief was systematically provided, besides which there were numerous charity balls of which Princess Pauline Metternich was a leading organiser.

At the other end of the social spectrum there were equally significant if less dramatic changes. When Emperor Franz I relinquished the crown of the Holy Roman Empire in 1806, the aristocratic German families, other than those of the hereditary Habsburg lands, gradually left Vienna. The Magyar nobility returned to their estates in Hungary after the Compromise of 1867.

Despite these changes, the composition of society was remarkably static. Walburga, Lady Paget, a shrewd observer of the Viennese social scene in this period, was quite clear as to what constituted society. In her essay *Vanishing Vienna*, she wrote: 'The line was clear and firmly drawn, and when Viennese society is spoken of, it must be understood that it means the score or so of noble families and that no exception is made to this rule'.

Those in society, almost one large family, spent the winter in old-fashioned stateliness in Vienna and the summer in extreme simplicity at their country houses. With the expansion of the railway system, the inclination to remain on their estates became much easier to indulge. Lady Paget caustically remarks that few of them were good administrators. To this caste, reverence for good birth was a religion, and to penetrate it almost impossible; mere wealth counted for nothing.

Lady Paget was prepared to admit that 'a Second Society does exist; it is wealthy and very fashionable and said to be amusing'. This 'Second Society' of bankers, merchants, architects, engineers, artists, actors, *employés* and officers, and their families, was more diverse. Broadly speaking, it comprised the *nouveaux riches* of high finance, the old burgher class, the 'good' Jewish bourgeoisie and those connected with the arts in one form or another. The title of Baron had, by this time, become almost synonymous with the Jewish financier and was unknown in aristocratic circles. In spite of their often vast wealth, they did not overstep the invisible but very real line separating the classes.

The core of 'good society' was the old burgher class: men such as Ludwig Bösendorfer, the pianoforte-maker, or Ludwig Lobmeyr, the second generation of a great firm of glass-makers. The latter, confident in his class and in himself, refused

9

Museum Photo

10

Museum Photo

11

Foto Marburg

Fig. 11 **The Hofburg, Vienna.** *This is part of the nineteenth-century wing of the Imperial Palace, completed in 1893 by Ferdinand Kirschner. It was dedicated to the Emperor Franz Josef, throughout whose reign it was the centre of the official life of the Austro-Hungarian Empire.*

12

H.-H. Kossatz Photo

Fig. 12 **Allegory of sculpture** *by Gustav Klimt (1862–1918), Vienna, 1896. Lithograph. One of the founders and most talented members of the Vienna Secession, Klimt challenged contemporary taste with the strong sexual element in his work. (Manfred Gerlach Collection.)*

to assume a title of nobility but accepted the freedom of the City of Vienna. Also of this upper-middle class were the ministers and high functionaries who had the right to go to Court, who were *hoffähig*. Despite this privilege, they did not mix with the higher nobility, who also went to Court.

Next came the lesser bourgeoisie, the butcher, the baker, the greengrocer, the chimney-sweep and the tinker, who found themselves under increasing economic pressure from the large, mainly Jewish enterprises which were crushing the small man out of business. This class found its champion in the form of Dr. Karl Lüger, whose politics took the form of an anti-semitic Christian Socialism. Despite repeated refusals, the Emperor was ultimately forced, in 1897, to sanction his election as Burgomaster of Vienna and he gave a powerful impulse to the middle-class attitude of the government of the day.

Meanwhile, Vienna danced to the music of Strauss at the two magnificent court balls of the season, at the many charity balls such as the popular Artists' Ball, at the 'picnic' balls for which the wealthy Count Pallavicini was renowned, or merely at one of the great dance-halls which carried on the tradition of the famous Sperl.

Music and opera found as fanatical a following. The composers resident in Vienna at this time bridged three generations, from Brahms and the younger Strauss through Mahler to Schönberg and Berg. Concerts were held in the Bösendorfersaal, where Chopin, Liszt, Brahms and Rubinstein had played, or at the less popular Musikverein. The Opera, where Mahler was director from 1898, was always packed for modern works such as Massenet's *Manon* (with Vandyke and Mademoiselle Renard), or for Wagner, but was by no means over-subscribed for the classics such as Mozart.

The wave of artistic renewal which swept Europe in the last decade of the century did not meet with unquestioning acceptance in Vienna. Indeed, something different happened there, and it was typically Viennese that the new movement had a specific beginning in time and space. The Wiener Secession (Vienna Secession) was founded in 1897; it had an official journal, *Ver Sacrum*; it also had a permanent home in the shape of the Secessionhaus designed by J. M. Olbrich and completed in 1898.

Of the Secessionstil painters, the most considerable talent was that of Gustav Klimt (1862–1918). He challenged contemporary taste by the strong sexual element in his work, but his style was not abstrusely modernistic. The new art, however, was beyond the comprehension of the critical Henry Wickham Steed who stigmatised the Viennese as a people 'that has lately adopted with snobbish alacrity the unintelligible canons of "modern art"'

Sally Thompson

1 2 3

Thonet Photo Thonet Photo Thonet Photo

Heading: ***Trademark** of the firm of Thonet.*

Fig. 1 ***Chair No. 1** by Thonet for the Palais Schwarzenberg in Vienna, 1850–59. Bentwood and laminated wood with cane seat. (Gebrüder Thonet A.G., Frankenberg-Eder.)*

Fig. 2 ***Armchair** by Michael Thonet, Boppard am Rhein, Prussia, 1836–40. Laminated wood with cane seat. In his earliest days, Thonet experimented with chairs made almost entirely of laminated wood. (Gebrüder Thonet A.G.)*

Fig. 3 ***Chair No. 14** by Thonet, from 1859. Bentwood with cane seat. By 1910 about fifty million chairs of this design had been made, and the pattern is still available to this day. (Gebrüder Thonet A.G.)*

A brilliant innovator, businessman and designer of furniture, Michael Thonet produced cheap bentwood chairs by the million, many of which are still best sellers today

The career and achievements of Michael Thonet (1796–1871), craftsman, designer, technician and *entrepreneur*, are unique in the history of design. He was without question the most successful furniture-manufacturer of his time, probably of all time. He invented a series of new techniques for bending and shaping wood and much of the machinery for applying those techniques to mass production. Most remarkably, he designed chairs of such universal and timeless appeal that forms thought suitable for a palace in the middle of the nineteenth century are used still with equal propriety and only slightly modified in modern interiors; in the meantime they have appeared in the cafés of every capital of Europe and in the dwellings of aristocrats and revolutionaries, peasants and bourgeoisie, rich and poor alike. Renoir drew one; Picasso has been photographed with one; Le Corbusier, in 1925, more than fifty years after Thonet's death, chose one to represent the spirit of the new age at the Paris Exhibition.

Yet, in spite of the acclaim of the *cognoscenti*, there is no indication that Thonet's simple and elegant designs were the product of anything more spiritual or aesthetic than the profit motive. If he revolted, it was not so much against the values expressed by the florid and pretentious products of his contemporaries as against the difficulty of mass-producing such products. Indeed, as catalogues of his time show, he was not averse to producing the florid and pretentious himself.

Yet, ironically, it was Thonet, not the idealist William Morris, who really created something approaching the 'decorative, noble, popular art' for which Morris, arch-enemy of mass production, strove. Certainly Thonet did more than anyone to eliminate 'waste, pomp and insolence' from the home and to give 'every man his share of the best', producing durable and elegant furniture more cheaply than anyone would previously have thought possible. His most popular chair was sold in Austria-Hungary during the 1860s for the same price as three dozen eggs.

Michael Thonet was born in 1796 in Boppard am Rhein, the son of a tanner. As a youth he was apprenticed to a carpenter and at the age of twenty-three achieved the status of master carpenter, opening his own small workshop in

4

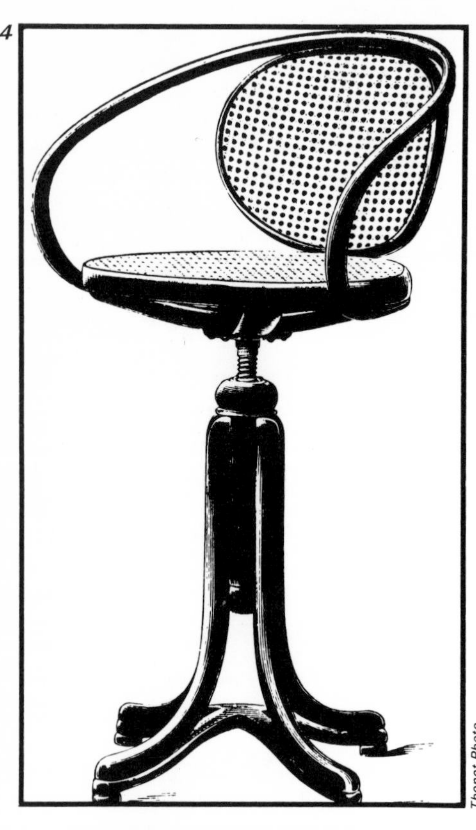

5

Thonet Photo

Thonet Photo

8

6

7

Thonet Photo

Thonet Photo

Fig. 4 ***Swivel chair No. 5601** by Thonet. Engraving. Early twentieth century. (Gebrüder Thonet A.G.)*

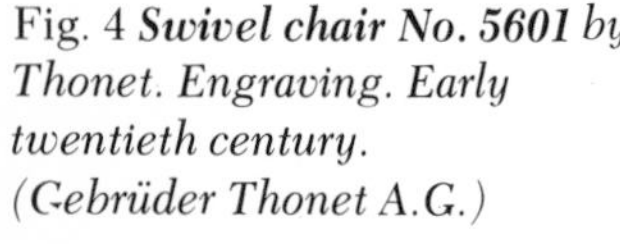

Fig. 5 ***Chair** by Michael Thonet, Boppard, 1836–40. Laminated wood with some carved decorations and tapestry seat. (Gebrüder Thonet A.G.)*

Fig. 6 ***Chair No. 25** by Thonet. Engraving from the 1911 catalogue. This model was made from both laminated wood and bentwood. (Gebrüder Thonet A.G.)*

Boppard. At first he produced furniture by traditional wood-working methods, but from 1830 onwards, in an effort to economise on labour and materials, he began to look around for new techniques for shaping furniture without carving and jointing the wood in the usual manner. Wood was already bent in a limited way in the construction of boats and carriages by the application of heat and water. Thonet decided that greater flexibility could be achieved by using thinner wood, so he began to experiment with the thin strips normally used for veneers, bending them and then gluing them together to achieve the necessary thickness and strength for furniture-making (Figs. 2 and 5). From this point he went on to make further experiments such as tying the strips together and boiling them in glue, and by 1841 he was ready to take out patents in France, England and Belgium. In the same year he showed his work at an exhibition in Coblenz, where it was brought to the attention of Prince Metternich, and his designs were introduced to the Austrian Court at Johannisburg Castle.

The following year Thonet and his family emigrated to Vienna, partly, it is thought, at the invitation of Metternich and partly as a result of severe financial difficulties in Boppard. He was awarded a patent from the royal court in Vienna and worked first for the firm of Franz List, making chairs of bent, laminated wood, and then, between 1843 and 1849, under Carl Leistler on the furnishing of the Palais Liechtenstein (Fig. 9).

The interior decoration of the palace was under the general supervision of an English architect,

Museum Photo

Fig. 7 **Café Daum Chair (No. 4)** *by Thonet, Gumpendorf, Vienna, 1850. Bentwood with carved vestigial capitals and tapestry seat. (Gebrüder Thonet A.G.)*

Fig. 8 **Café Griensteidl**, *Vienna, by Rudolf Volkel, 1890. Water-colour. All the chairs in this café are Thonet's chair No. 4, the model which had been used at the Café Daum (Fig. 7), but here it has a wicker seat. (Städtische Museen, Vienna.)*

P. H. Desvignes, and it is assumed that at least some of the chairs Thonet produced, whether traditionally cut and carved or exploiting the new techniques, were of his design. Those made of laminated wood strips were of great delicacy and quite free from the slight air of contrivance found in some of his earlier pieces.

In 1849 Thonet founded a firm bearing his own name in the Gumpendorf district of Vienna; chairs produced from this time until the opening of the first Thonet factory in 1858 are likely to have the words 'Thonet Wien Gumpendorf' stamped on the bottom of the seat-frames. It is thought that one of the firm's first commissions was to supply chairs for the Café Daum in Vienna (Fig. 7), the first of many public establishments to find Thonet's light-weight, yet sturdy, constructions ideally suited to their needs (Fig. 8).

But Thonet was still a long way from mass production. Some of the chairs of this period still had legs carved from a single piece of wood; most had front legs with at least vestigial capitals which had to be carved by hand. When Thonet sent some of his products to the Great Exhibition of 1851 in London (Figs. 10 and 11), they were shown in the section described as 'Luxury Furniture' and were closer in spirit to those he made for the Palais Liechtenstein than to the 'consumer chairs' he was making by the end of the decade.

He was in fact still searching for a simpler and cheaper method of achieving his aims. Laminations served well enough but were by no means ideal, a point which became plainer still when he began to export furniture to the Americas and it was found

9

Thonet Photo

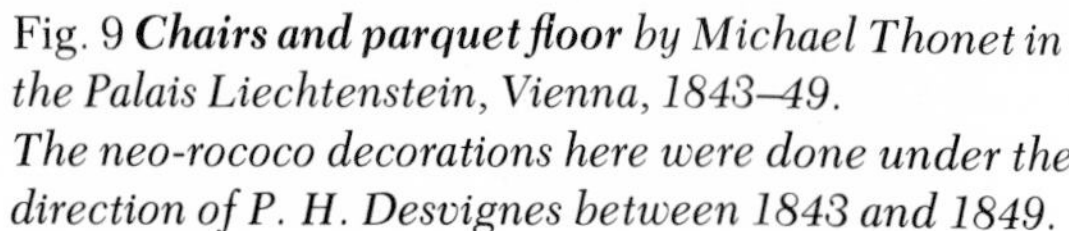

Fig. 9 ***Chairs and parquet floor*** *by Michael Thonet in the Palais Liechtenstein, Vienna, 1843–49. The neo-rococo decorations here were done under the direction of P. H. Desvignes between 1843 and 1849.*

Fig. 10 ***Rosewood and walnut table*** *by Michael Thonet, c.1850, from* Art-Journal Illustrated Catalogue, *1851. Engraving. Note the intricately inlaid top and bent legs.*

11

10

Mansell Collection

that the glue used to secure the laminations dissolved in hot and humid weather conditions. He addressed himself in earnest, therefore, to the problem of bending solid pieces of wood of the necessary thickness into the shapes he required.

When wood is bent, the fibres on the outside of the bend break first. Thonet worked out a method of attaching wood, which had already been steamed, to a metal strap secured by clamps at each end. Metal and wood were then bent together, the metal on the outside and the wood on the inside of the bend. The metal, which was of course stronger yet more flexible, took the strain and it became possible to force both into a cast-iron form. The whole thing was dried for several days in a heated room, then straps, clamps and form were removed, leaving the wood set permanently in the desired shape.

Thonet first used members formed in this way in conjunction with members from laminated strips, and his chairs for the Palais Schwarzenberg in Vienna, produced some time in the 1850s, are notable examples of this combination (Fig. 1); but, from roughly 1859 onwards, furniture parts were made from bentwood only. The consolidation of this new technique marks Thonet's breakthrough from super-craftsman to big businessman. It made the dream of mass production, never quite possible with the laminating method, a reality.

In 1853 Thonet had taken his five sons, Franz, Michael, August, Josef and Jacob, into the firm, which was renamed Gebrüder Thonet. Three years later, in 1856, they all assumed Austrian citizenship and the first Thonet factory, designed by Michael Thonet himself, was opened at Koritschan,

12

Fig. 11 ***Table** by Michael Thonet, c.1850. Bent rosewood legs with brass marquetry. This table, together with eight chairs, a sofa, the table illustrated in Figure 10 and various other pieces, was sent to the Great Exhibition in London in 1851. The pieces were classed as 'Luxury Furniture' and were highly praised. (Gebrüder Thonet A.G.)*

Fig. 12 ***Demonstration chair** by Thonet, 1870. Bentwood, constructed entirely of three pieces. Of the many experimental chairs made at this period, this model was the most practical. (Technisches Museum für Industrie und Gewerbe, Vienna.)*

Moravia, on the edge of the copper-beech forests which were to provide their raw material. This wood was used because it was relatively knot-free, with fibres that were quite long, thin and pliable.

Machinery, frequently of the Thonets' own invention and design, and new business methods, also often of their own invention, were introduced. But, although methods changed, designs remained very much the same during the early years of the new regime. The very first chair produced at the Moravian factory was similar to those made earlier for the Palais Schwarzenberg. The third had a back inset similar to the chairs sent to London for the Great Exhibition; the fourth was like the Café Daum chairs. One distinguishing feature of the new factory-made chairs is that they were equipped with circular stretchers between the legs, and most were also given strengthening braces between back and seat-frame.

All Thonet's pieces – chairs, tables, sofas, *chaises longues* and so on – were given production numbers from this time on; these were used in the catalogues and indicate the chronological order in which they went into mass production. The most successful and popular of all was the chair with the production number '14' (*c.*1859) (Fig. 3). On sale to this day in modern furniture shops, it was used by the Austrian architect Adolf Loos in the decoration of the Viennese coffee-house, Café Museum, in 1899. From 1869, when Thonet's patents expired, this design was copied in every furniture-manufacturing country in the world, and it is estimated that by 1910 at least fifty million had been made. Chairs made in Thonet's own factories were marked in some way with the firm's name; sometimes they were stamped or impressed, but often they were merely labelled and the labels were, of course, frequently lost or removed.

The chair which perhaps marks the height of Thonet's achievement for its perfect fusion of form and function is his Writing Chair No. 9 (*c.*1870). Le Corbusier found nobility in it, but architects today, one supposes, might equally admire it for its classlessness. It was composed of six elements only: one piece formed the arms and the top of the back, two more the front legs, another the inside of the back and back legs, a fifth the seat-frame, and a sixth the stretcher.

Yet Thonet remains perhaps best known for his rocking-chairs. In the middle of the nineteenth century, the rocking-chair was already popular in America but almost unknown in central Europe. Thonet, looking for ways of exploiting his discoveries, realised that here was a form for which bentwood was ideally suited. The first, which had a buttoned leather back and seat, went into production in 1860. The refinements which took place during the next ten years are characteristic of the perfectionism that illuminated Thonet's work. The Child's Rocking Chair No. 10, which is thought to be one of the last forms that he designed, has a logic and clarity that would be difficult to fault.

By the time Michael Thonet died, in 1871, four factories had been established. By the end of the century two more had been added and the firm was employing six thousand workers producing four thousand pieces of furniture daily. Many thousands more were produced to his designs by his numerous imitators. There is no doubt that the sheer quantity of his furniture would be quite enough to make him a significant figure in the history of interior decoration. Happily, the quality was also quite outstanding.

Michael Thonet's influence on twentieth-century designers has almost certainly been greater than that of any of his contemporaries, and he anticipated the famous axiom of the modern movement – 'less is more' – by over fifty years. Most important of all, perhaps, he showed that industrialisation could be harnessed for pleasure as well as profit, and that things of beauty could be produced mechanically as well as manually.

MUSEUMS AND COLLECTIONS

Thonet's bentwood furniture may be seen at the following:

AUSTRIA

Vienna: Technisches Museum für Industrie und Gewerbe

GREAT BRITAIN

London: Bethnal Green Museum

FURTHER READING

Bentwood Furniture – The Work of Michael Thonet, exhibition catalogue from the Bethnal Green Museum, London, 1968.

Form from Process – The Thonet Chair, exhibition catalogue from the Carpenter Center for the Visual Arts, Harvard University, Cambridge, Mass., 1967.

Il Caso Thonet by Georgio Santoro, Rome, 1966.

Das Biegen des Holzes by Wilhelm Franz Exner, enlarged and revised by G. Lauboeck, Leipzig, 1922.

1

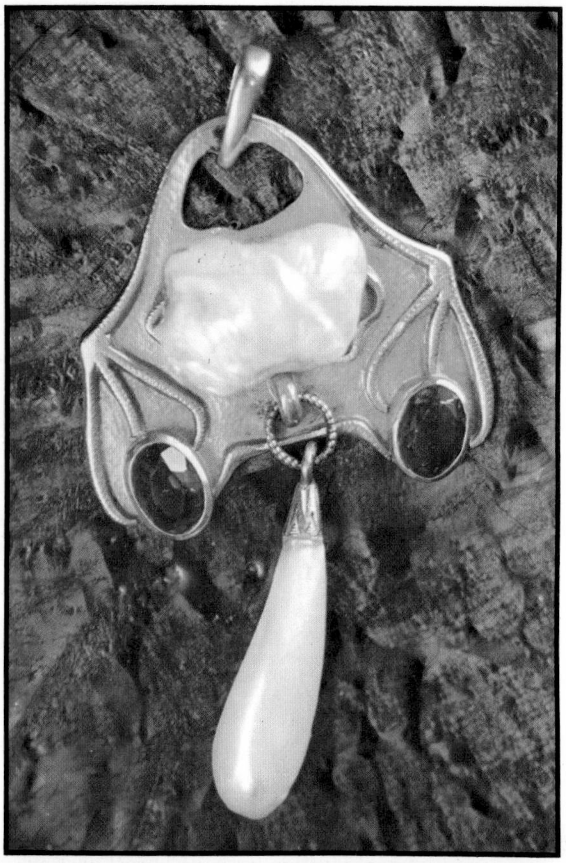

2

3

Albert Berger

Dennis Frone

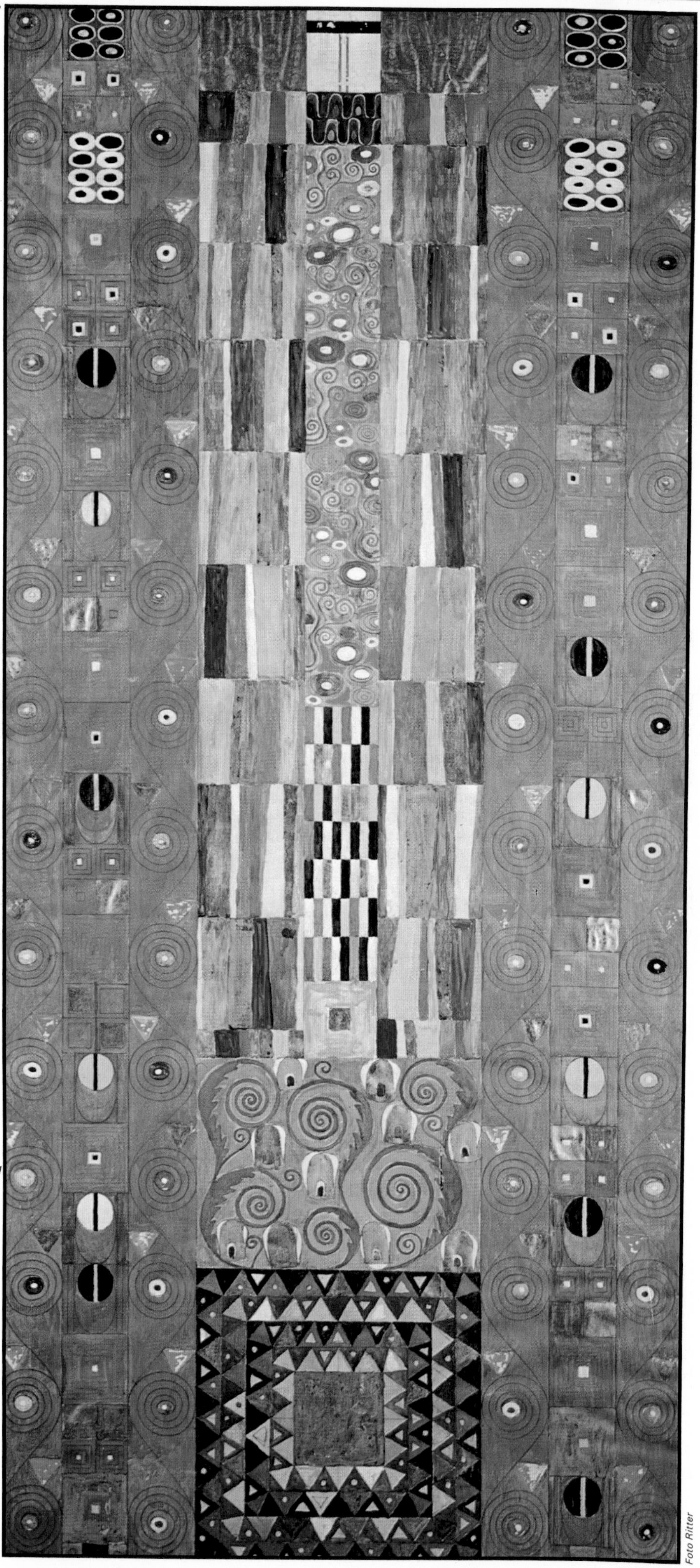

Foto Ritter

Fig. 1 ***Pendant*** *by Joseph Maria Olbrich, c.1900. Pearls and amethysts set in gold, height $2\frac{5}{8}$ ins.*
(Private Collection.)

Fig. 2 ***Flatware*** *by Josef Hoffmann (1870–1955), 1904. Silver-gilt.*
Many of Hoffmann's designs prefigure the functional austerity of Bauhaus work from the 1920s.
(Private Collection.)

Fig. 3 ***Design*** *for a mosaic in the dining-room of the Villa Stoclet, Brussels, by Gustav Klimt, 1908–11. Tempera, water-colour, gilt and silvered bronze, chalk and lead pencil, 6 ft. $5\frac{1}{2}$ ins. x 2 ft. $11\frac{3}{4}$ ins.*
(Österreichisches Museum für angewandte Kunst, Vienna.)

HOFFMANN AND THE SECESSION

Horst-Herbert Kossatz

In 1897 progressive artists in Vienna founded the Secession, and at the exhibitions they organised were displayed not only advanced painting and sculpture but also futuristic furniture, fabrics, metalwork, jewellery and ceramics

Foto Ritter

Fig. 4 ***Desk and armchair*** *designed by Josef Hoffmann and made by the Wiener Werkstätte, 1905. Black-stained and waxed oak with white metal mounts. (Österreichisches Museum für angewandte Kunst.)*

The groundwork for the Vienna Secession, which was the nucleus and breeding ground for Viennese Jugendstil (as Art Nouveau was known in Austria and Germany), originated in exploratory discussions during 1896 between disillusioned members of the Vienna Genossenschaft der bildenden Künstler (Society of Visual Artists), as well as members of various intimate coffee-house and wine-parlour coteries, students and colleagues of Otto Wagner – the influential architect and guiding inspiration behind the new Viennese school – and a group surrounding Gustav Klimt.

The Society had been formed with the object of acquiring its own exhibition premises. The fact that the competition for modernising the residential quarter facing the Museum for Art and Industry had been won in 1892 by a member of the association, Julius Mayreder, together with his brother Karl, goes a long way toward explaining why, through the third brother, Alderman Rudolf Mayreder, it submitted to the Municipal Council an application for the erection of an exhibition pavilion on that site. The day following the Municipal Council meeting at which the project was approved (3 April, 1897) saw the formal foundation of a new group of artists entitled 'Vereinigung bildender Künstler Österreichs' (Association of Austrian Visual Artists). In consequence of the disapproval by the older Society of this move, several artist members walked out of the Society on 24 May, 1897.

It was not until the following day that Josef Hoffmann announced his resignation and he, in turn, was followed by a further five artists. For his formal qualifying project – a neo-classical forum described enthusiastically as a 'masterpiece' by his teacher, Otto Wagner – Hoffmann had been awarded the Rome Prize of the Academy and had left in July 1895 to spend one year in Italy. After his return, he had worked at the offices of Wagner, who was a past master in exploiting to the full the talents of students and colleagues alike on his numerous projects. For example, he entrusted Joseph Maria Olbrich with the architectural design of the Metropolitan Railway; Olbrich was the creator not only of the numerous decorative columns on this railway, but also of the designs for the Hofpavillon and the Karlsplatz Station.

Despite the fact that Hoffmann had been on friendly terms with Olbrich, who had played a leading role in the founding discussions of the Association when he was still in Italy, Hoffmann did not actually join the Association until 2 July, 1897. It is possible that he was somewhat disenchanted by the fact that the new group had immediately entrusted the design of the exhibition building to Olbrich. This theory is supported by the fact that Hoffmann was duly asked to design the Council Chamber in the exhibition building.

Fig. 5 ***Poster** for the Fifth Exhibition of the Vienna Secession, by Koloman Moser, 1899. Colour lithograph, $39\frac{1}{8}$ ins. x $25\frac{3}{4}$ ins. A winged genius is depicted holding the emblem of the Association of Austrian Visual Artists. (Staatliche graphische Sammlung Albertina, Vienna.)*

Fig. 6 ***Poster** for the Fourteenth Exhibition of the Vienna Secession by Alfred Roller, 1902. Colour lithograph. $37\frac{1}{8}$ ins. x $24\frac{7}{8}$ ins. Roller's poster, in comparison with Moser's seen in Fig. 5, demonstrates the increasing use of geometric stylisation in Secession decoration. (Private Collection.)*

Olbrich produced numerous draft designs which can be classified into various phases of development. Lack of building permits then delayed construction and ultimately a site was used which was different from that originally envisaged. Time and again, Olbrich was obliged to revise his project, which explains the clarity expressed in his final concept. By this time, however, the Secessionists had intended to open the new centre at the beginning of 1898, in order to launch the extensive festivities planned in celebration of the fiftieth anniversary of Emperor Franz Josef's accession with a major exhibition. However, as this proved impossible – the centre was not ready for opening until 15 November, 1898 – the association rented premises from the Horticultural Society in order to acquaint the Viennese public with the work of leading artists from other European countries – work which at that time was virtually unknown in Vienna. The exhibition opened on 24 March, 1898, and was a sensation overnight; it marked the start of the reorientation of the Viennese arts.

The Secessionists were inspired by English examples

Only a short time after the resignation of the new Secession from the original Society, on 6 June, 1897, Felician Freiherr von Myrbach, appointed Director of the department of graphic arts at the School of Applied Arts in the Austrian Museum of Art and Industry, became a member of the new group. Myrbach, who, from 1881 until the rebellion of the Secession, had lived in Paris where he had gained a reputation as an illustrator of important books and periodicals, was a master of all the graphic media of his day. After his appointment on 25 February, 1899, to the post of provisional Director of the School of Applied Arts, the first appointment Myrbach made, in April, was of Josef Hoffmann to the directorship of the architectural department. Subsequently he managed to enlist the services of Alfred Roller, Koloman Moser, Rudolf von Larisch, Carl Otto Czeschka and the prominent educaţionalist Franz Cižek. In this way numerous young artists studying at the School of Applied Arts were won over to the objectives of the Secessionists.

The Secessionists were, to a considerable extent, inspired by English artists. The revival of the minor arts which had been promoted by the Arts and Crafts Movement led to the establishment of the Arts and Crafts Exhibition Society, of which the leading lights – Charles R. Ashbee and Walter Crane – were revered by the Viennese artists as shining examples. In Vienna, however, discussions had at that time already been held into theoretical principles which extended beyond Art Nouveau.

The alacrity with which the Secessionists familiarised themselves with the fundamentals of the new graphic style which had evolved in other European countries is illustrated by Koloman Moser's poster for the Fifth Exhibition of the Secession in 1899 (Fig. 5). The depiction of a winged genius holding the emblem of the association embodies all the stylistic elements which are characteristic of the Art Nouveau school: the symbolic character of the representation, the floral linearity of the drawing, the stylisation of the natural model, the combination of positive and negative tonal forms, the script which still retains such freedom despite all the ornament.

In 1899 Joseph Maria Olbrich joined the Artists' Colony founded at Darmstadt in that year by the Grand Duke Ernst Ludwig of Hesse, and his departure signalled the start of a major migration of young artists to Germany; Emil Orlik, Carl Otto Czeschka, Richard Luksch and Franz Metzner were a few of the many who believed that Germany offered better financial scope for their talents. In Darmstadt, Olbrich was lionised; one of his creations there was the pendant illustrated in Figure 1, in which the natural pearls are set off by the artistically mounted amethysts.

Already, before the departure of Olbrich, Josef Hoffmann stood out as the leading exhibition designer, but his most important work in this respect is the design of the Fourteenth Exhibition of the Secession (1902). In homage to Max Klinger, this exhibition gave pride of place to his recently completed *Beethoven*.

This piece of sculpture was the central point within a spatial concept in which all the artists accepted subordinate roles. Gustav Klimt created his famous Beethoven frieze especially for this exhibition; Alfred Roller, who at that time was President of the Secession, supplied a massive backdrop in the form of a stencilled painting with metal inlay and mother of pearl tarsia, *Die sinkende Nacht* (*Nightfall*), a section of which is shown in the poster for the exhibition (Fig. 6). By comparison with Moser's for the Fifth Exhibition, this poster illustrates the change in creative direction which had occurred in Vienna in the intervening period. The patterns used in such work can often be found in the principal handbook on historical ornament – Owen Jones' *The Grammar of Ornament*, published in London in 1856. At this exhibition, to a hitherto unequalled degree, surface decoration approached the austerity of the objects' forms and a mosaic-like treatment began to gain acceptance.

Of their contacts with British artists, those with Charles Rennie Mackintosh and his group in Glasgow were fostered with particular cordiality. Hoffmann and Moser are particularly indebted to that circle for inspiration. Following the model of Ashbee's Guild and with the advice of Mackintosh, the Wiener Werkstätte (Vienna Workshop) was founded in June 1903 by Hoffmann, together with Koloman Moser and the banker Fritz Waerndorfer, with the object of applying artistic design to the widest possible range of articles. Remarkably, the first works of Hoffmann for the Werkstätte included extraordinarily bold and almost cubist designs for vessels and furniture which were scarcely encountered again until the Bauhaus was moved to Dessau – and then not usually with the same elegance.

Immediately after it was established, the Werkstätte was entrusted with the construction of the Sanatorium at Purkersdorf. The original form of the structure has not been preserved, but the grid upon which Hoffmann based his designs can be recognised from the dining-room ceiling.

The clarity and utility characteristic of Hoffmann's approach are also apparent in an oak desk and armchair produced by the Werkstätte in 1905 (Fig. 4). White colouring has been rubbed into the grain of the black-stained and waxed wood; the recessed handles are of white metal and the black cowhide seat is self-supporting. This treatment imparts to the surface of the material a uniform

Albert Berger

6

Albert Berger

finish. The Werkstätte has repeatedly produced fabric designs (Fig. 7) which have been sold throughout the world and which not only inspired the leading fashion artists of its day but also induced the Werkstätte itself to set up a fashion department.

A trend toward greater refinement in Hoffmann's designs can be substantiated by a cabinet made between 1910 and 1914, the front of which is adorned with tarsia strips of mother of pearl and panels of boxwood and ebony. This costly piece of furniture is a worthy descendant of the type of showcase used for the display of *objets d'art* in the late renaissance period.

After the departure of Klimt and his followers from the Secession on 10 and 13 June, 1905, the Wiener Werkstätte became a collecting point for the progressive forces displayed in the Kunstschau (Art Show) of 1908–9, a complex of buildings designed by Hoffmann. At that time Hoffmann, in collaboration with the best people in the Werkstätte, was building his most important design, the Villa Stoclet in Brussels (1905–11). The house was constructed in a black and white scheme typical of Hoffmann; the outer surface was clad in slabs of white marble surrounded by borders of black granite. The external appearance of the structure and the decoration of the 1910–14 cabinet adhere to the same design approach.

The entire furnishings and fittings for the structure were produced in the Werkstätte and assembled room by room in Vienna before being shipped to Brussels, where twenty-one joiners from the Werkstätte had been waiting from the beginning of 1908 to install the components on site. The calculations which the Werkstätte had made for this building proved totally erroneous and it was necessary to impose repeated additional demands for money on the patron who, in turn, demanded progressively more luxurious appointments. In due course, the services of Gustav Klimt were also called upon and he designed a magnificent

Fig. 7 **Furnishing fabric,** *Wiener Werkstätte, early twentieth century.*
The design of this material, while unmistakably belonging to the early twentieth century, would not look old fashioned in a modern setting.
(Österreichisches Museum für angewandte Kunst.)

Foto Ritter

frieze for the dining-room.

The design for the narrow side of this room (Fig. 3) shows an almost abstract rendering of a man on a pedestal, and is one of Klimt's most free representations. Here, Klimt's design, with its grid-system, is akin to the approach of Hoffmann, but at the same time the general severity of the scheme upon which the design is based is somewhat attenuated by the floral ornamentation. The entire frieze was executed in marble slabs two metres high and it required a year and a half to complete. Each slab was first reinforced from the back with a second slab and then hollowed out to the depth required for the laying of the mosaic by Leopold Forstner. All the metal parts of the mosaic were chased in the Werkstätte and enamelled in the School of Applied Arts at Vienna. The butterflies and birds are ceramic and the glass parts of the mosaic have been ground out of coloured glass. The frieze was installed in November 1911 and this completed the project.

With this approach Klimt crossed the threshold of his painting style, dubbed '*Malmosaik*' (painted mosaic) by his contemporaries, and entered the realm of arts and crafts. The inlaid ceramics impart physical depth to this mosaic, but, far beyond this, there seems to be a pictorial world solidified and calcified according to laws of decoration without its organic origins being in any way disowned.

MUSEUMS AND COLLECTIONS

Examples of the work of the Vienna Sesession may be seen at the following:

AUSTRIA

Vienna:	Graphische Sammlung Albertina Österreichische Galerie Österreichisches Museum für angewandte Kunst

GREAT BRITAIN

London:	Victoria and Albert Museum

WEST GERMANY

Berlin:	Stiftung Preussischer Kulturbesitz Kunstbibliothek
Darmstadt:	Hessisches Landesmuseum
Hamburg:	Museum für Kunst und Gewerbe
Munich:	Die Neue Sammlung Museum Stuck-Villa

FURTHER READING

Die Wiener Secession by Robert Waissenberger, Vienna and Munich, 1971.

'The Vienna Secession and its early relations with Great Britain' by Horst-Herbert Kossatz in **Studio International**, January 1971.

Gustav Klimt – Dokumentation by Christian M. Nebehay, Vienna, 1969.

Lötz and Austrian Glass

Gawain McKinley

1

The Art Nouveau glass of Lötz and his Austrian contemporaries, although influenced by the designs of Tiffany, was individual and often superb in its own right

Austria's contribution to Art Nouveau although not entirely divorced from the international movement was not submerged in the general style. It was one of the last countries to begin practising a version of the style, and it was perhaps the first to give notice of the future developments towards purism in design and architecture. A great variety of work in all fields of design went under the cloak of the Secession. This was in particular true of glass-making.

Austrian glass has suffered the disadvantage of being dismissed by many writers on Art Nouveau as merely the poor man's version of the finest wares from the more renowned centres in France and America. It is arguable that much of this criticism is due to the lack of information available and also to the poor quality wares of the period which, for want of a better description, are called 'Austrian'.

The great quantity of scholarly writing on American Art Nouveau, and in particular on iridescent glass, is hardly matched by the literature on the eastern European product. Scholars and collectors are fortunate, however, in the existence of a book by Dr. Gustav Pazaurek called *Moderne Gläser* (1901) in which he gives an account of the major developments in techniques, and also reviews the achievements of the national schools. Pazaurek discusses the work of no less than fourteen Austrian factories and schools of design, but many were still working in the styles popular twenty or thirty years earlier.

The industrial revolution was slow to start in

Sperryn's Ltd

Fig. 1 ***Vase**, signed 'Loetz Austria'*, c.*1900. Ruby glass with green and silver swirls and silver overlay of a sort more typical of Adolf Zasche, Gablonz, height 9 ins. (Sotheby and Co., London.)*

Austria, and it was not until 1873 that the first International Exhibition was held in Vienna. It was at this exhibition, according to the American publication *Crockery and Glass Journal*, December 1905, that 'the first examples of iridescent glassware were exhibited by Lobmeyer, the Austrian glass manufacturer . . . where the beautiful colour play of the ware attracted general attention'. The article goes on to describe the accidental origin of the iridescent glass which, it said, occurred in the Hungarian town of Zlatno during a festival in 1850 at a glassworks where fireworks were exploded in a furnace. However apocryphal this description, Lobmeyer scored a great success, and his glass was immediately copied by Thomas Webb and Sons of Stourbridge, England, from whom Louis Comfort Tiffany derived much information in perfecting his processes of producing iridescent glass. Tiffany in his turn lost a worker – and the secrets of his furnaces – to the most famous Austrian firm of Lötz.

Austrian iridescent glasses of this period are perhaps the best known, and they are the most easily available. Pazaurek devotes an entire chapter to what he calls '*Metallreflexe*', the word deriving from the fact that metallic oxides incorporated into the surface of the glass, on being reduced, produce a lustrous effect. The most important manufacture in this field took place at the factory of Lötz in Klostermühle, Bohemia. The factory came under the control of Johann Lötz in 1830 and, although he died in 1848, the firm continued under the direction of his widow; hence came the name 'Lötz Witwe' The grandson of Johann Lötz, Max von Spaun, a Viennese designer, took over guidance of the factory in 1879, and within a few years had brought to the firm international fame for very fine quality glasses imitating precious stones such as agates and aventurine. The firm was awarded a Prix d'Honneur in Brussels in 1888 and a Grand Prix in Paris in 1889.

Lötz shared the Grand Prix at Paris in 1900

Tiffany's U.S. patent for the processes he perfected in the manufacture of iridescent glass was issued as early as 1881. Through the shop of S. Bing in Paris, his glass soon became widely known in Europe, but it was not until 1898 that Max von Spaun took out his patent. The Lötz factory was not slow in developing the technique, for in 1899 their glass was awarded a gold medal, and in 1900 Lötz shared a Grand Prix at the Paris Universal Exhibition with the foremost glassmakers of the time: Daum, Gallé and Tiffany. Other Austrian glassmakers were well placed: Graf von Harrach won a gold medal, Ludwig Moser and Sons a silver, and Bakalowits a bronze.

Although Tiffany's range of glassware was much wider and the products were in many cases finer, the best productions of Lötz, mainly designed by Von Spaun, have a very distinct character and are frequently very sumptuous (Figs. 2 and 3). That Von Spaun copied Tiffany's designs is obvious, but so did many American companies. It is most likely that the copies were made in order to capture some of Tiffany's market, for while the American was an artist and a dreamer with no great degree of business sense, Von Spaun was a businessman and his prices were much lower than Tiffany's.

The matter of quality in Lötz glass is worth mentioning, for, unlike Tiffany and Gallé, there are no personal or extravagant signatures to distinguish the very fine wares. Most Lötz glass is unsigned but there exist about four versions of signatures, the most common of which seems to be 'Loetz Austria'. Though it may command a considerably higher price, the signature is no guarantee of quality, for there are many relatively indifferent signed pieces. It has been suggested that Tiffany insisted on Lötz glass bearing a signature when sold alongside his own wares, and this may account for the English spelling. More confusing is the mark of crossed arrows within a circle and the 'Lötz, Klostermühle' signature, for almost identical glasses may differ only in that one will be signed in this way. It is instructive to compare the pieces shown in Figures 1 and 5: of the three vases of related form, with similar basic colour and decoration, two bear different signatures and one is unsigned, and yet the quality of each is very high. On the other hand, the rather uninspired

2

Sperryn's Ltd

ribbed jar on the left in Figure 5 bears the crossed arrows and 'Lötz' signature, but the similar, smaller vase, so much more successful, is unsigned.

The value of the signatures is in the positive identification they provide in a field in which Lötz had imitators who did not sign their work; in which Lötz copied other Bohemian glassmakers' lines; and in which other factories' pieces were made at the Lötz glasshouse. In Pazaurek's *Moderne Gläser* there are illustrated four 'lustre glasses' made in Klostermühle for E. Bakalowits and Sons of Vienna.

Fig. 2 ***Lamp,*** *Lötz,* c.*1902. Opalescent green and gold glass, mounted by Julius Alexandrovich Rappoport at Fabergé for Czar Nicholas II's yacht Standard, height* $11\frac{1}{4}$ *ins. (Sotheby's.)*

Fig. 3 ***Vase and plate,*** *designed by Max von Spaun for Lötz, 1899. Iridescent glass, height of vase* $11\frac{3}{4}$ *ins., diameter of plate* $12\frac{1}{4}$ *ins. The plate is similar to one in the Museum für angewandte Kunst in Vienna, which was made for the 1900 exhibition in Vienna. The influence of Tiffany's designs is obvious in both plates. (Author's Collection.)*

Fig. 4 ***Three vases,*** *designed by Max von Spaun, Lötz, Klostermühle,* c.*1900. Iridescent glass, height (*left to right*)* $11\frac{1}{4}$ *ins.,* $14\frac{1}{4}$ *ins., and* $10\frac{1}{4}$ *ins. (Author's Collection.)*

Fig. 5 ***Four vases,*** *Lötz,* c.*1900. Iridescent glass; that on the left signed on the base with crossed arrows within a circle and 'Lötz'; those on the right obviously from the same 'glass batch' as Figure 1; heights,* back left $7\frac{3}{4}$ *ins.,* back right $8\frac{1}{2}$ *ins.,* front left $8\frac{3}{4}$ *ins.,* front right *9 ins. (Victoria and Albert Museum, London, and Author's Collection.)*

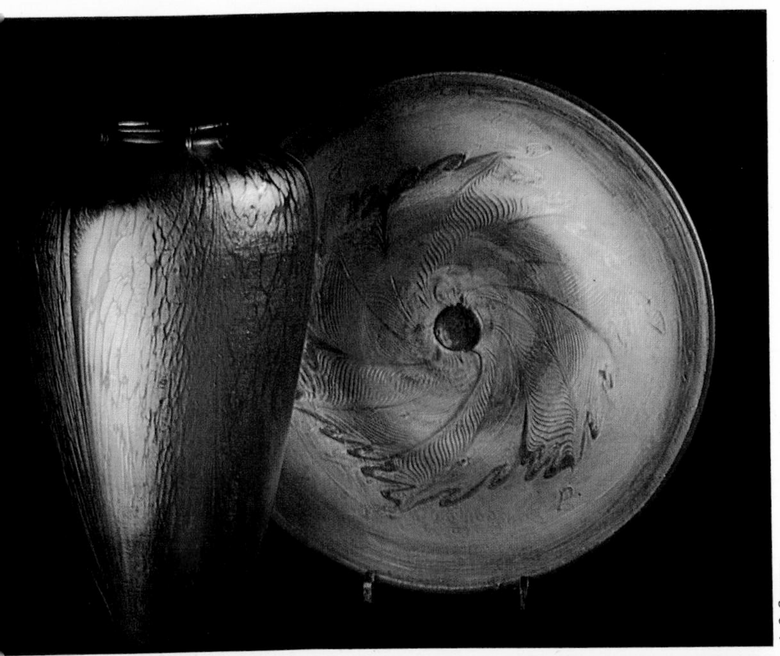

A. C. Cooper

4

A. C. Cooper

A. C. Cooper

Fig. 6 ***Two vases,*** *attributed to Professor Rudolf Bakalowits of Graz, c.1902. Iridescent glass;* Left: *mounted in a parcel-gilt bronze mount, height* $11\frac{3}{4}$ *ins.;* Right: *resting on a bronze base, height* $14\frac{3}{4}$ *ins.* *(Private Collection and Editions Graphiques, London W.1.)*

Fig. 7 ***Two vases,*** *attributable to Lötz or Adolf Zasche, c.1900. Iridescent glass, that on the left with a bronze mount of three girls, heights* $5\frac{3}{4}$ *ins.* *(Editions Graphiques and Private Collection.)*

The shapes and decoration of these pieces are hardly distinguishable from glasses which dealers and collectors would confidently ascribe to Lötz.

With the aid of Pazaurek's book, we are in a better position to ascribe certain glasses to the Bakalowits factory. Professor Rudolf Bakalowits of Graz is given as the designer of an identical glass to the piece illustrated on the right in Figure 6. He was assisted on this particular series of vases by a designer, Brendt, of the factory of E. Bakalowits of Vienna. The similarity of the golden vase on the left speaks in favour of its attribution to the same source, for the close, regular festoons in the decoration on the glass seem to be a feature of Bakalowits. The shapes of Bakalowits glasses are odd, but the good quality of manufacture and the large ground pontil mark on the base (a more or less constant feature of attributable Lötz) have led to many pieces being ascribed to Lötz. It is to be hoped that the original trade catalogues will one day be published.

Illustrative of the confusion which exists over similar lines of manufacture, the dark vases with string-like trailing (Fig. 10, right) are claimed by some authorities to be definitely by Lötz. But similar glasses are sometimes attributed to Joseph Palme König. Pazaurek illustrates fairly similar glasses under the name of Palme König. The other two glasses in Figure 10 are of a type sometimes referred to as 'early Lötz'; but there hardly seems to have been sufficient time, between Von Spaun's obtaining a *privilegge* (patent) in 1899 and the prize-winning exhibitions, for distinct stages of development to have taken place, and perhaps they can be reasonably ascribed to Palme König.

A glassmaker who is possibly less well known than any other and whose glasses seem always to be confused with Lötz is Adolf Zasche. The factory of Zasche, situated in Gablonz, produced glasses of simple forms with iridescent splashes decorating their bodies. A designer, Lederle, is responsible for the distinguishing feature of galvanized silver overlay. The overlay tended to be simple and of characteristic whiplash inspiration. It is likely that the factory was responsible for a series of glasses

6

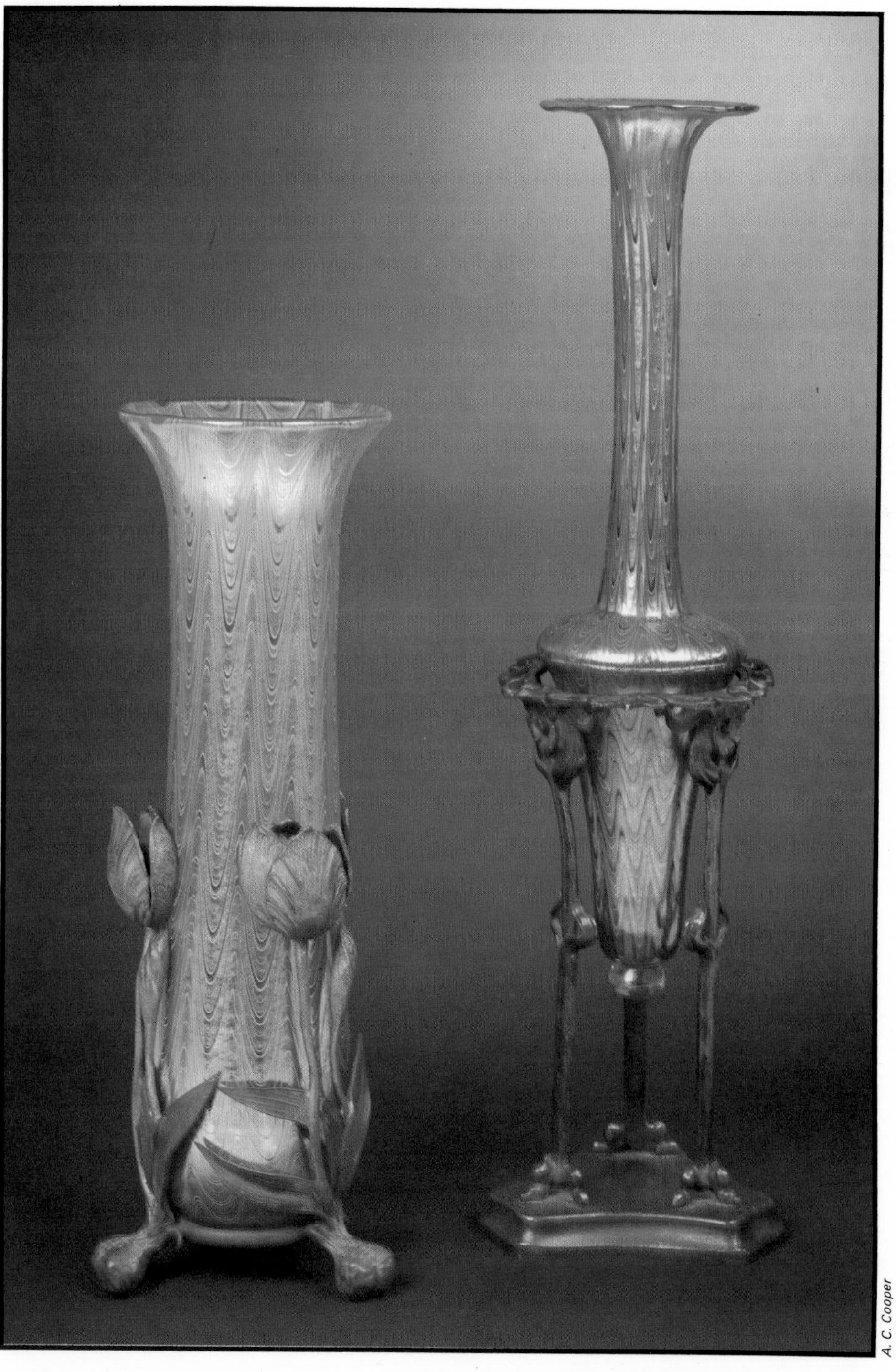

A. C. Cooper

7

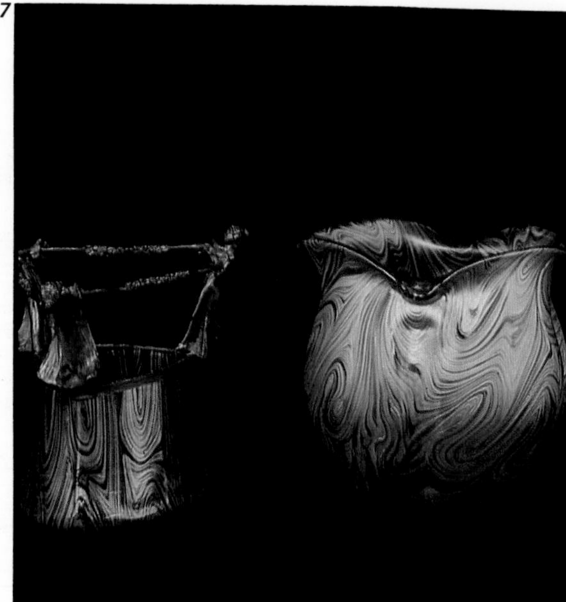

8

A. C. Cooper

Fig. 8 ***Vase,*** *L. Moser & Sons, Karlsbad, c.1900. Overlaid, carved, etched and enamelled glass. Height 7 ins. (Editions Graphiques.)*

Fig. 9 Left: ***Candlestick*** *by A. Zasche (?) Height $6\frac{1}{2}$ ins.*
Centre: ***Vase,*** *Lötz, designed by Michael Powolny (?), Vienna. Height $4\frac{1}{2}$ ins.*
Right: ***Dimpled vase,*** *by Graf von Harrach (?), Neuwelt Height $5\frac{3}{4}$ ins. (Private Collections and Malcolm Hillier Collection.)*

Fig. 10 ***Four vases*** *by either Lötz or Joseph Palme König, c.1900. Maximum height $12\frac{3}{4}$ ins. (Judith Downie Collection and Author's Collection.)*

decorated with simple overall splashes which were then mounted in brass or bronze in a more austere style. The candlestick illustrated in Figure 9 (left) is part of a table-setting which could be attributed to this factory. Gablonz (now Jablonec in Czechoslovakia) has a museum containing many examples of glass from this area.

The glassworks of the Graf von Harrach are not now well known, although they were highly regarded at the time. Harrach produced perhaps the most skilful imitations of Tiffany's non-iridescent wares, particularly the tall glasses with combed lines and alternating bands of transparent and opaque glass (Fig. 9, right). He manufactured ruby-glass vases of pleasant form with flowing floral ornament in polychrome matt enamel, and opaque milk-glass with a blue overlay which was then etched. Harrach's cameo or cased glasses are uncommon, and are usually signed with his name. As with Lötz's attempts in this field, the floral motifs are usually of one colour, widely spaced, rather crudely carved, and are quite similar to the industrial work of Gallé.

A. C. Cooper

A. C. Cooper

Moser and Sons, of Karlsbad, were the most successful makers of carved and cameo glass in Austria at this time. They do not appear to have made any lustre or iridescent glass, but concentrated on two types of manufacture: the most usual was a series of heavy purple glass vases cast in moulds with gilt friezes of plants or dancing figures; the other – more interesting – was a crystal-type glass, sometimes overlaid here and there in green and purple and then carved and etched. The example illustrated in Figure 8 is a fine example of this aspect of Moser's work. It is stylised without being stiff and combines enamelling, overlay, carving, etching and faceting without the vulgarity which spoils so many similar undertakings by the factory. As the most usual overlay colours were purple and green, it is not surprising that the most common floral motif on these vessels is the iris.

After 1900, the Austrian Art Nouveau movement developed very much more in the direction of purism. Flowing plant forms in decoration began to be replaced by geometric shapes, with an emphasis on contour. The luxurious glittering surfaces, which Lötz glass so well characterised, were abandoned and in place of these there was a growing insistence on the simple contrast of black and white. The vase illustrated in Figure 9 (centre) is an example of this intermediate stage; it could even be said to mark the first step towards the triumph of the purity of form, in which faceting, enamelling and acid etching of simple cased glasses became the rule of the day.

Glassmakers such as Lötz and Bakalowits were able to adapt to the changes in taste, but eventually they ceased production of art glass. Moser of Karlsbad (Karlovy Vary) is the only manufacturer of that period to have survived the passage of years, and it is interesting that they were still making, until recently, the huge, heavy, vases decorated with friezes of plants or figures.

MUSEUMS AND COLLECTIONS

Examples of Lötz glass may be seen at the following:

AUSTRIA
Vienna: Kunsthistorisches Museum; Österreichisches Museum für angewandte Kunst
GREAT BRITAIN
Bristol: Bristol City Art Gallery
London: Bethnal Green Museum; Victoria and Albert Museum
U.S.A.
Corning, N.Y: Corning Museum of Glass
WEST GERMANY
Darmstadt: Hessisches Landesmuseum
Düsseldorf: Kunstmuseum der Stadt Düsseldorf
Munich: Museum Stuck-Villa

FURTHER READING

The Book of Glass by Gustav Weiss, London, 1971.
Internationales Jugendstilglas, a Museum Stuck-Villa catalogue, Munich, 1969.
Art Glass Nouveau by R. and L. Grover, Rutland, Vermont, 1967.
Moderne Gläser by G. E. Pazaurek, Leipzig, 1901.

Swiss Enamelling

Kenneth Snowman

Fig. 1 ***Design for a Swiss enamel,*** *c.1800. Water-colour. Conventional floral motifs of this sort were much used by the Swiss painters. (Author's Collection.)*

Fig. 2 ***Plaque*** *by Alexandre de la Chana, 1745. Enamel on copper, signed and dated, diameter $2\frac{1}{2}$ ins. This still-life of fruit was probably the first of a long series of similar enamels on watch-cases,* bonbonnières *and snuff-boxes produced throughout the nineteenth century. (Musée d'Art et d'Histoire, Geneva.)*

Nowhere was the Swiss national genius for meticulous attention to detail more apparent than in the brilliant enamels produced throughout the eighteenth and nineteenth centuries

The traditional linking of the art of the enameller with Geneva may be historically traced as far back as the sixteenth century. It was in the next century, however, that the craft, by then organised into a powerful brotherhood, established itself as a vital expression of national life in Switzerland.

The earliest object we know to be signed and dated in Geneva is, unsurprisingly, a fragment of a watch-case, now in the Louvre. It bears the inscription 'P. Huaud p à G. 1672'

It is a matter of regret that the limpid, unself-conscious clarity of the Blois school was not maintained, and that this innocent eye was inevitably to develop over the next hundred and fifty years (not only in Switzerland) into a more calculating gaze.

The search for realism in both decorative and narrative themes occupied the talents of many native enamellers; Jean Petitot with Jacques Bordier concentrated on bringing the art of enamel portrait-painting in miniature to an astonishing degree of perfection. Petitot's expression took the form of speckled brush-strokes.

Geneva has traditionally served as a convenient jumping-off ground for her local artists. The enameller Paul Prieur, for example, became attached to the Court of Denmark from 1656 to 1681 and also worked successfully elsewhere in Europe, notably in England and Russia.

Alexandre de la Chana, popularly regarded as the successor of the Bordier-Petitot combination, produced in 1745 what would appear to be a unique plaque enamelled with a still-life subject composed of fruit (Fig. 2). It is illustrated here not so much for its artistic merit, but because it may well have been the first of a long series of similar enamels which decorate watch-cases, *bonbonnières* and snuff-boxes produced throughout the nineteenth century and which reached their apogee in the products of Messrs. Piguet and Meylan.

In this same year, a portrait of Maria Theresa by the Geneva enameller Jean Mussard presented the pale Imperial features against a background of a rather unfortunate milk-chocolate hue; this innovation might well have presaged the subsequent inclusion of this oblique reference to an important national product in the much enlarged enameller's palette of the next century.

Jean-Etienne Liotard (1702–89) of Geneva was typical of both his time and his town in that he travelled and worked throughout Europe and even got as far as the Middle East.

It has been necessary to emphasise the persistent activity of the Swiss enameller, both in and out of his own country and for hundreds of years, in order to demonstrate the sheer professionalism which they have invariably brought to this most testing of crafts.

The nineteenth century, with its rich opportunities for technical exploitation and mercantile advantage, was seized with eager hands by the indefatigable men at the bench in towns all over Switzerland. No traveller touring the cantons was immune from the temptation of adding just one watch or snuff-box to his baggage, proclaiming in hard brilliance the inevitable pink reflected lights on snowy peaks and the alleged blue of the lakes.

These scenic motifs appeared as naturalistic backgrounds in the enamelled portraits of Jean-François Soiron; and Marc-Théodore Bourrit, a pupil of Thouron, is known to have made detailed studies of glaciers and mountain scenery in general although none of these has apparently survived. It may thus be concluded that it was at the opening of the latter half of the eighteenth century that landscape became a legitimate subject for the enamel-painter's brush.

Richter's work stands out for its elegance

Jean-François Blay exhibited a View of Mont Blanc in Geneva in 1787 and his *Vue de la Mer de Glace* (Fig. 8) in the Musée d'Art et d'Histoire in that city must have contributed substantially to the artistic development of the most outstanding artist in this genre, namely Jean-Louis Richter (1766–1841). His teachers were the brothers David-Etienne (1758–1832) and Philippe-Samuel-Théodore (1756–1805) Roux, whose work was concerned with the enamelling of jewels and *objets de vertu* such as watches and gold boxes. None of their work has been identified with certainty.

Many of Richter's enamelled scenes on gold boxes are signed in a cursive script, and they are distinguished by an elegance and a serious attention to detail which puts them in an entirely different class from the seemingly inexhaustible stream of slapdash examples from inferior hands which consistently plague the collector in the auction-room. The lake pictures of the eighteenth century Swiss painter Ludwig Aberli (1723–86) seem to have inspired a number of Richter's enamels (Fig. 8).

The international aspect of the Swiss craftsman's

Author's Photo

2

Albert Grivel

attitude to his job has already been touched upon, but the export drive in watches and boxes designed specifically for eastern markets really got into its stride during the first quarter of the nineteenth century.

It is recorded that there were no fewer than seventy-seven enamel-painters in Geneva in 1789. Their number was certainly not diminished in the ensuing thirty years, especially with the rise of La Chaux-de-Fonds as another centre; the group merely became less distinguished as the craft declined. It is perhaps understandable that the majority of these commercial artists preferred to remain anonymous and the names of none of these enamellers appear to be recorded.

With the interest and patronage of Napoleon, a brief Indian summer took place which warmed the art of enamelling into a short-lived revival. François Soiron became extremely popular in Paris and carried out many ambitious projects in enamel among which special mention should be made of the equestrian portrait of Napoleon of 1806 and those of the Emperor and the Empress Josephine which were completed two years later. His work graced decorative panels and vases used at the new court and a pair of gilt-bronze candelabra enamelled in translucent *bleu de roi* figured at Napoleon's coronation.

The neo-Classicism of the period inspired some of the ugliest snuff-boxes ever seen. It was one thing to have palatial *salons* hung with vast grandiloquent canvases by David – they at least imparted an impressive sense of scale to an Imperial banquet or conference – but quite another to bring out of one's pocket a shiny little box with a crudely painted representation of some obscure classical tragedy on the cover.

Boxes for Turks, set with half pearls

The sentimentalised scenes of Arcady or the harbour scenes painted for eastern markets are surely less offensive since they are less pretentious.

'Turkish market' boxes, as they are popularly known, enamelled with coats of many colours and often ribbed and scalloped, appeared in numerous forms. They were liberally decorated with trophies, floral garlands and flags (Fig. 5), often set with half-pearl borders and sometimes even showered with a profusion of diamonds or other precious stones in order to boost their value and appear more attractive to the unsophisticated oriental taste. The enamelled backgrounds were generally in rather original pastel shades which had previously not been popular among the makers of gold boxes, who had restricted their palettes to a more sober range.

Enamelling itself is an extremely hazardous operation requiring the most skilled and patient practitioner. The medium is a form of glass which is applied by fusion to a metal surface and subsequently fired. This varnish, in its colourless state, is known as 'flux'. The enamelling is then burnished with a wooden wheel, a process which must be carried out with the greatest care, in order to ensure the smoothest surface possible and to polish away any irregularities. The work is then finally completed with a buff.

The Swiss brought the technique of enamel-painting on gold to an extraordinary pitch of excel-

1738

Rodney Wright-Watson

6

Author's Photo

Author's Photo

Fig. 3 ***Group of watches,*** *their gold cases enamelled by Swiss artists, with half-pearl motifs occasionally intruding into the design.* Centre: *musical automaton watch,* c.*1830.* Clockwise from the top: *nineteenth-century clock-watch; cylinder watch* c.*1830; cylinder watch* c.*1820; musical watch* c.*1790; cylinder watch* c.*1820; cylinder watch.* *(Sotheby and Co., London.)*

Fig. 4 ***Snuff-box*** *in the form of a trout by Bautte et Moynier, Geneva,* c.*1800. Enamelled gold and half pearls, length* $3\frac{1}{2}$ *ins. (Author's Collection.)*

Fig. 5 ***Design for a Swiss enamel,*** c.*1800. Water-colour. (Author's Collection.)*

Fig. 6 ***Design for a Swiss enamel,*** c.*1800. Water-colour. Possibly intended for the eastern market, this* chinoiserie design is *reminiscent of Louis XV work. (Author's Collection.)*

lence. A neutral colour *fondant* was spread evenly and thinly over a prepared gold panel and fired; the scene was then painted in enamels on this matt surface and fired again before a final and protective transparent glaze of flux was applied and polished.

The name of Jean Coteau of Geneva has come to be connected with the most brilliant *tours de force* in the craft of translucent enamelling. Among other technical achievements, this artist is said to have introduced the coloured and gold *paillons* which enrich so many Louis XVI boxes. These are small pieces of foil cut into different shapes, rolled extremely thin in gold, silver or colours and fired between two layers of translucent enamel; they serve to add interest to a large area of colour, often royal blue, in the way printers' flowers enliven a printed page. Coteau was born in about 1739 and was still active as late as 1812 – the precise year of his death is not known. Naturally enough, his compatriots, as well as the French, made widespread use of his discoveries which added so much to the repertoire of the working enameller.

Apart from their natural talent for enamelling, another preoccupation of the Swiss craftsman had traditionally been the manufacture of tiny watch-movements, often of extremely complicated design. These two expressions of national genius, both demanding the same meticulous attention to detail, were stretched to the fullest extent when they produced what has come to be known as the 'form' watch. This was generally designed as a pendant jewel for a lady. They reached their zenith in the early years of the nineteenth century in both Switzerland and Austria when quantities of small, brightly enamelled musical instruments, cherries, insects and shells – to enumerate just a few of the subjects chosen – all concealing ingeniously planted watch-movements, were manufactured and exported to all parts of the world.

'Chinese' duplex enamelled watches, occasionally to be found cased in pairs, were a particularly successful line in the commercial armoury of the diligent Swiss craftsmen. William Ilbery of London introduced the *montre chinoise*, and it was not long before Bovet of Fleurier was producing the same vividly coloured and decorated time-pieces for export. The circular enamelled plaques and the dials were usually bordered by a frame of half pearls. This same technique was applied very often, as we have noted, to the snuff-boxes of the period, and the pearls occasionally spilled into the main design where there was a decorative justification (Figs. 3 and 8).

This encroachment into the enamelled area was especially liable to occur in the case of *fantaisie* boxes. These provided the sort of challenge beloved of the Swiss craftsman who was free to design his box in the form of an animal, butterfly, fruit or anything else that his imagination proposed. The silhouette of the box would follow the contour of

7

8

Albert Grivel

9

Author's Photo

Fig. 7 ***Vue de la Mer de Glace*** *by Jean-François Blay, c.1787. Enamel on copper, 3½ ins. x 2¾ ins.*
An early example of the introduction of the Alpine scene into Swiss enamelling, this view was painted after an engraving by J. P. Linck.
(Musée d'Art et d'Histoire.)

Fig. 8 ***Four snuff-boxes*** *by Jean-Louis Richter (1766–1841), 1800–10. Gold with enamelled and half-pearl decoration.*
Richter was the most successful Swiss painter to involve himself in the craft of enamelling.
(Musée d'Art et d'Histoire.)

Fig. 9 ***Working design*** *for a Swiss enamelled snuff-box, c.1800. Water-colour.*
The drawing indicates clearly where the half pearls are to be set and gives a good indication of the method of chasing to be adopted by the goldsmith.
(Author's Collection.)

Fig. 10 ***Signatures*** *of the Geneva artists Jean Coteau (1739–after 1812) and Jean-Louis Richter (1766–1841).*
Coteau's name is connected with a most brilliant tour de force *in the craft of translucent enamelling – he introduced the use of* paillons. *The successful enameller Richter often signed his work in this cursive script.*

his chosen theme and the usually shallow body of the box itself would be naturalistically enamelled to give a generally agreeable or amusing effect. The snuff-box in the form of a trout in Figure 4 is rather an unusual object which evokes pictures of cosy *stübli* parties thronged with happy anglers absorbing *glühwein*.

Enamelled boxes in the form of books are not uncommon although many more are found in this design in plain engine-turned gold of French Empire origin.

The Swiss were responsible at this time for the production of the most elaborate singing-bird boxes (and even singing-bird pistols), the gold examples lavishly enamelled on all surfaces. They produced musical boxes, some divided into various compartments and others designed as *nécessaires*, knives and telescopes and a seemingly unending range of automata including the Magician's Box, which answered questions put to it – a sort of precocious Alpine computer.

The craft flagged badly as methods near to mass-production were adopted; the work itself became slovenly and cloying – the decay brought on by too much sweetness.

MUSEUMS AND COLLECTIONS

Swiss enamelling may be seen at the following:

FRANCE
Paris: Musée du Louvre
GREAT BRITAIN
London: Victoria and Albert Museum
Wallace Collection
IRAN
Teheran: Melli Bank
SWITZERLAND
Geneva: Musée d'Art et d'Histoire
U.S.A.
New York: Metropolitan Museum of Art

FURTHER READING

Objects of Vertu by Howard Ricketts, London, 1971.
Eighteenth Century Gold Boxes of Europe by A. Kenneth Snowman, London, 1966.
European and American Snuff Boxes, 1730–1830 by Clare le Corbeiller, London, 1966.
Les Peintres sur Email Genevois au XVIIe et au XVIIIe siècle by Pierre F. Schneeberger, Geneva, 1958.
Antique Gold Boxes by Henry and Sidney Berry-Hill, New York, 1953.